D1570468

Existentialism and sociology

Existentialism and sociology

A STUDY OF JEAN-PAUL SARTRE

IAN CRAIB

CAMBRIDGE UNIVERSITY PRESS

CAMBRIDGE

LONDON·NEW YORK·MELBOURNE

Published by the Syndics of the Cambridge University Press
The Pitt Building, Trumpington Street, Cambridge CB2 1RP
Bentley House, 200 Euston Road, London NW1 2DB
32 East 57th Street, New York, NY 10022, USA
296 Beaconsfield Parade, Middle Park, Melbourne 3206, Australia

Library of Congress catalogue card number 75-44579

ISBN: 0 521 21047 X

First published 1976

Printed in Great Britain at the
University Printing House, Cambridge
(Euan Phillips, University Printer)

CONTENTS

FOREWORD

The publication of Ph.D theses seems to be a hazardous business, and revising the present manuscript for publication only eighteen months after completing it, I begin to see why. From the standpoint of a new situation, new arguments, a further eighteen months' reading, I can find, beyond the embarrassments of style, problems glossed over, problems never raised, answers that should be questions, dead-ends never followed sufficiently far to become apparent as such. Moreover, intellectual argument seems to have produced a surprising anonymity: in a work concerned with 'reflexive sociology' I can find very little direct evidence of myself. Obviously, academic career requirements were no small influence on the decision to seek a publisher. I hope a brief attempt to fill in the missing 'reflexivity' might add a more honourable dimension to the apology.

On the most general level, I found reading Sartre a most exciting experience. I discovered a method of argument that seems to be rarely understood or tolerated in Anglo-Saxon countries yet one which I find infinitely more rigorous than much of what passes for sociological theory, and, further, one which is able to root the most abstract theorising in the most immediate personal experience. For that reason alone, not to mention Sartre's role in the development of Western thought over the last 50 years, I think he should be known to and taken seriously by sociology, yet in the literature references to him are few and very general. I am certainly not demanding that he be accepted; indeed a serious intellectual rejection of his position could benefit sociology more than the somewhat naive acceptance that I can now find at times in the present work. My first justification, then, is that Sartre ought to be known.

On an autobiographical level, I, like many friends of around the same age, came to sociology as a Marxist, desiring to be an informed Marxist, only to find after a while that my Marxism was disappearing in a host of different, apparently more powerful ideas amongst which I was rapidly losing myself. Sartre led me back to Marxism, but of a very different sort to that I had left. He offers a Marxism able to learn from its critical activities rather than simply reject its opponents, one that does not have to turn away from intimate personal experience, and one that can recognise the importance of 'theoretical practice' without abandoning its demand for political commitment. Eventually, it was a Marxism that enabled me to regain a minimum intellectual coherence and to begin to make sense of what had by then become my chosen subject: sociology.

Of course, over the last few years, there has been an increasing access to Marxist writers of a sophistication that puts to shame both sides of the traditional Anglo-Saxon debate about Marx, and the complexity of Marx's work itself seems to have been rediscovered. To an extent, it was 'accidental' that I should have discovered Sartre before, say, Althusser or Marcuse; but, having done so, it seems to me that Sartre occupies a central position within modern Marxist thought, one that can eventually embrace the rigorous scientific analysis of a Poulantzas or an Althusser and the critical dialectics of an Adorno. From my current position, the greatest lack in the present work is that there is no attempt even to begin to explore the problems involved in the construction of such a Marxism; nevertheless, I believe its possibility is apparent in what follows, and that is my second justification.

May 1975   IAN CRAIB

ACKNOWLEDGEMENTS

I would like to thank those members of staff and postgraduates of the Sociology Department at Manchester University who contributed directly or indirectly to the working out of my ideas while I was a student there; in particular, I would like to thank Dr David Morgan, my supervisor, for his continuous help and patience. His specific suggestions that have been incorporated into the text are too numerous to mention.

I am grateful also to those colleagues and students at Essex, and to Jeremy Mynott of the C.U.P., whose comments have helped me in revising the text for publication, and to the secretaries in the Essex Sociology Department for efficiently typing a difficult final manuscript.

The research for this study was carried out whilst in receipt of a 3-year SSRC postgraduate award.

Introduction

An examination of the relationship between philosophy and sociology would appear at first glance to be a task which should be
carried out in general terms, any one writer being important only
insofar as his work throws light on the general relationship. The
justification for choosing to approach it through the work of one
writer, and for choosing Sartre in particular, must lie to a large
extent in what we can learn from the examination itself. All we can
do at this stage is offer a prima facie case for the enterprise, and
this will take the form of a general 'overview' of Sartre and his work:
his relationship to the school of philosophy with which his name
has often (and wrongly) become synonymous, and the development
of his work in relation to the development of the world in which
he has lived.

1. The concerns of existentialism

Existentialism is notoriously difficult to define and even
those writers covered by the term do not always acknowledge it.
According to Simone de Beauvoir (1968: 45–6) '. . . we took the
epithet that everyone used for us and used it to our own purposes'.
However, although we can find the origins of his work in Husserl,
Hegel and Marx, there are illuminating affinities between Sartre and
'existentialism' as a general descriptive term. Jean Wahl (1969), for
example, argues that existentialism is best described as 'an atmosphere, a climate' and the categories he uses to convey this atmosphere include Existence, Being, Transcendence, Possibility and
Project, Situation, Choice and Freedom, Nothingness and Dread,
Authenticity, the Unique, Paradox, Tension and Ambiguity. These
are certainly categories that we find in Sartre's work and he also
shares the concerns that other commentators have chosen to
characterise existentialism: a concern with 'integral' man against
philosophies that portray men as purely rational creatures (Barrett,
1961) and a concern with the concrete, the specific as a means of
approaching the general, more often than not the specific and the

concrete being the writer's own personal experience (Warnock: 1970; McIntyre in O'Connor: 1964). We shall see in fact that the development of Sartre's work only makes sense in the context of the development of his private and public life and that it is rigorously rooted in everyday experience.

Sartre's work also shares the features of existentialism that run counter to traditional Western philosophy: it is concerned with movement and change and particular truths rather than general eternal essences, and it is Sartre's combination of these concerns with methods and ideas taken from philosophers within the mainstream tradition that is a source of his originality and of the paradoxes of his thought which will become apparent in what follows. The basis of his position is immediate experience as much as intellectual argument, and as Tiryakian (1962) points out, the usual criteria by which arguments are judged, meaningfulness and logic, are likely to become hopelessly confused.[1] Thinking is seen as a secondary process, inverting the Cartesian cogito to 'I am therefore I think', but at the same time the only way in which this can be argued is by means of logical thought.

A sociological description of the rise and development of existentialism is beyond the scope of this study, but it is important to note that, as Tiryakian (1962: 76) also points out, it grew up in opposition to an increasingly rational industrial and democratic society, against what Weber was to see as the dominant trend in modern society: bureaucratic rationality. In other words it was opposed to a society in which sociology was establishing itself as an integral part. To begin with, then, we have situated Sartre very much in opposition to sociology, both historically and in terms of his concerns and approach. To get a clearer idea of his relevance it is necessary to move on from the 'atmosphere' of existentialism in general to Sartre in particular.

II. Sartre: a general view

No discussion of Sartre can ignore the close connection between his work and his own life, and, particularly after the Second World War, political developments, both internationally and in France. The logic of the development of his thought lies as much in the situation in which he was writing as in his work itself.

---

[1] Some idea of what is meant can be gained from Sartre's own statement concerning his reading of Marx in the 1930s: 'It was about this time that I read *Capital* and *The German Ideology*. I found everything perfectly clear and I really understood absolutely nothing. To understand is to change, to go beyond oneself' (1963b, 17–18).

However this development has by no means been a straight line leading to a conclusion. He has not attempted to present a total theory of man or existence which is true for all time, he claims to be no more than a moment in the dialectical process that he is attempting to describe, and he has never attempted to give an explicit unity to his work. He has produced volumes of philosophy, novels, plays, literary criticism, political tracts and studies of individual writers and artists, each of which must be placed in the context of his personal development and the rest of his work before it can be fully understood. This study will focus on his philosophical work because it is here that we can get closest to the presentation of his ideas as a 'totality', but as we will see, even here there are various breaks and jumps that will present us with problems. There have been a number of dead ends, abortive 'projects' and works that have lost their importance once published.[1] Nevertheless, it is possible to discern overriding themes and to trace a line of development. This is not intended to be a fully worked out study in the sociology of knowledge or literature, although the beginnings of such a study will inevitably appear. It is intended, rather, to provide a 'map' on which those parts of his work that we will look at more closely later can be situated and on the basis of which we can establish the prima facie case for studying Sartre.

It is the first part of his work, up to and including *Being and Nothingness* (1957a) that is involved most intimately with his 'personal' as opposed to his 'political' development.[2] In most cases a philosopher or any academic writer works within a system of thought that has been established by others and in which he achieves a considerable degree of anonymity: his personality remains hidden behind the words and methods he uses to achieve 'scientific objectivity'. Sartre, however, adopts ideas and concepts from other writers without working in their tradition and he gives them a highly individual meaning. This is particularly true in his treatment of Descartes, and, to a lesser extent, of Husserl. One result of this isolation from an established tradition is that 'influences' such as personal history and class position, that in other writers remain in the background, can be fairly easily discerned in his work.

[1] Amongst promised works that have never appeared are a fourth volume to the *Roads to Freedom* series of novels (although extracts were published in *Les Temps Modernes*) (1949a) a volume of ethics to follow *Being and Nothingness*, and a second volume to the *Critique*. One work – *Existentialism and Humanism* – was partially disowned after publication.

[2] 'Personal' and 'political' are in inverted commas because, as we will see, the implication of Sartre's work is that the distinction between the two is a false one.

The dominant themes of his early work are freedom and contingency. Man is seen as contingent, as having no reason for being
in the world, and as a 'nothingness' in relation to the solidarity of
the world around him. The 'nothingness' is the source of man's
'total freedom': he is not subject to any laws, he is the source of
all values and morality (there is no God) and he cannot justify his
actions by reference to anything outside himself. He apprehends
his freedom in anguish and tries to escape it by means of bad faith.
Ian Birchall (1970: 21) offering a Marxist 'explanation' of this
period of Sartre's thought sees it as the expression of the world view
of a bourgeoisie stripped of its usual mystifications; it is:

a response to the development of capitalism after the First World War.
Two distinct and somewhat opposite trends were taking place. On the
one hand war and revolution were showing that the existing social order
was not eternally established, but fragile and temporary. But at the
same time monopoly capitalism was replacing competition, the old vision
of the harmonious interplay of competing individuals was replaced by a
world in which the individual becomes insignificant.

The problems of this as an explanation reveal one of the major
themes of Sartre's work that we can illustrate in relation to Sartre
himself. No doubt the general trends outlined by Birchall were
taking place, but there were many thousands of intellectuals living
through them and only one produced Sartre's work. If we are to
understand the meaning of his early work, then we must look for
the specific mediations through which the trends described by
Birchall reached Sartre, and the way in which he reacted to them.[1]
Simone de Beauvoir approaches the heart of the matter when she
writes (1965: 21): '. . . it was our conditioning as young petit-
bourgeois intellectuals that led us to believe ourselves free of all
conditioning whatsoever'.
She describes the 'freedom' that they experienced:

At every level we failed to face the weight of reality, priding ourselves
on what we called our 'radical freedom' . . . we possessed a practical,
unimpeachable intuitive awareness of the nature of freedom. The
mistake we made was in failing to restrict this concept to its proper
limits . . .
We were unaware of any cloudiness or confusion in our mental
processes; we believed ourselves to consist of pure reason and pure
will. (1965: 15–16)

[1] The problem is summed up in Sartre's statement: 'Valéry was a
petit-bourgeois writer, but not all petit-bourgeois writers were Valéry.'
The Problem of Method presents a rigorous criticism of the type of
over-generalising Marxism practised by Birchall.

We will have occasion later (Chapter 5) to consider the 'ideological' nature of Sartre's early concept of freedom. The immediate point is that it is less a 'demystified bourgeois ideology' than an ideology of a petit-bourgeoisie which realises the inadequacies of bourgeois ideology; at the same time it is unable to identify with Marxism and remains confident of its own academic or literary future. We will see that the concept of freedom outlined in *Being and Nothingness* does not necessarily carry these ideological connotations, but we can only understand their nature and importance in the light of Sartre's personal development and the way in which he was read by his audience. We can explore the first more fully before we move on to the second.

In *Words* (1967b) Sartre attempts an analysis of his childhood, intended finally to break his literary 'destiny' and it is here that we find the theme of contingency emerging more clearly than it would in an analysis of the period and society in which he lived. His father died shortly after he was born (in 1905) and he was brought up at the home of his grandparents, under their control rather than that of his mother. His grandfather taught German and seems to have belonged to the intelligentsia rather than being an intellectual as such. He (Sartre) was generally sheltered from the outside world, only occasionally getting the impression that something was wrong: the breakdown of 'eternal values' does not appear to have reached him. In the death of his father, he finds another root of his idea of freedom:

The rule is that there are no good fathers; it is not the men who are at fault but the paternal bond which is rotten . . . If he had lived, my father would have lain down on me and crushed me . . . among the Aeneases each carrying his Anchises on his shoulders, I cross from one bank to the other, alone, detesting those invisible fathers who ride piggy-back on their sons throughout their lives . . . I am happy to subscribe to the judgement of an eminent psycho-analyst: I have no Superego. (1967b: 14–15)

He describes himself as a spoilt child who learnt to act in the way expected of him in order to please. The result was a sense of not *being* anything. He likens it to being asleep in a railway carriage, and, on being awakened by the inspector, finding that he had no ticket, no money to pay for one and no reason to be making the journey in the first place (1967b: 70). It was in writing, originally bound up with the act he was playing for the adults' approval, that he found his ticket.

The ideas of contingency and freedom which we find in Sartre's personal history and class position were mediated through a philosophical method that he discovered in Husserl and this will be examined in the next chapter. What is important at the moment is that we can illuminate these ideas and their later development through Sartre's own experience. Before we move on to this, however, we can note that the ways in which they are expressed in *Being and Nothingness* presents us, directly and indirectly, with a theory of the self and of consciousness which is intimately bound up with the concept of freedom: it is in this way that freedom leads us to sociological problems, as well as through the more obvious connections with the problem of freedom vs. determinism and the relationship of the individual to his class.

By the time that *Being and Nothingness* was published in 1943, Sartre was beginning to move beyond the positions contained therein. The Second World War had meant that the outside world had forced itself on him in no uncertain manner. For the first time he was faced with the possibilities of death and failure and he was forced to define his relationship with the outside society more clearly. Simone de Beauvoir writes (1968: 13):

[The war] had shown him his own historicity; and the shock of this discovery had made him realise how much he had been attached to the established order, even while he was condemning it . . . Relentless in his denunciation of this society's faults, he still had no desire to overthrow it. Suddenly everything fell apart; he found himself drifting aimlessly between a past of illusions and a future of shadows

There was another effect of the war:

His experience as a prisoner left a profound mark on him. It taught him the meaning of solidarity; far from feeling persecuted, he took great joy in this participation in a communal life.[1]

This is the first intimation that the Other, in *Being and Nothingness* a permanent threat and a mortal danger, might also offer salvation. The most immediate manifestation of this development in Sartre's thought was the idea of 'commitment' which appeared at the end of *Being and Nothingness* in an attenuated form. The idea is principally a moral one[2] although as we shall see (Chapters 4 & 11) it is

---

[1] For Sartre's own assessment of what he learnt during this period, see his 'Reply to Camus' and 'Merleau-Ponty' (1966b).

[2] 'Commitment' was never clearly elaborated, although we can obtain some idea of what it entails from Simone de Beauvoir's summary (1968, 205ff) of the last, unpublished volume of *Roads to Freedom*. It seems to involve an acceptance of one's own contingency and freedom and at the same time a free commitment of that freedom. It is encapsulated in two major characters who arrive at commitment from opposite directions. Matthieu, who, contrary to popular belief, was not killed in the third volume, is the petit-bourgeois intellectual, trying to

based on his philosophy and has serious consequences for any
sociology that might in turn base itself on his work.

On his return from the prisoner of war camp in 1941, Sartre made
an abortive attempt to form a Resistance group ('Socialism and
Liberty') and then concentrated on writing with fairly minor Resistance activities in co-operation with the Communist Party. His play,
The Flies, was performed during the occupation despite its message
of freedom. With the end of the war, the notion of commitment
led him into further difficulties. In his own words:

there was a very simple problem during the Resistance – ultimately,
only a question of courage. One had to accept the risks involved in
what one was doing, that is, of being imprisoned or deported. But
beyond this? A Frenchman was either for the Germans or against
them, there was no other option. The real political problems, of being
'for, but' or 'against, but,' were not posed by this experience. The
result was that I concluded that in any circumstances, there is always a
possible choice. Which is false. (1969b: 44)

As Raymond Aron (1969) has pointed out, after the war there is
a shift in Sartre's writing from the ontological to the ontic, from
emphasis on man as total freedom to men-in-the-world trying to
act, from a 'philosophical' to a practical freedom. He has been
accused at various times of abandoning himself to Marxism and of
having aligned himself finally with the Communist Party.[1] It seems
evident now that however close he came to the Communist Party
in the ten years after the end of the war, he can in no way be
accused of 'surrendering' to them and it will become apparent later

> protect his 'freedom' from his bourgeois origins and his communist
> friends. He finds himself in a vacuum until the war forces him to
> accept responsibility for what happens in the world. He finally dies in
> the Resistance. On the other hand, Brunet, a member of the
> Communist Party, tries to escape his freedom through bad faith,
> making himself a tool of the Party and History. He is forced to
> recognise his freedom after the Hitler–Stalin pact, but nevertheless
> maintains his commitment and meets a similar fate to that of Matthieu.
>
> [1] Mary Warnock (1970) and Ian Birchall (1971) both claim that Sartre
> had abandoned his earlier positions by the beginnings of the 1950s; the
> abandonment is usually associated with capitulation to Stalinism and
> the Communist Party (see the Cranston–Caute debate in *Encounter*,
> April and June 1962). For balanced accounts of this period see Caute
> (1960) and Burnier (1966). Simone de Beauvoir's *The Mandarins* (1960)
> provides a fictional account of the period although care should be
> taken not to identify the characters too closely with 'real people'.
> As far as Sartre's own work is concerned, an account of the period
> can be found in 'Merleau-Ponty' (1966b) and the work in which he is
> politically closest to the PCF is, without doubt, *The Communists and
> Peace* (1969a). The briefest perusal of this work should be sufficient to
> show that his support was, to say the least, unorthodox.

that Sartre's Marxism is by no means that of an orthodox Party member. If it is possible to sum up his attitude to the Party, it was one of strong sympathy, tempered with an intense dislike of Stalinism; he did not want to participate in the self-indulgence of attacking the Party at every opportunity and he was well aware that politics is no place for saints. He realised, slowly, the impossibility of 'moral behaviour' at least in the present political and economic system.

Throughout the post-war period Sartre was 'thinking against himself'. He wrote in some unpublished notes (de Beauvoir 1968: 272–3):

I discovered the class struggle in that slow dismemberment that tore us away from them (the workers) more and more each day . . . I believed in it, but I did not imagine that it was total . . . I discovered it *against* myself.

The result of this thinking was, on a personal and literary level, *Words*; on a theoretical level it was *La Critique de la raison dialectique* (1960a). The latter is not an attempt to integrate Marxism into his earlier work, at least on a formal level but rather to reintroduce freedom into Marxism.[1] We will discuss the relationship between his earlier and later work in Chapter 5, but there are certain similarities that we can note here: many of the concepts of *Being and Nothingness* are recognisable in the *Critique* albeit under different names, and fulfilling different functions. The For-Itself and In-Itself appear as praxis and the practico-inert. The concept of the project is carried over directly.

In the *Critique* we can recognise the personal and political problems that concerned Sartre after 1945: other people remain enemies but at the same time become the source of freedom; the class is seen as a complex network of social formations in which the Party (the 'institution') always has an ambivalent status, both expressing the 'class praxis' and distorting it, even on occasions trying to suppress it. All this will become clearer when we look at the work in detail; it is the later work which is most immediately relevant to sociology, in terms of its aims and its content.

The *Critique* aims at making explicit the philosophical basis of Marxism and of the social sciences. Both, Sartre argues, force the real world into their concepts and are thus incapable of 'understanding' human activity. His concept of understanding will be

---

[1] Merleau-Ponty (1947) made the first attempt to combine some form of existentialism with Marxism; later (1955) he presented a vigorous critique of Sartre's position in *The Communists and Peace* and the influence of this criticism is apparent in the *Critique*.

expounded and developed throughout the study and it will become apparent that it involves, as its base, the idea of freedom developed in his earlier work and that it is opposed to 'knowledge' considered as established truth. In the latter part of the work, the attempt to found Marxism leads him to deal with group formations ('the group-in-fusion', 'the organised group' and the 'institution') that are self-evidently the realm of sociology. It is Marx, in fact, who Sartre sees as having originally achieved the synthesis between the specificity of individual human existence and man as an 'objective reality' that he (Sartre) is attempting to elucidate (1963b: 14).

The period since the *Critique* has seen a steady move away from the PCF on Sartre's part, beginning with his condemnation of Moscow at the time of Hungary and culminating with the events in Czechoslovakia and Paris in 1968 (1965c; 1972c; 1972d). His major works – *Words* and the recently published *L'Idiot de la famille* (1971a; 1972a), a mammoth study of Flaubert running so far to three volumes – have established that he has in no way abandoned the ideas of his earlier work. The Flaubert study in particular employs together ideas from both of his major philosophical works and draws heavily even on his pre-war studies of the imagination (1949b; 1962c). The original concern with freedom and the individual has now become a concern with the free individual situated in a massive and oppressive social structure which limits and alienates his activities. He has abandoned what he would call his 'petit-bourgeois idealism' of his earlier work without surrendering to a deterministic Marxism.

It was suggested earlier that if we are to grasp the 'ideological' aspect of Sartre's earlier work then we must not only look at his personal history but at the way in which his work was read by his public, the meaning that they gave it. There seems in fact to have been considerable differences between what he thought he was doing and what he was thought to be doing, particularly in *Being and Nothingness*, which have given rise to all sorts of confusions and misinterpretations, not only by the media (from which he suffered considerably in the post-war period) but also amongst academic philosophers and serious critics.[1] His later adoption of Marxism only succeeded in confusing his critics to a greater extent.

Again, we find in Simone de Beauvoir an acute assessment of what was happening that is well worth quoting in full:

[1] A full list of inadequate commentaries would take too long, and several will be mentioned in passing in the course of the study. Significantly, perhaps – and with some notable exceptions – the most unreliable commentaries up until the mid-1950s were those produced by Roman Catholics and orthodox Communists.

His petit-bourgeois readers had lost their faith too, in perpetual peace,
in eternal progress, in unchanging essences; they had discovered
History in its most terrible form. They needed an ideology that would
include such revelations without forcing them to jettison their old
excuses. Existentialism, struggling to reconcile history and morality,
authorised them to accept their transitory condition without
renouncing a certain absolute, to face horror and absurdity while still
retaining their human dignity, to preserve their individuality. It seemed
to offer the solution they had dreamed of . . . Sartre seduced them by
maintaining, on the level of the individual, the rights of morality; but
the morality he meant was not the same as theirs. His novels presented
them with an image of society which they rejected; they accused him of
sordid realism, of 'miserabilism' . . . When confronted with the Marxist
dialectic, they clamoured for their freedom; but Sartre went too far.
The freedom he offered them implied wearisome responsibilities; it
could be turned against their institutions, against their mores; it
destroyed their security. He invited them to use this freedom in order
to ally themselves with the proletariat, they wanted to enter History,
but not through that door . . . He was speaking their language, and
using it to tell them things they did not want to hear. They came to
him, and came back to him, because he was asking the questions that
they were asking themselves; they ran away because his answers
shocked them. (1968: 47)

Many misinterpretations of Sartre stem from the fact that he was
working in no particular tradition and by choice excluded himself
from the academic world. It was his earlier work which was most
popular amongst the public at large and produced most commentaries. Paradoxically, as his mass popularity declined with his move
towards Marxism, he has not been accepted generally as a Marxist
thinker. His influence over Marxists has, on the whole, been
implicit and in terms of a following amongst Marxist theorists at
the present time, he is very much in second place to Althusser, one
of the few to have developed a serious critique of his position. Over
the years he has collected a few writers around him who have
intelligently expounded and used his ideas, Simone de Beauvoir,
André Gorz and Francis Jeanson most notably but, with the possible
exception of the first, no one has developed his work in any
fundamental way. The vast amount of literature that has appeared
around his work has by and large been in inverse proportion to the
number of serious attempts to come to grips with his thought. In
this country, his greatest influence has probably been through the
'existential psychoanalysis' developed in the work of R. D. Laing
and David Cooper, but this has tended to emphasise only certain

aspects of his thought; his Marxism in particular has by no means been explored in depth by these writers.[1]

III. Sartre and sociology

The case for looking at Sartre should now be more apparent. The directly opposing emphases of sociology and existentialism, the former on the objective, on what can be scientifically known, the latter on what cannot be scientifically known, make each a topic for investigation by the other, and on a general level, the importance for existentialism of the writer's own experience indicates that we might find crucial lessons for what has become known as 'reflexive sociology'.[2] But the term 'existentialism' covers a vast range of writers whose differences are as important as their similarities and the major attempt to date by a sociologist to come to grips with existentialism – that of Tiryakian (1962) – has been very general indeed. Of all the 'existentialists' it is perhaps Sartre more than any other who stands out as being relevant to sociology. His early work is self-evidently of some concern to the sociology of interpersonal relationships that has developed so rapidly over recent years, and his later work deals with the type of social formations that have been the province of traditional sociology; his later work is also an attempt to 'found' Marxism, to provide Marxist concepts with the roots that have been lacking hitherto, and insofar as he succeeds Sartre offers us a Marxism which is open and developing, which can take account of the work of non-Marxists and which promises a compensation for sociology's general neglect of Marx. Furthermore it should by now be clear that the experience of which Sartre is trying to make sense is the experience of most of Europe over the past half century; as such, what he has to say is relevant to any attempt, whatever its nature, to understand the modern world, and that sociology makes this attempt – at least on occasions – can hardly be disputed.

Despite this, Sartre has received scant attention from sociologists – he might be mentioned in passing as the source of an odd idea[3]

[1] On existential psychoanalysis, see Laing (1967; 1971a; 1971b); Laing and Cooper's (1964) summary of the *Critique* bears the doubtful distinction of being at least as difficult to read in English as the French original. It is in this work that their reluctance to deal with Sartre's Marxism is most apparent.

[2] 'Reflexive sociology' is by no means a clear term; it is used here in Gouldner's (1971) sense of a sociology that is conscious of its own 'domain assumptions' – or rather those of the sociologist in question. The relationship between the sociologist, his values and personal experiences and his work will be a major theme of this study.

[3] Jack Douglas (1971) is particularly guilty; Friedrichs (1970) gives Sartre slightly more attention, but in both cases their source seems to be

but little more; even Tiryakian concentrates on only one section of *Being and Nothingness* – that on being-for-others – which cannot properly be understood in isolation. A writer of Sartre's complexity needs to be taken as a whole, before we can draw any conclusions about his relevance to sociology or the relationship between his type of philosophy and sociology. Our discussion, then, will be at least initially on the 'philosophical' or 'theoretical' level, and one aim will be to develop a conception of 'theory' different to that usually employed in sociology. This will be done not by comparing Sartre with the major sociological theorists – which would be a mammoth task – but rather by investigating the implications of his work for sociological practice. To this end several existing empirical studies will be re-analysed from a 'Sartrian' position and this by itself should convey a good idea of his originality.

The empirical studies that will be re-analysed – Goffman's *Asylums* (1968a), some studies by Garfinkel and Gouldner's *Patterns of Industrial Bureaucracy* (1954a) and *Wildcat Strike* (1954b) – have been chosen because they are fairly well known and in the first two cases at any rate represent what appear to be increasingly popular approaches in sociology. The criticisms that we make of them are by no means applicable across the board to all sociological research and theory, but at the same time it is not possible to fit Sartre into any one existing sociological approach; it will become apparent that he cuts across all of them. It is however possible, as a crude, preliminary 'situating', to envisage him as developing a very sophisticated Weberian position which can be used as an underpinning for a Marxist structural analysis, attempting to combine a methodological individualism and a methodological holism in a unified theory. Insofar as much of the history of sociology can be seen in terms of a division between these two approaches, Sartre's relevance is self-evident.

iv. The plan

The study will be divided into two parts, the first concentrating on *Being and Nothingness*, the second on the *Critique*, in both cases presenting an exposition of Sartre's work and following it up with the re-analysis of an empirical study. The first half is concerned primarily with showing the relevance of Sartre's phenomenology

(*n 3 continued*)
Desan's (1966) commentary rather than Sartre's original. Alfred Adler's article (1950) suggesting the 'operationalisation' of some of Sartre's concepts contains a fundamental misunderstanding that should become apparent as the study continues.

and ontology to sociological studies of the self and interpersonal interaction. A linking chapter (5) will attempt to look at the relationship between Sartre's early and later work in more detail and it is here that the nature of 'theory' will come to the fore; the second part will be concerned primarily with ways of conceptualising 'social structures' and the structures of groups and group actions, the relationship between the society as a whole and individuals and groups within it. Throughout both parts there will be an ongoing attempt to look at the organisation and practice of sociology itself in the light of Sartre's work and to develop a solid theoretical base for a reflexive sociology. The conclusion will attempt to bring together the diverse strands of the arguments in the body of the book.

Sartre's work is by no means easy to grasp and given the limitations of space and time, it is not possible to start the discussion from first principles; there are innumerable commentaries that do so and the reader will be referred to these as the occasion arises. There is no such thing as a 'simple' way of expounding Sartre's work. His central concern is to indicate the vast complexity of what he is talking about and many of his ideas undergo a continuous development – in some ways the earlier work only falls into place in the light of the later work. In this sense, the study should be read as a whole rather than as a collection of parts.

2

Consciousness

Being and Nothingness is a difficult book, very far from what is usually regarded as sociology; we will attempt to present it here in such a way that the sociologist may begin to draw lessons from it, concentrating on its central conceptions. There are a host of expositions of the work of varying degrees of quality and the reader will be referred to these on less important or more philosophically esoteric issues.[1]

Beginning with the 'ontological proof' which provides us with a means of grasping Sartre's methods, we will go on to discuss his 'categories of being' – the For-itself, the In-itself and Being-for Others, and the notions of the situation and the project. In the process we will steadily draw nearer to terrain more familiar to sociologists, and there will be an ongoing attempt to draw out the sociological consequences of the work, finally bringing these together in the concluding section in such a way that we can move forward.

1. The ontological proof

Sartre's debt to Husserl is undeniable, and although a full exploration of their relationship is not possible here, one or two brief comments are necessary if we are to understand Sartre's starting point.[2] There are two notions of Husserl's that are important in this context: that of the *intentionality* of consciousness, and the phenomenological *reduction*.

Husserl aimed to develop a rigorous inductive philosophy that would provide the foundations for the sciences, that would seek the

---

[1] Perhaps one of the best, in that it manages to summarise Sartre fairly intelligibly without sacrificing too much complexity, is Desan (1954). The organisation of the first two sections of this chapter was suggested by Desan's commentary.

[2] For a discussion of Sartre's relationship to Husserl, see Spiegelberg 1960; Natanson (1951a) argues that Sartre's phenomenology owes more to Hegel than to Husserl; his debt to the latter – particularly in the ontological proof – cannot, however, be doubted.

roots of knowledge in the way in which phenomena appear to consciousness. Consciousness is intentional in the sense that it is always directed towards something, it is always consciousness *of*; to an extent of course this is self-evident: to be conscious of nothing is to be unconscious. All phenomena that appear to consciousness are given an equal priority: dreams and imaginary objects are on a par with 'real' objects. This suspension of assumptions about the reality or otherwise of phenomena is what is known as the 'reduction'. Amongst the objects that appear to consciousness and therefore fall within the reduction is the ego – the 'I' with a specific structure, history and position in the world; what is left after the reduction is the 'transcendental ego', crudely a sort of minimal ego, which is the source of the unity of my past and present thoughts and which organises my world, constituting through its activity the objects of consciousness, including the empirical ego.[1]

Sartre introduced the work of Husserl to French philosophy, applying and modifying the latter's ideas in several works published before *Being and Nothingness*.[2] His two major modifications were the elimination of the transcendental ego, leaving consciousness 'empty' and thoroughly impersonal, and secondly a move from phenomenological description of the way in which phenomena appear to consciousness to ontological conclusions, statements about the nature of Being. These statements are however very different from everyday assumptions about reality or unreality that Husserl placed in suspension; they are reached at the end of the phenomenological description rather than assumed at the start.

The ontological proof (1957a: ix–xii) starts from the point that all consciousness is consciousness *of* something. If this is the case, then consciousness can either be constitutive of that of which it is conscious (as Husserl at least implied) or it must be facing a transcendent Being. If the first alternative is correct, then that being of which consciousness is conscious must be consciousness itself, i.e. it can have no existence apart from consciousness and is therefore nothing. However, consciousness cannot be consciousness of nothing and the first alternative cannot be the correct one. Con-

---

[1] For an elaboration of the idea of intentionality, see Spiegelberg 1960; for a straightforward discussion of the transcendental ego, see Warnock 1970.

[2] Sartre is generally regarded as having introduced Husserl to France; see in particular his work on the imagination (1949b, 1962c), the emotions (1963e) and, in particular, *The Transcendence of the Ego* (1957b).

sciousness must be opposed to a transcendent Being of which it is conscious: the 'For-itself' is opposed to the 'In-itself'.[1]

Most of *Being and Nothingness* is devoted to an exploration of the relationship between consciousness and this transcendent Being by means of the method used to arrive at the above conclusions: phenomenological description. The actions of consciousness are described and the question asked: 'what must consciousness be for such action to be possible?'. We shall see that Sartre does not attempt to describe all acts of consciousness and his examples are certainly selective but the selectivity does not matter; the important points are: is the action possible? if it is possible, what does it tell us about the nature of consciousness?

II. The for-itself and the in-itself

Our initial concern will be with consciousness, the For-itself. The most important act of consciousness, the one that leads us directly to the heart of its structure, is *negation*, the ability to say no.[2] Negation is present in any act of consciousness: If I am conscious of a cup on the table in front of me, then there are three negations or 'nihilations' (néantisations) involved. First, my consciousness posits itself as *not being* the cup or the table; secondly it posits the cup and the table as *not being* the rest of the world; thirdly it posits the cup as *not being* the table. The 'nihilation' might, in terms of Gestalt psychology, be expressed in terms of figure and ground: the perception of the figure involves the nihilation of the ground. The importance of what might appear at first glance to be no more than an exercise in sophism will emerge as we continue and it will be seen, for example, that the first nihilation in particular is of fundamental importance to any sociological conception of 'the self'.

It is consciousness itself which introduces the possibility of negation into the world. Matter – Being-In-Itself – does not become nothing, it only undergoes structural changes and modifications. It

[1] R. E. Butts (1958) claims to have found a logical fallacy in the proof insofar as Sartre excludes (*a priori*) the possibility that consciousness can be conscious of itself; Sartre, however, avoids this criticism by arguing for the primacy of the pre-reflective cogito (1957a: l–lvi). A frequent criticism of Sartre is that he creates too wide a gap between consciousness and Being, but it will become apparent later that they are inextricably involved with each other. See in particular Ames (1950) and Natanson's reply (1951b). This issue was a prominent feature in Sartre's later dispute with Merleau-Ponty.

[2] Kenneth Burke (1966) includes the ability to say 'No' as a basic element in his 'definition of man', but for him it remains a property peculiar to symbolic systems, with no reference to consciousness. He seems to follow closely the approach of Bergson whom Sartre criticises in his first chapter.

is only consciousness which can differentiate between the different structures of matter and say that there is 'nothing there' and it does so through a series of nihilations. The possibility of asking questions which have a negative answer is of a fundamental importance since it means that consciousness is able to dissociate itself from any mechanical chain of causality: it is capable of imagining a situation which *is not yet* the case and which, because a question is asked about it, might not become the case.

The answer to the question 'what is consciousness', then, is that it is defined by a negation: 'it is what it is not', i.e. it is not what it is consciousness *of*. In the sense that it is consciousness of a transcendent being, then 'it is not what it is': my consciousness of the cup is not the cup but neither is it a 'pure' consciousness, independent of the cup. It is in Sartre's words, a nothingness, a 'hole' in Being which is no more than a relation to that Being, a nihilation of it.

It is this 'nothingness' that separates consciousness from the world, that consciousness *is* in the world, that constitutes human freedom. At the moment it is still an abstract freedom, and its full meaning will appear when we discuss the situation and the project; it is perhaps best understood as the ability of man to separate himself from the mechanical laws of matter in order to question them, to find out what they are, and we can illustrate this by means of an argument which could be used against Sartre.

It might be argued that what Sartre calls our freedom is in fact an incomplete knowledge of what determines our behaviour and at some stage in the future we might discover that our behaviour is determined to the last detail by external or even 'internal' forces such as the structure of the brain and the organism, etc. This very argument, however, is an example of freedom in the sense that Sartre uses the word: it nihilates the present state of what we call 'knowledge', where the freedom/determinism argument is unsettled and posits a state in which it is settled; it then nihilates the future state as not yet existing. Using a much simpler example, that of imagining an individual in a room, Sartre (1957a: 27) describes the freedom implied in such an act of consciousness:

If in terms of my perceptions of the room, I conceive of the former inhabitant who is no longer in the room, I am of necessity forced to produce an act of thought which no prior state can determine nor motivate, in short, to effect in myself a break with being.

If my image of the prior inhabitant were determined then:

Inasmuch as my present state would be a prolongation of my prior state, every opening by which negation could slip through would be completely blocked.

But we have seen that the act of imagining the prior inhabitant, or of positing a future, and different state of knowledge, involves an act of negation. To say that Sartre's argument might, at some time, be open to a scientific proof of its rightness or wrongness is in fact itself a proof that his argument is correct. This raises the problem of how we are to judge his arguments, and we find the answer in the other actions from which he derives his idea of freedom.

We do not recognise our freedom only through a phenomenological description of the actions of our consciousness but we have an immediate intuition of it in various forms of anguish. The experience of vertigo provides a good example. This is not simply a fear of falling: fear has an object out in the world, an object that threatens me. Vertigo however involves no threatening object, it is a fear that *I* will fall, and this in turn involves a recognition of falling as one of my possibilities, a possible free choice. Vertigo does not even involve a danger of falling, rather it simply requires that I be in a high place and recognise that I could make myself fall.

It is in this argument that we can recognise the meaning of Tiryakian's comments about the confusion of meaningfulness and logic. The adequacy of Sartre's arguments refers us firstly to our own experience: it depends on their ability to enable us to understand our own experience. This is as true for the argument about negation as it is for the description of vertigo. The logical contradictions, if there are·any, only become important as faults if they do not reflect contradictions in experience. The logic involved here is a logic of experience, what we will see later as a 'dialectical logic'. In relation to sociology, it will become important when we go on to discuss the nature of theory and the requirements of a reflexive sociology.

We will return to freedom later;[1] we can now look in more detail

---

[1] See section IV of this chapter; when we come to the 'situation' and the 'project' we will see that the idea of freedom becomes more complex. Its 'ideological' content perhaps consists in a simple transference of this absolute 'ontological freedom' to a practical level; as Sartre seems to do, for instance, in *The Flies* (1962b) and to a lesser extent in *Bariona* (In Rybalka & Contat 1970). An important idea here, for Sartre's ethics but not for this exposition, is that of 'bad faith': at one and the same time, consciousness recognises its freedom and tries to deny it by identifying with its being-for-others or its facticity (see below). It is perhaps in contrast to bad faith that 'authenticity' and 'commitment' can be best understood. See in particular his play *Lucifer and the Lord* (1965a).

at the structure of the For-itself. The first feature that we can note is that it is *impersonal*. Sartre's main systematic criticism of Husserl concerned the transcendental ego for which, he argues, there is no need. We have seen that consciousness is always conscious *of* something; what gives a unity to its activities is not an abstractly posited 'transcendental ego' but firstly the objects – the transcendent being – of which it is conscious and secondly what Sartre calls a 'transversal intentionality', the fact that previous acts of consciousness can become objects for present acts of consciousness (Sartre 1957b). There is nothing 'in' consciousness, it is a simple awareness of, a relationship to, Being. It does not 'constitute' its objects but recognises itself in relationship to them, and, of course, there are different sorts of relationships to Being. What we usually call an 'emotion', for example, is an immediate relationship to Being, a consciousness of the world which attempts to change it magically.[1]

Consciousness, then, is not a container which is empty at first and fills up in the course of experience, nor does it contain from the start any content that is responsible for its activities. The importance of this will emerge when we come to discuss sociological concepts of the 'self' and of language in the next chapters. Consciousness is a *lack* of Being and a relationship to Being and at the same time a desire *for* Being. It seeks to become Being, in other words to give itself its own justification; it seeks what we will refer to from now on, in Sartre's terms, as 'value'. This 'value' is the original source of all other values, which are created in the way in which the original value is sought.[2]

In the same way that the For-itself introduces nothingness and value into the world, it also introduces *time*. Being, the In-itself, is simply there, complete with no future and no past, no subdivisions and no distinctions. The For-itself *is* nothing, it is a nihilation of Being and a pursuit of value. The past is the relationship to Being that the For-itself was, a relationship which as soon as it is grasped by a 'present' act of consciousness, takes on a being as an object, it falls into the In-itself. There is no present as such (although as we will see there is such a thing as an instant) rather the For-itself

[1] See *A Sketch for a Theory of the Emotions*. In general, Sartre shows a distinct rationalist bias when he discusses the emotions, regarding them as inferior to a rational consciousness. Anders-Stern (1950) takes him to task for this, arguing that an emotional consciousness as a 'magical' attempt to change the world, may sometimes succeed. In this connection, see also R. D. Laing (1967).

[2] The being that the For-itself seeks is a Being-in-itself-for-itself, or God, a being which gives itself its own justification for existing. The For-itself as such is contingent, and this should become clearer later. The flight towards value is in fact the 'project'.

is simply a flight from the previous relationship towards 'value'. 'Value', of course, is never achieved, the For-itself is a perpetual flight. It is this flight which accounts for the unity of time, nothing else can link together apparently disparate 'moments'. The future is the sum total of possibilities which the For-itself might become in its pursuit of value, and it reaches back into the 'present' as the condition of action, and into the past, to which it gives a meaning. What this means fundamentally is that to understand an individual's 'present' action, we must understand his future possibilities (1957a: 109ff.; 1955: 79–87).

Sartre concludes his description of the For-itself by elaborating the relationship between the reflective and pre-reflective consciousness, and this throws some further light on the above discussions. The pre-reflective consciousness is simple consciousness *of* something, the reflective consciousness is consciousness of being conscious of something; the whole argument has been, of necessity, on the reflective level since words, 'logic' etc are a means of reflection; we cannot argue on a pre-reflective level. What we have been describing however is the pre-reflective relationship of the For-itself to Being; nihilation, the flight towards value are all pre-reflective relationships, in which consciousness, as it were, loses itself in its object (1957a: 150ff.).

Sartre likens the relationship between the two to two mirrors perpetually reflecting each other. There are two sorts of possible reflection: pure and impure. Pure reflection grasps the pre-reflective consciousness as a simple flight towards Being and value, as a translucent relationship to the world. Impure reflection hypostatises the flight of the pre-reflective consciousness as 'character traits', as a 'personality'. This is one way in which consciousness may attempt to achieve value: by giving its flight an existence in substantive qualities. This is a false solution and one which is half-way to a very important but rather different false solution that we will be looking at soon: the attempt to find my being in the eyes of others.

The difference between pure and impure reflection is akin to the difference between phenomenological description and introspection. The former is a disciplined investigation of consciousness which brackets off assumptions about reality; the latter is an assumption about reality. Any criticism of Sartre's 'subjectivity' needs to take account of this and his arguments cannot legitimately be contested in terms usually used when we talk about or try to exercise 'introspection'. Again the importance of this for any discussion of the self will become apparent.

We have already indicated the nature of the In-itself, of Being, and there is little more that need be added here. It is sufficient to say that it simply *is*; it is brute, massive, undifferentiated being. Divisions within it in terms of space, time, qualities, potentialities etc. come to it through the For-itself – we have already examined the way in which time is introduced and the other qualities appear in the same way, through the pursuit of value. The essential bridge between the For-itself and the In-itself is 'knowledge'. Sartre uses the term to express the pre-reflective awareness that 'there is Being', the nihilation that we described earlier, the awareness that Being is 'not me'. This is the only certain knowledge that is possible and its consequences will be further explored in Chapter 5. For the moment it is important to note that it is a very different knowledge to that usually considered in epistemological studies. The latter is reflective, expressed in concepts, a matter for thought. Pre-reflective knowledge is prior to words, it is an awareness that involves our very certainty of being alive, of existing.[1]

The inadequacies in the presentation of these ideas and the restrictions of space should not be allowed to obscure the fact that they emerge in the course of a rigorous discussion and argument based on the phenomenological method. They represent, perhaps, the farthest point from conventional sociology that we will reach in this study, and although we have tried to indicate the way in which they are important for sociology, this will only become fully apparent over the next sections and chapters.

III. Being-for-others

i

Being-for-others, as a third type of being different from the In-itself and the For-itself, is revealed through an immediate intuition, that of shame.[2] Shame is a way of being conscious of myself in the world. It is pre-reflective but subject to reflection: I can be conscious of my consciousness (of) shame, and it is intentional, but the object

---

[1] We have seen that there can be various ways in which the For-itself is present to the In-itself: it is the nihilation of being, the revelation of being, the desire for being etc. Desan (op. cit. p. 50) provides a valuable chart showing the possibilities. In each case, however, it is knowledge which unites the two.

[2] Natanson (1951a) and Marcuse (1947) both argue that at this point Sartre drops phenomenology for psychology, but as we will see the discussion continues in the terms developed in the earlier phenomenological description and is basically a description of the Other as he appears to my consciousness. It is interesting that Natanson (1970) some twenty years after his original criticism, adopts Sartre's argument. This latter work contains an excellent exposit ion of the phenomenological method.

to which it is directed is myself, a particular 'version' of myself – that version which appears to others as 'the real me' my Being-for-others. Shame is inconceivable without the existence of other consciousnesses, yet the problem of their existence Sartre argues (1957a: 221ff.) is usually approached as if our first apprehension of the Other were the perception of his body, i.e. the Other-as-object. If this were so, however, the existence of another consciousness similar to my own would always remain on the level of probability, there is nothing in the simple perception of the body that signifies consciousness. Yet nobody adheres to solipsism as anything more than an intellectual sophistry. We are all, in our everyday activities, certain of the existence of other consciousnesses.

We have discovered our intuition of the Other's existence in shame. More generally we discover it in his *look*. The look has nothing to do with the Other's eyes: '. . . my apprehension of a look turned towards me appears on the ground of the destruction of the eyes which "look at me"' (1957a: 258).[1] It transforms by Being-for-myself into my Being-an-object-for-the-Other. My Being-for-the-Other is in the form of the In-itself: it is there, I have not created it, it is the product of the freedom of the Other and I have to assume it. The appearance of the Other is the appearance of a new centre around which the world is organised and in this world I take on an outside, I acquire a 'nature'. My flight towards the future, my possibilities, which for me are open, become, in the eyes of the Other, probabilities, a matter of statistics. By myself, my reflective consciousness can never hypostatise the pre-reflective consciousness since because of the nature of the latter, there is always some aspect of my 'character' that escapes me. The intervention of the Other is necessary for me to grasp myself finally as an object,[2] although as we shall see, this, too, is eventually a failure.

Face to face with the Other, there are two alternatives, each based on the internal nihilation described above (I am *not* the table):

Either I make myself not-be a certain being, and then he is an object for me and I lose my object-ness for him; in this case, the Other ceases to be the Other-Me – that is, the subject who makes me be an object by refusing to be me. Or else this being is indeed the Other and makes himself not-be me, in which case I become an object for him and he loses his own object-ness. Thus originally, the Other is Not-Me-not-object (1957a: 285).

[1] Sartre has sketched the beginnings of a 'phenomenology of the face'. See 'Visages' (in Rybalka & Contat: 1970).
[2] This is one form of 'bad faith'. Thus, in *Roads to Freedom*, Daniel, seeking to *be* a paederast and thus to avoid the responsibility of choosing to be one, eventually finds comfort in the eyes of God. God, of course, is the Other *par excellence*.

If, however, I attempt to grasp myself as an object-for-the-Other and nothing else, then I must transform the Other himself into an object. If he remains a free subject then he must change his view of me, my being is not safe in his hands. Immediately I transform him into an object, however, I rediscover myself as subject and myself-for-the-Other becomes no more than one of his subjective impressions. I have stopped assenting to his view of me. Thus there is a possibility of a perpetual conflict arising between myself and the Other, the perpetual transformation of myself and the Other into subject and object by each of us.[1]

This permanent possibility of conflict is of self-evident importance for a sociology of interaction and for the relationship between the sociologist and those he studies, and it will become a major theme throughout what follows. We will explore the self-Other relationship again later, but before we can continue we must look at some other implications and extend some of those already indicated.[2]

ii

The essential differences between by Being-for-myself and my Being-for-others lies in the future. Consciousness is a relationship to Being and a pursuit of value, but this is still an abstract description. It must pursue Being in a particular and specific way (or ways) and it is this particular pursuit of value which is the project. No project is determined; as we have seen consciousness is a freedom, a nothingness in the midst of Being. It must therefore choose its project, the particular way it will seek value, from amongst the choices offered to it by the world.[3] In the course of this project – the fundamental project – other more immediate choices will

---

[1] It is at this point that Sartre comes closest to Hegel, with the important difference that Sartre, at this stage, offers no eventual synthesis. For a good discussion of his relationship to Hegel, see George Kline in Lee and Mandelbaum (1967).
For excellent literary representations of what Sartre is talking about here, see Sartre (1958) and Violette Leduc (1968), particularly the relationship between Thérèse and Marc.

[2] This type of conflict is strangely often overlooked by sociologists. G. H. Mead (1952) whose 'I/Me' dichotomy bears a superficial similarity to Sartre, does not consider it. His 'Me' is very close to Sartre's 'Being-for-Others' with the fundamental difference that for Mead the intervention of the Other is not necessary. I realise myself-as-object initially through my physical contact with the world. Sartre's position on this will emerge shortly.

[3] This will become clearer in Section IV of this chapter. Choice is both contingent in that it is eventually undetermined, and necessary in that the nature of the For-itself as nothingness and flight means that it cannot choose not to choose.

present themselves, some of an everyday nature, some which come at what may be called 'crises' in my life trajectory. It is in this second case that the possibility of changing my 'fundamental project' presents itself. In both cases, however, at the time of choice, these possibilities present themselves to me as open: I can choose any one of them and although there are reasons for choosing this one rather than that one and vice versa, I can choose between the reasons as well. This is an everyday experience of choice which may come with a greater or lesser intensity and importance for the future.

For the Other for whom I am an object, however, these possibilities become probabilities. I become a physical object – a body – with a set of properties which include a 'character', a tendency to act in certain ways, a particular view of the world and a future which although it may not be fixed, may be predicted in what is essentially a mathematical way. In this sense, my flight towards value becomes objectified in, or rather merged with, the In-itself. Even if the Other envisages the 'chance' that I may change in some fundamental way, or admits my 'unpredictability', it still remains for him a probability or a trait of my 'character' which the Other grants me, which I do not produce or experience myself, except insofar as I make myself a particular kind of object for him.

It is possible now to attempt to describe in general terms the position of the sociologist, who presents us with an ideal example of the Other as not-me-not-object, as the one who looks. In various ways, the sociologist carrying out a study is treating those he studies as particular types of object. He looks for certain qualities 'possessed' by whoever it is he is studying – a particular view of society, of work, aspects of behaviour etc.; in some cases, the aim may actually be a statistical correlation for purposes of prediction, but in the next two chapters we will look at sociological studies which are at the opposite extreme to statistical studies and we will see that there too, those studied are seen as objects, albeit very complex ones. It is important to remember that my Being-for-myself cannot be grasped by myself, it is a nothingness, and it does not fill up with something as a result of Being-for-Others. The 'outside' that I receive through the Other only appears solid through its free assumption by myself. And this 'solidarity' is frail: as soon as I try to confirm it, it disappears. This will have obvious consequences for any conclusions reached by the sociologist or any other social scientist.[1]

The second implication that we can develop here has implications

[1] Much of Laing's work, already referred to, is based on the self-Other dialectic.

for our earlier discussion of the For-itself; it has to do with the way in which the body is experienced. Consciousness is neither founded (caused) by the In-itself, nor is it its own foundation; we have seen rather that it is the constant attempt to become its own foundation. At the same time, its necessity, the fact that it is a point of view on the world, means that it must be situated in the midst of the world, and this situation is provided by the body. We are, then, not talking about 'consciousness in general' in a Hegelian way, but of specific consciousnesses and I do not have access to any 'consciousness in general', only, directly and in its full complexity, to my consciousness. Thus when we argued earlier that Sartre's work was to be judged by the illumination that it shed on the reader's own experience, this was not an unfounded observation: the only criteria that is available to him is his own experience.

The 'situating' of the For-itself in a body (which Sartre calls its 'facticity') has consequences for the way in which the body is experienced. This particular part of Sartre's work (1957a: 303ff.) will not be referred to very often in what follows but self-evidently it would be relevant to any study of social action directly concerned with the body – sexual activity, for example.

Whatever instruments I may use on the world around me, they all refer to a 'key' instrument which is my body, but I never actually experience my body as an instrument. I see the Other's body as his instrument and as an object and through him I experience my body as an object. This, if you like, is my 'normal' reflective knowledge of the body – a knowledge fundamentally similar to that of the doctor who treats me. But I also experience my body in a different way. When I write, I use my pen as an instrument but I am not conscious of using my hand as an instrument on the pen; in Sartre's words 'I am my hand'. On the pre-reflective level, I am only conscious (of) the world around me and I *live* my body as I live my relationship to the world. I am typing in the half light, during a power cut. I am aware of my typewriter in front of me, and of the words I am putting on paper, beyond that of my work as a whole; on the horizon of my awareness there is a discomfort, a floating 'unease' which, looking up and breaking off writing, I suddenly discover to be a pain in my eyes. I live the pain as I live my hands when I am typing; the pain becomes attached to my eyes, and I see myself as manipulating my hands only on reflection, when I grasp my body as an object for myself.

My body, then, is not a screen between myself and the world nor a tool I use on the world; it is, rather, the expression of the individuality and the contingency of the For-itself in its relation to the world. At the same time the Other can only grasp what I am, what I am doing through the position of my body as an object in the world and its relationship to the world.

iii

It is now possible to give a brief outline of a more complex self–Other dialectic; Sartre discerns two contradictory basic attitudes to the Other (361ff.) that may lead to each other and in this sense we are perhaps describing a circle rather than a dialectic: there is no synthesis. The essential contradiction in each attitude is that between my grasp of myself as subject and my grasp of myself as object: the more I try to establish myself as an object in the eyes of the other the more I am thrown back on my own subjectivity; the more I try to transform the other into an object, the more he reveals his subjectivity.

The first attitude towards the Other is *love*: I posit myself as a privileged object for the beloved, one which is the whole world for him, in an attempt to seduce his freedom. I demand that he loves me, but also that he loves me freely, not because I demand it. But if I am successful, then he must experience me as the subject for whom he is the privileged object: I am thrown back on my own subjectivity. As a result I try to transform myself into a simple object for the beloved: love becomes masochism, but the more I try to suppress my subjectivity the more I must become aware of its existence.

The failure of love may lead to the adoption of the second attitude, although each is a fundamental reaction to the Other's existence. The second reaction is *indifference*: I refuse to recognise the transcendence of the Other's subjectivity and build up my subjectivity on that refusal.[1] I remain within my subjectivity with no way of seeing myself-as-object, but the danger of being transformed into an object for the Other haunts me as a vague and uncertain possibility; *sexual desire* may be seen as a half-blind attempt to capture the Other's freedom – the danger that I refuse to recognise – by incarnating it in his flesh. But as soon as I possess that flesh, it becomes one instrument amongst others and again I am thrown back on my own subjectivity. This is the origin of *Sadism* – an attempt to trap the Other's freedom in his body by forcing him to manifest his humiliation, to display his cowed freedom. But

---

[1] 'This state of *blindness* can be maintained for a long time, as long as my fundamental bad faith desires . . . there are men who die without ever having suspected – save for brief and terrifying moments of illumination – what the Other is' (p. 381).

the moment of submission is decided by the Other, it is not a determined result of my torture: his very humiliation is an exercise of his freedom.[1]

The final refuge from this circle is *hate*: the recognition of the Other's freedom for what it is and the desire to destroy it; I seek his death. Yet this, too, fails: I might destroy his existence but I cannot alter the fact that he has existed. In his earlier work, Sartre does not discuss whether it is possible to break out of these circles,[2] confining himself to a brief discussion of the 'Us-object' and 'We-subject'. The former is produced as the result of myself and the Other coming under the gaze of a third and the latter is a 'psychological construct' on the basis of the 'Us-object' but it is not a fundamental structure of the For-itself. In the '*Critique*' we will see that he roots the conflict we have just described in material conditions and proposes 'reciprocity' as a fundamental human relationship. His failure to take account of such a relationship in *Being and Nothingness* may be seen as one of the 'ideological' failings of the work, since there is nothing in it that is incompatible with his analysis of consciousness.

These descriptions are useful in several ways. Firstly they are excellent examples of Sartre's type of phenomenological description. It must be emphasised that the names that he gives the relationships are only of marginal importance – 'love' or 'infatuation', it doesn't matter. Nor is he saying that they encapsulate the whole of human experience. Rather he argues that such relationships do exist, that their structures are experienced, under whatever name (and this again refers us to the readers' experience) and that they comprise all (or most, in view of his omission of reciprocity) that can be said about human relationships on an *a priori* level, in terms of the categories developed as a result of the previous descriptions of the In-itself and For-itself and Being-for-others.

In the second place they convey a notion of the transformations of, and the complexity in, the structures of interpersonal relation-

[1] As is often the case, this point is illustrated dramatically in Sartre's fiction in a somewhat more illuminating way than in his philosophy. See in particular the short story 'Erostratus' (1960b) and the play *Men Without Shadows* (1962d).

[2] For a discussion of the same problem in a different philosophical context but one which throws light on this discussion, see Marcuse's (1968) critique of Norman O. Brown. In a footnote (1957a, p. 412) Sartre says that 'the possibility of an ethics of deliverance and salvation' is not excluded but can only be achieved by a 'radical conversion'. It is, presumably, this conversion that is executed in the *Critique* but as we shall see it involves abandoning ethics altogether (but not as Mary Warnock (1970) claims the whole of his earlier analysis).

ships that the sociologist can come across in his work, and offer an alternative to the conventional conceptualisation of interpersonal relationships as a matter of characters, 'definitions of the other' etc.

Thirdly they enable us to extend, albeit in a fairly limited way, what we said earlier about the position of the sociologist as the one who looks, who grasps those he studies as some kind of object. It can now be seen that the attitude is very close to what Sartre calls indifference, but as such it takes on a relativity – transformations are possible. For obvious reasons it is unlikely (although not out of the question) that it will break down into sexual desire, but it might in individual cases, be possible to identify a 'sociological sadism' or a 'sociological masochism' or even a 'sociological love'. The nature of such relationships could, however, only be determined in a study of an individual sociologist and that is beyond the scope of the present work. More importantly, implicit in the possibility of a transformation, is the possibility that those studied might 'look back', reject the sociologist, transform him into an object. In certain areas – the sociology of race relations, and of development – this may be seen to be happening.[1]

iv. The situation and the project

We can now look at the freedom of the For-itself in more detail. We have seen that it is a nothingness, free from outside determination and a flight into the future, towards value, an ideal Being. In its very nature then, it is a nihilation of what is (Being) and the positing of a future situation which is not yet (value), in other words it is *action* – an attempt to change the world. We have also seen that it is a particular point of view on the world, that it is individualised and situated in its facticity (the body) and that it pursues a specific flight towards value, that it tries to found its being in a specific way, and this is its fundamental project, in the light of which the world is revealed to it:

It is in the light of the project that we can understand causes and motives. Causes are usually seen as being in some way 'objective', as laying outside and 'behind' the action, pushing it forward. It is true, argues Sartre, that they are objective in the sense that they lie outside of consciousness and in the world, but:

. . . the world gives counsel only if one questions it, and one can question it only for a well determined end. Therefore the cause, far from determining the action, appears only in and through the project of an action. (1957a: 448)

[1] For a good articulated expression of this transformation covering both of the fields mentioned, see Frantz Fanon: *A Dying Colonialism* (1970).

Motives, on the other hand, lay within consciousness and the project – in a sense they are the project. A will to power, for example, or a desire for wealth are ways of aiming at a possession of Being, at value. It is in the light of the motives that causes are discovered. Thus, to use Sartre's example, Clovis' conversion to Roman Catholicism finds its cause in the (objective) power of the Catholic Church in Gaul and in its opposition to Arianism. But this state of affairs only becomes a cause of his conversion in the light of his project to rule Gaul. Other projects would reveal other causes.

The project is a unity of 'causes', 'motives' and 'ends': it is the flight of the For-itself and it cannot be 'known' in the way in which the world outside of consciousness may be known, in terms of scientific concepts and laws; it can only be described: understood. To say that the choice of the fundamental project is a free choice is not to say that it is gratuitious or capricious; the For-itself *has* to choose, but it does not *have* to choose this or that fundamental project: its choices are set out for it by the world around it, sometimes, as in the case of Genet, in a very limited way indeed;[1] the fundamental project is 'irrational' in the sense that it is not externally 'caused' but it is intelligible in the sense that we can understand and discover it through the surrounding world. It must be emphasised that we are talking about a *pre-reflective* choice and not a 'rational' reflective choice, and that it is not a random whim or easily revocable. Using the words in a conventional, non-Sartrean way, it is 'a commitment of my whole being' – a commitment which I am not free to avoid but which I must make freely.

We understand the project in a double movement of progression and regression. We can understand an immediate action by reference to its end, the state of affairs that it is trying to bring about. The reference to the future is a fundamental difference between what Sartre calls 'existential psychoanalysis' and a Freudian psychoanalysis.[2] Then: '. . . by a regressive psychoanalysis one ascends

---

[1]   *Saint Genet* (1963d) is perhaps the best of Sartre's individual studies in
      which to see the ideas of *Being and Nothingness* in action, specifically
      the tracing of the fundamental project. Less successful is *Baudelaire*
      (1948b).
[2]   The central difference between Sartre's psychoanalysis and that of
      Freud lies in the concept of the unconscious – the 'censoring'
      mechanism which Freud sees as repressing or sublimating the drives of
      the 'id'. In Sartrean terms this would be some sort of strange object
      within consciousness, dividing it from itself, and in the light of the
      earlier arguments, this is inadmissible. Repression, Sartre sees as an act
      of bad faith.
      The progressive–regressive method will be seen to be fundamental in
      Sartre. Thomas Wilson (In Jack D. Douglas, 1971) describes a similar
      method of comprehending action when he is elaborating on Garfinkel,

back from the considered act to my ultimate possible; and by a synthetic progression one re-descends from this ultimate possible to the considered act and grasps its integration in the total form' (1957a: 460).

The 'ultimate possible' is of course the particular form of value that I am aiming at. The relationship between any particular choice and the ultimate possible is not determined: the former cannot be derived from the latter. The relationship is rather that of a part to a synthetic whole: neither can be fully understood without reference to the other; a number of apparently self-contradictory choices can only find their unity in the ultimate possible.

The original choice may change; it will still be a pursuit of value but the specific form of the union with Being that it seeks is changed. This is what in conventional terms would be called a 'conversion', a sudden and radical change in character; it is this possibility that is manifested most acutely in anguish. The past of the For-itself falls back into the In-itself, and is nihilated in the onward flight towards value, thus a radical divorce from the past is always a possibility. It is this occurrence that has given rise to the idea of an 'instant' – a moment of time which is a 'whole ' rather than a progression. There is no 'present' as such: the 'instant' occurs if the end of one project coincides with the beginning of another – it is bounded by the nothingness that follows the end of the former project and that which precedes the beginning of the later one.[1]

This, then, is the 'project': it is chosen in a context, it is selected from a field of possibles presented by the world. It is free but it is free 'in situation'. The situation is ambiguous: it is in part the brute In-itself in which the For-itself is situated in its facticity, of which it is a revelation and a nihilation. In part it is the In-itself which has been formed and given a meaning by others in the world; and in part it is the way in which the In-itself is revealed through the project of the For-itself. By situating the For-itself we move away

(*n 2 continued*)
but in this case the regressive movement is to an 'underlying pattern' of 'indexicality' and the progressive movement forward to what that underlying pattern would indicate to be the future course of the interaction. This approach is only possible with linguistic interaction however, and a critique of this limited use will be developed later. See below, Chapter 4.

[1] It could be argued that at least some hallucinatory drug experiences mark the end of one project and the beginning of another which aims more directly at an ideal being; its inevitable failure would help us to understand, for example, the observations on 'youth culture' made in a very different context by Hunter Thompson (Rolling Stone, 103, 2 March 1972).

from the ontological freedom that was the starting point of our analysis, towards its practical manifestations: '. . . the empirical and practical concept of freedom is wholly negative; it issues from the consideration of a situation and establishes that this situation *leaves me free* to pursue this or that end' (1957a: 486).

The situation comprises everything that surrounds the For-itself including the body, 'nature', the social structure, Others, etc. Sartre discusses several of these aspects in detail (489ff.) and these will illustrate the concept more clearly.

My *place* reveals the ambiguity common to all aspects of the situation. My original place in the world was both necessary – since I have to be born somewhere – and contingent, since I did not choose to be born there, I just found myself there. My present place is the result of my own free choice – whether I have stayed in the place in which I was born or moved, I have used it in order to achieve an end, I have lived it in a particular way. This is true even if I have never been aware of a possibility of moving: by living it I assume it and make myself responsible for it. On the other hand, however far I might have moved, I am constantly referred, when I ask why I am here, to the place where I was before, and so on back to my original place, the contingency of which I can never escape.

My *past* is rather different. We have seen that the past falls back into the In-itself in the course of the flight of the For-itself and that a radical break is possible. The past, unlike my place, is not contingent – it is the product of my past choices, but it is necessary in that it cannot now be changed. It is however the future, the flight of the For-itself, that gives the past its meaning, as something to be broken away from, to be identified with and honoured, something which is a stage on a consistent journey forward or something which is an aberration – 'not really me at all'. The meaning of the past is never fixed until death and even then it falls into the hands of others and their actions.

It is with the natural *environment* that the brute In-itself is most in evidence. It is *there*, revealed, but not created, by the For-itself in the course of its project; but it is revealed as being-there *in a particular way*. The For-itself endows the In-itself with a 'co-efficient of adversity' or a 'utilisable instrumentality'. Thus, for example, that mountain is only steep if I want to climb it or if climbing mountains is a possible project for human beings. In the same way, soil is only fertile if the growing of crops is a possibility.

As far as the sociologist is concerned, the most important aspects of the situation to be considered by Sartre are subsumed under the heading of 'My Fellow Men'. We have seen that there are Others in the world in to which we are born and we have an immediate intuition of their existence. One of the consequences of this is that I face in my situation instruments which already have a meaning endowed by Others with whom I have no contact. These meanings, far from being created in the course of my project, take on the nature of the In-itself and present themselves to me as 'there-to-be-assumed' by me if I am going to belong to any of the possible human collectivities.

Perhaps the most important of these techniques is language. Language as a structure is already given when I come into the world, yet each sentence I speak is an original creation, at least to the extent that each situation is original, and it is a free act of designation: I don't *have* to speak this particular sentence or speak it in this particular way, I don't even have to speak at all. When I do speak, it is my project which gives a unity and meaning to the string of words that come from my mouth. When I hear the Other speak, I grasp his 'meaning' through his project and his situation and vice versa; I only see it as a structure when I look at it in a particular way, when I see it as conforming to certain grammatical or other rules. It is there before me, and presents the world to me in terms belonging to Others, but in my project I make it mine and give it an original specificity of meaning. Insofar as I express my project (my 'being') through words, I make myself into words, dissolve myself in them; insofar as they belong to Others then I am alienated in them. We will come across this basic contradiction and alienation several times in the course of the study.[1]

Through my assumption of language, I make myself a member of 'humanity'. Humanity, Sartre argues, is not some pre-existing essence which finds its specific manifestation in each new individual, but, like language, it is sustained through its assumption in free individual projects. By assuming a particular language I make myself a member of a particular nation, by assuming language in an even more specific way – in the form of a dialect for instance – I make myself a member of more specific collectivities.

[1] In structuralist terms, my project defines the position of the words I speak on the systematic plane. Sartre has returned to language as a problem at several points of his career, usually under attack from the structuralists, and has steadily elaborated this analysis without abandoning its essentials. Particularly interesting elaborations are to be found in *Saint Genet* and 'L'Ecrivain et sa langue' (1972d); the latter will be referred to at several points. His most sophisticated treatment is to be found running through *L'Idiot de la famille*, an exposition of which is well beyond the scope of this study. For his earlier conceptions see in particular Iris Murdoch (1967). For a study of Sartre's own use of language, see Fredric Jameson (1961).

The techniques that are presented to me and which I assume are lived in much the same way as the body is lived, and, just as the body takes on an 'outside' and becomes an object through the existence of Others, so these techniques become structures through the existence of Others. Rules of grammar, for example, are only important because Others speak as well as myself; when I speak they become the inessential means to communication.

It is the Other who confers on me not only techniques such as language but more 'personal' meanings that are attached directly to me. I find myself, through my Being-for-Others, defined as a Jew, a black, a worker, a bourgeois, etc. These meanings represent true limits to my freedom, but they are limits presented by Other freedoms – only freedom can limit freedom. They are presented to me from the outside and I have to be them, to live them. But as we have seen, the For-itself cannot *be* anything. I am defined as a Jew and all that that entails, and I have to live my Jewishness as a project. I cannot escape the definition even by rejecting or ignoring it – if I were not a Jew I would not have to reject or ignore it. The Other imposes this limit on my freedom but I can never reach that limit insofar as I can never *be* a Jew.[1]

The final aspect of the situation that Sartre explores at length is *death*. Death is what places my life finally into the In-itself and the hands of the Other. It is not one of my possibilities (I am bound to die sometime, suicide is only a choice of time) but rather it is the possibility that I should have no possibilities. It is not a limit to my freedom in the sense that an electrified fence is a limit to my movement, but rather the destiny of all my projects, a destiny over which I have no control whatsoever.

The For-itself, then, can only exist in relation to a situation and is only free in relation to a situation, as a relation to the In-itself and a pursuit of value. At the same time the In-itself can only 'be-there' as it is revealed to the For-itself. In this way Sartre claims to have transcended the idealism – materialism debate: the situation is not 'subjectively' defined since it is made up of objects out-in-the-world, but neither is it 'objective' since it is only revealed in the light of the project.

The foregoing has a rather more obvious relationship to conventional sociological problems. Nevertheless it depends on and is an

---

[1] This conception can provide a base for an analysis of group relationships. In particular see Sartre's *Anti-Semite and Jew* (1948a) and Simone de Beauvoir: *The Second Sex* (1953). In his later work he would regard all relationships with the Other as mediated by matter. See below, Chapter 7.

extension of the earlier arguments. In what follows, it will be seen
that establishing Sartre's relevance to sociology does not consist in
arbitrarily taking one or two ideas from his work and showing how
they can be used by the sociologist, but rather in establishing the
fundamental importance of his method and his subject matter for
sociology. Before we can move on to this, however, it is possible to
bring together one or two of the loose ends of the current chapter
and extend some of the arguments.

v. Conclusion

We have already tried briefly to describe the sociologist as
the Other, the one who looks. We can also describe him as 'in
situation' and as a project. The discovery of the project in its full
complexity and individuality is of course a matter for investigation
in each individual case, but we can suggest at least one possible
project which can be regarded as a sociological project: that of
possessing the world through knowledge. To know something is to
make it mine (Sartre, 1955), to give it an existence in my head as
well as in the world. The project of possessing the world through
knowledge reveals my situation, including the Others in it, as
something there-to-be-known. At the moment we are talking about
knowledge as opposed to understanding, a knowledge which seeks
to know its object *as* an object. In the latter half of the study, this
will be known as analytic knowledge, and we will look at it in the
context of the social formations that produce and support it. For
the moment, we must look at it solely in terms of the individual
project.

The conception of the sociologist in terms of situation and
project leads us to the problem of values and value-freedom in a
new way. Even when they receive a comparatively sophisticated
treatment – for example, in Friedrichs (1970) – values tend to be
treated as qualities, somehow possessed, consciously or uncon-
sciously, by the sociologist affecting his activity from the outside. Our
argument here, however, suggests that values are better conceived
of as standards created by the project, as ways of acting: the project
of value-freedom itself creates its own values, is itself an expression
of value. The project of being a sociologist is one possible expression
of the project of possessing the world through knowledge, and
within that expression, there are different alternatives, different
types of sociologist that I might become. In each specific case we
need to trace and render explicit the most general and the most
specific values created and expressed in the project, and this must
be done before we are able to meet any requirements of a reflexive

sociology and before we can fully understand the work of the sociologist under consideration. And, in turn, to understand the project and the values it creates, we need to grasp his future possibilities, his practical possibilities in terms of his life and career and his ultimate possibility.

We have already argued that Sartre provides us with the means of grasping the complex transformation of interpersonal relationships, and with a conception of interpersonal conflict, both of which are often missing in conventional sociology. With the notion of the ultimate project, we also find a means of grasping the unity of contradictory actions, of different levels of action – rational, emotional, imaginary – and the unity of activities in very diverse areas of life. Each action – however different from the others it might appear – is at the same time the project itself and a manifestation of the project.[1] Here, we can move beyond the 'ideal type' models of rational action developed by Weber and Schutz, and beyond the limits of role analysis, both of which tend towards a breaking up, a compartmentalisation of the personality. In the terms of G. H. Mead and symbolic interactionism, we have developed a clearer and more elaborate description of the 'I' which all too often tends to become a residual category. It must be emphasised again that the description of the 'I' – consciousness, the source of originality, of creativity – is essentially a matter for philosophy; it is presupposed by any other type of investigation. Consciousness is what investigates and questions the world, but it is not itself found *in* the world. Since we cannot talk about consciousness in general, any questioning of consciousness by itself must be a questioning of *my* consciousness by myself, a matter of asking the question 'How am I conscious of the world and other consciousnesses in it?'.

Obviously, it is out of the question that the sociologist should carry out a full scale existential psychoanalysis of everybody he studies; more general analyses are possible and several will be attempted in the following chapters. However, it should not be thought that the foregoing is a way of saying, in a rather complex language, that we should look for 'the actor's definition of the situation'. This presupposes an 'objective' situation and a 'subjective' assessment of it, taking place on the reflective level. The concept of situation employed by Sartre carries the implication of *creation* in and by the

---

[1] For example, Genet's writing was his project, but so was his homosexuality and his thieving. Their unity is found in an ultimate possibility that was originally coincidence with being and which, through failure, transformed itself into pure negativity (Sartre, 1963d).

project, as opposed to a definition, from the outside, which in turn leads to the project. Finally, the concept of understanding that we have developed here is that of a progressive–regressive movement: from situation to project and from project to situation – a *movement* as opposed to the *state* of shared rationality, shared meanings implied in Weber and Schutz. The movement of understanding is grounded in the structure of consciousness itself as a project from a specific point of view on the world, and this basic structure of project-situation is common to each consciousness. This is what Sartre calls 'human reality', the nearest we can come to a 'human nature', and it means that all human action is, in principle, understandable.

3
The substantive self

1. Introduction

In this chapter, we will examine Goffman's conception of the 'self' as it is presented in *Asylums* (1968a) with the initial aim of drawing out its assumptions and discussing its adequacies and inadequacies in its own terms. We will then attempt to relate this criticism to the discussion of the previous chapter and sketch out a re-analysis in terms of the concepts developed there. Goffman has been chosen because he is perhaps the one sociologist whose name is almost automatically linked to the study of the self and because, at least at first glance, his conception of the self is very much like the conception that we could derive from Sartre. *Asylums* has been chosen because it deals with the self in a comparatively limited and structured context rather than cutting across a wide variety of contexts (as is the case, for example, in *Stigma*) or dealing with the self in a very open context (as in *The Presentation of Self in Everyday Life*). It thus facilitates a fairly close and coherent examination of the relationship between self and situation that would not be available from the other works.

Goffman espouses no systematic theory of the self; his theoretical statements tend to be made either as additions to his empirical descriptions (1968a: 154), prefaces to them (p. 119), or, less often, as suggestions derived from them (p. 280). It is possible to discern two conceptions of the self, which sometimes he employs together, sometimes separately; each implies that the self is some substantive entity or form, that it is possible to *do* something to the self, build it, destroy it etc. in the way in which we *do* something to a material object, and that it is possible to *possess* it as one possesses an item of clothing.

In the first conception, the self is presented to the individual by the network of institutional relationships of which he is a part, in some respects it *is* this network. It is something that is built *for* the individual. We find this conception in three essays: 'On the Characteristics of Total Institutions', 'The Moral Career of the

Mental Patient', and 'The Medical Model and Mental Hospitalisation'. The second conception sees the self as something built by the individual, and 'presented' as a way of gaining acceptance from others or used as a means of avoiding domination by others, of maintaining some area of independent control. In this latter case the self *becomes* this area of independent control. This second conception is used in conjunction with the first in the essay on total institutions and is dominant in 'The Underlife of a Public Institution'.

We are not trying to argue *a priori* that Goffman sees the self in a contradictory or confused manner; this is something that we must investigate in the course of the study. There is no immediate reason why both conceptions should not be appropriate on different occasions, nor even why they should not be used together: the materials for the self are presented by others and selected, united and used by the individual in particular ways. This could correspond to Mead's (1952) view of the relationship between the 'I' and the 'Me', and more importantly has immediate similarities with what was said in the last chapter about my being-for-myself and my being-for-others. The extent of the similarity remains to be discovered. Each conception will be studied separately since each is self-sufficient independently of whether it is used in conjunction with the other.

ii. The self as the product of others
i. *The self inside and outside the institution*
The category of 'total institutions' unites a number of institutions, as varied in their functions as monasteries, armed services and mental hospitals, into the same group because of their 'total' nature. They remove the usual barriers between work, sleep and play that divide up the life of the individual in outside society; they involve the bureaucratic organisation of large numbers of people and a consequent division of inmates into a controlling and controlled group each of which develops a usually unfavourable stereotype of the other. The bureaucracy must organise schedules covering the lives of the inmates for twenty-four hours a day. For Goffman these similarities outweigh the wide differences in function.

His discussion of the 'inmate world' is the most relevant to his conception of the self; entrance into the institution, he argues, entails a radical restructuring of the self:

The recruit comes into the establishment with a conception of himself made possible by certain stable social arrangements in his home world. Upon entrance, he is immediately stripped of the support provided by these arrangements. In the accurate language of some of our oldest total institutions, he begins a series of abasements, degradations, humiliations and profanations of self. His self is systematically, if often unintentionally, mortified. He begins some radical shifts in his *moral career*, a career composed of progressive changes that occur in the beliefs that he has concerning himself and significant others. (p. 24)

One element involved in mortification is the denial of the autonomous control over his activities that the individual enjoys outside of the institution. We will deal with this autonomous aspect of the self in the next sections; what concerns us now is the self as it is presented to the individual by others, and the immediate question we can ask is whether entrance into the total institution involves as *radical* a change in that self as Goffman implies. Large areas of outside life are bureaucratically organised, if to a lesser extent, and no element of Goffman's original definition of the total institution is specific to total institutions; we find it more intensively inside rather than outside but that is all. The State and industrial organisations organise and define large numbers of people accord-ing to a 'lowest common denominator' in the same way as 'total' institutions, only perhaps, in some cases, using different criteria: impersonal factors such as age, sex, marital status, earnings, hours worked, quantity produced, etc. are frequently employed and each involves a 'mortification' of the self in Goffman's terms.[1]

When Goffman goes on to consider the emergence of a new self around the system of rewards and punishments in the institution, we find a similar exaggeration in the comparison with the outside world:

punishments and privileges are themselves modes of organisation peculiar to total institutions. Whatever their severity, punishments are largely known in the inmate's home world as something applied to animals and children . . . And privileges in the total institution, it should be emphasised, are not the same as perquisites, indulgences or values, but merely the absence of deprivations one ordinarily expects not to have to sustain. (p. 53)

Again it cannot seriously be argued that outside of total institu-tions, punishments are only applied to animals and children. There is a vast and costly system of law enforcement which is geared to ensuring that those who break the law are punished, and the very existence of some total institutions is a 'punishment'.[2] It is possible

[1] In the case of autonomy as well, it can in no way be claimed that there is a complete freedom outside of the hospital; again it is a matter of degree.
[2] It could be argued – probably not very convincingly – that the function of law enforcement is 'protection' or even 'rehabilitation' and certainly

also to argue that the entire world of work is based on a system of reward and punishment: too little work or unsatisfactory work leads to a loss in wages, possible dismissal or at least the threat of it; satisfactory work is rewarded sometimes as such, but more fundamentally any sort of work receives some reward and at the lower levels of the income scale it is almost certainly true that this reward is 'merely the absence of deprivations one ordinarily expects not to sustain'.[1] It is not being argued that this is a sufficient analysis of the wage system – obviously it is not – rather that 'normal' life can just as easily be interpreted in the terms Goffman uses to portray institutional life; nor is it being argued that the world is one big asylum, merely that the differences between the 'inside' and 'outside' are not as radical as Goffman would have us believe.

We find the same tendency to exaggeration in the final essay 'The Medical Model and Mental Hospitalisation' in which Goffman looks at mental hospitalisation as a 'personal service occupation'. Briefly he argues that the problems of supplying a 'personal service' in a bureaucratically organised situation and in an institution that has a clear custodial role confronts the physician with conflicting demands (pp. 282–8). Most importantly for our present purposes, Goffman goes into the consequences of applying the personal service model to the patient: the latter is supposed to be an independent client but is often being kept in the hospital against his will. The physician has to 'redefine' the patient:

The key view of the patient is: were he 'himself' he would voluntarily seek psychiatric treatment and voluntarily submit to it, and, when ready for discharge, he will avow that his real self was all along being treated as it really wanted to be treated. (p. 326)

All of the patient's activities have to be re-interpreted in this light: they become a sign of his 'illness' and his 'recovery' and not a rational response to a situation:

The response of the patient to hospitalisation can itself be nicely handled by translating it into a technical frame of reference, whereby the contribution of the hospital to the patient's trouble becomes incidental, the important thing being the internally generated mode of disturbance characteristic of the patient's conduct. Interpersonal

(*n 2 continued*)
not, intentionally, punishment, but this would not affect our argument. Much of what Goffman calls 'punishment' is not necessarily seen by those involved as such, particularly in mental hospitals where it would be regarded as treatment.
[1] It would seem reasonable to ask whether what Goffman regards as 'normal' in outside life is normal only for the white middle-class male. We will return later to his conception of the self in outside society.

happenings are transferred into the patient, establishing him as a relatively closed system that can be thought of as pathological and correctable. (pp. 326–7)

and later:

I am suggesting that the nature of the patient's nature is redefined so that, in effect if not by intention, the patient becomes a kind of object upon which a psychiatric service is performed. (p. 330)

On the whole, the essay can be regarded as an exercise in the sociology of knowledge: a study of the way in which a particular social group, the physicians, in a particular structure, the mental hospital, comes to see its position. The important point here is that the way in which the patient is viewed is *not* specific to physicians or even to those working in the hospital. The view of actions and mental illness outlined in the above quotations is implicit in the very existence of *mental* hospitals and would appear to be widely current in society at large; part of Goffman's own originality is that he disputes this commonly held view. It is certainly everyday practice to transfer interpersonal happenings into the individual: I talk about somebody as being aggressive, kind, happy when he has been aggressive *towards* me, kind *to* me, happy *with* me; in each case something in our relationship is projected into him. And the implication of many acts of social policy, including the setting up of mental hospitals, is that the individual is a relatively closed system which can be worked upon – an assumption that in some respects is prevalent in the education system as well.

If there is a radical change involved in entering a total institution – and we are not arguing against that possibility – then it does not lie in the view of the self that is offered to the individual by the institution. That view is not qualitatively different from the one offered by other institutions, by the State, and the one prevalent in society at large. All that can be said about it is that *in some respects* it becomes more obvious and is applied to a greater area of an individual's life. If we regard the self as being a product of the institutional network of which he is a part, whether or not we combine this conception with some other, our explanation or understanding will be inadequate because it is difficult to attribute any *specific* role to a particular institution: many institutions would appear to define the self in much the same way.

We can go on, briefly, to question Goffman's assumptions about the self in the outside society. Here, it seems, the self is normally stable, created and maintained by a stable life and relationships. This is explicitly stated in the first quotation above, and it can be immediately questioned: it seems very likely that entrance into some total institution – the mental hospital and prison in particular, the armed forces during periods of unemployment, war or conscription – is due to the very fact that life outside is *unstable*. And, of course, there are people who display the greatest reluctance to leave total institutions for fear of the 'stability' of outside life – even when that institution is prison. We can go further and ask how we judge stability: does a relationship that continues over a long period automatically constitute a stable relationship? If not, do we have to judge the 'quality' of the relationship, and how do we do that?[1]

We find another example of Goffman's rather naive assumption about outside life in one of his examples of the 'demoralisation' of the self inside the mental hospital: there is what he calls a 'marriage moratorium' (p. 152): an absence of the usual restrictions on extra-marital affairs. Yet it seems reasonable to suggest that such a 'moratorium' exists in many situations in which marriage partners are separated, whether it be for a short period of time – weekend conferences, business trips – or longer periods – wars, or when the husband (or the wife) works away from home,[2] and that it is in no way specific to total institutions or mental hospitals.

It would seem, then, that the conditions under which an individual receives a stable self-image from his relationships are problematic, and that Goffman can only argue that the total institution radically redefines the self-image on the basis of a naive view of what happens outside. It is also possible to suggest that the self or the self-image presented to the individual by his network of institutional relationships plays a much more problematic, and possibly less important role than is often assumed.

ii. The moral career
We can discover further problems with this conception of the self in Goffman's essay on the 'moral career' of the mental patient (pp. 119–55). The choice of the concept of 'career' is significant not so much for the advantages that Goffman sees in it – its 'two-sidedness', enabling the student to move back and forth between self and felt identity and institutional and social life – but for its implications that the self can be seen in terms of a continuous development, moving,

[1] Again it seems reasonable to suggest that a 'stable' life as Goffman seems to envisage it is specific to certain social groups, *Asylums* p. 152.
[2] It is also likely that such a 'moratorium' would apply to men more than to women. Goffman gives no indication of whether this is the case in the mental hospital. He mentions 'shipboard or vacation romances' but only to liken these to total institutions in their isolation from the world.

as it were, in a straight line which is bent by changes in the external situation.

It is in this essay that we find our first conception of the self stated most explicitly:

Each moral career, and behind this, each self, occurs within the confines of an institutional system, whether a social establishment such as a mental hospital or a complex of personal and professional relationships. The self, then, can be seen as something which resides in the arrangements prevailing in a social system for its members. The self in this sense is not the property of the person to whom it is attributed, but dwells rather in the pattern of social control that is exerted in connection with the person by himself and those around him. This special kind of institutional arrangement does not so much support the self as constitute it. (p. 154)

The process of hospitalisation and the social forces that determine life in the hospital are seen not only as taking people from widely varying backgrounds and situations and creating a common fate for them but also as making them into very similar characters (p. 121). The concept of the self that he uses here prohibits him from taking into account the variations in the responses of the patients that he considers in the other essays and that we will be looking at later.

In what he calls the pre-patient phase, Goffman sees the self as a function of the individual's relationships to those who are responsible for his hospitalisation. If the person who takes the first step towards commitment is a close relation or friend ('next-of-relation') of the individual concerned, then the future patient is likely to feel betrayed; if, moreover, the next-of-relation appears to be in collusion with the agents more directly responsible for commitment – the psychiatrist, for example – the pre-patient will not only have his feeling of betrayal intensified, but will experience himself as being plotted against by significant others. This will result in emphasising the gap that the pre-patient who has become an in-patient will feel between himself and the outside world, and may lead to a withdrawal from contact with others, involving behaviour that will confirm the in-patient's 'sickness'.

Thus the pre-patient's self is transformed in the nexus of the personal and professional relationships in which he is involved. But it should be immediately obvious that a feeling of betrayal and withdrawal are not the only possible reactions. Why should not the collusion of the next-of-relation and the medical authorities be experienced as beneficial, as it is portrayed by those involved – an interpretation often eventually accepted by the in-patient? (p. 334)

Why should the patient react by withdrawing from contact with others rather than rejecting the next-of-relation whilst submitting to 'the hospital version of himself, or by rejecting and overtly opposing both? There seems to be no *a priori* reason why such reactions should not occur, and the same set of relationships could be used to 'explain' all of them.

The withdrawal appears to link the pre-patient phase with the in-patient phase in a continuous line, in accordance with what is normally implied by a 'career'. The break, however, comes at the end of the withdrawal, which Goffman does not attempt to explain at all in terms of the 'self' – it just seems to happen:

Usually the patient comes to give up this taxing effort at anonymity, at not-hereness, and begins to present himself for conventional social interaction to the hospital community. Thereafter he withdraws only in special ways . . . or he withdraws only at special times. (p. 136)

On entering the hospital, the patient's self is debased according to the mortification process outlined above. He finds his physical environment closely tied to the institution's definition of his personality: the worse the ward, the worse his condition and vice versa, and the link, not usually so extreme in outside society, is reinforced by the official psychiatric interpretation of the patient's behaviour, conveyed via the staff and by such mechanisms as the case history which systematically records only such behaviour as can be considered 'symptomatic' of his 'illness'. Any attempt by the patient to build up an alternative version of his actions tends to be systematically destroyed by the staff[1] and this eventually dismantles the patient's sense of 'what a person ought to be' (pp.149–50). Goffman goes on:

Behind these verbally instigated ups and downs of the self is an institutional base that rocks just as precariously. Contrary to popular opinion, the 'ward system' ensures a great amount of internal social mobility in mental hospitals, especially during the inmate's first year . . . Each of these moves involves a very drastic alteration in the level of living and in available material out of which to build a self-confirming round of activities, an alteration equivalent in scope, say, to a move up or down a class in the wider class system. Moreover, fellow inmates with whom he has partially identified himself will similarly be moving, but in different directions and at different rates, thus reflecting feelings of social change to the person even when he does not experience them directly. (pp. 149–50)

[1] Of course, this too happens in outside society, but less obviously. There are socially constructed and accepted ways of explaining one's activities and failure to comply with them is likely to lead at least to one's being thought 'odd'.

Goffman seems uncertain about the results of this rapid fluctuation; on the one hand, the in-patient:

learns about the viability of taking up a standpoint – and hence a self – that is outside the one which the hospital can give or take away from him. (p. 151)

and on the other:

This setting, then, seems to engender a kind of cosmopolitan sophistication, a kind of civic apathy. In this unserious, yet oddly exaggerated moral context, building up a self or having it destroyed become something of a shameless game, and learning to view this process as a game seems to make for some demoralisation, the game being such a fundamental one...

Once he learns what it is like to be defined by society as not having a viable self, this threatening definition...is weakened. The patient seems to gain a new plateau where he learns that he can survive while acting in a way that society sees as destructive of him. (pp. 151–2)

It is not clear, then, whether the patient loses his self, and becomes demoralised and apathetic, or whether he creates a new self out of vastly impoverished materials, or whether apathy and demoralisation constitute a new self. We can get an idea of the problem involved by looking at another example of what Goffman regards as the 'demoralisation' of the self. He points out (pp. 152–3) that on the lower wards, where there is little material out of which to build a self, where discreditings of a patient's self-image are frequent, and where, at the same time, there is little scope for punishment, patients are able to stand up to staff with little fear of the consequences, and, in some cases, a kind of 'jaunty gallows-humour' develops. Is this humour a result of demoralisation or is it not equally understandable as an element of a 'new' self which assets itself against staff definitions? Again Goffman's concepts are so vague they can explain everything.

The concept of the institutionally defined self as employed by Goffman seems, then, to be unable to explain the difference between life inside and outside the institution, and so general that it is able to explain any action whatsoever inside, it is unable to account for the specificity of individual reactions.[1] Further, Goffman is unable

[1] It should be emphasised that we are not arguing that the concept of the institutionally defined self is of no use *at all*, nor that it is not, in some situations, very important. The first few years of a child's life, for example, is the period in which he is presented with definitions of himself out of which he forms his fundamental project. But this definition is passed on in very specific ways, in the way in which the mother handles the child, the noises that she makes, the way in which she looks at it. See in particular *L'Idiot de la famille*.

to sustain the notion of 'career' that goes with the concept. If, however, the concept of an 'institutionally defined self' can be related to and used in conjunction with a concept of the 'autonomous' self, built by the individual out of his institutional surroundings, then we might have an adequate conception with which the sociologist could operate. We must now examine the other aspect of Goffman's work.

III. The self as produced by the individual
i. *Responses to mortification*

Goffman goes on to consider the re-assembly of the self around the various systems of rewards and punishments inside the institution. There are various responses available to the new inmate: he may withdraw from interaction completely, interact with others but remain intransigent in the face of the institution's definition of his self, he may build himself a life as stable and contented as the situation allows ('colonisation') or he may accept totally the institution's definition of him ('conversion'). Each of these represents a coherent course of action but it is rare for any one of them to be followed through consistently:

In most total institutions, most inmates take the tack of what some of them call 'playing it cool'. This involves a somewhat opportunistic combination of secondary adjustments, conversion, colonisation and loyalty to the inmate group, so that the inmate will have a maximum chance, in the particular circumstances, of eventually getting out physically and psychologically undamaged. (p. 64)

These alignments are seen as ways of handling the tensions that arise from the differences between the home world and the institutional world. When it comes to why one should be chosen rather than another or even why none of them seem to be pursued very far, however, Goffman has very little to say. The only indication he gives is in the following paragraph:

The basic facts about self in this report are phrased in a sociological perspective, always leading back to a description of the institutional arrangements which delineate the personal prerogatives of a member. Of course, a psychological assumption is also implied; cognitive processes are invariably involved, for the social arrangements must be 'read' by the individual and others for the image of himself that they imply. But, as I have argued, the relation of the cognitive process to the other psychological processes is quite variable . . . (p. 50)

Presumably it is to psychological processes that we must refer if we are to understand why one alignment should be adopted instead of another. What exactly they entail is unclear but obviously fundamental: for example, if it is just a matter of physical perceptual processes that happen to work in one way rather than another, then the institutional definition of the self is all-important since it is the only means we have to understand self-images. If on the other hand the 'psychological processes' include something like a Freudian unconscious or various 'complexes' then the institutional definition of the self may be swallowed up and transformed in the individual's perception of it. Here, then, Goffman offers no adequate way of understanding how the self can be selected and built from the materials presented to it. Further he offers us a 'dispersive' conception of the individual: here we learn that the individual is a collection of, or possibly just one, psychological process; later we learn that he also has emotions, and can develop affective relationships with others. There is, however, no coherent conception of the 'individual' as a basic unit in the study. In the essay on underlife (pp. 159–266), he gives us a much more complete picture.

ii. The underlife

Goffman begins by arguing that any formal organisation not only prescribes a round of activities for its members but also presents them with an implicit conception of their self. On entering the organisation the individual incurs the obligation to act in a particular way whilst carrying out the prescribed activities, and by so doing he accepts the self that the organisation prescribes. Activity in compliance with the prescriptions, Goffman calls 'primary adjustments'. Secondary adjustments, on the other hand, are:

any habitual arrangement by which a member of an organisation employs unauthorised means, or obtains unauthorised ends, or both, thus getting around the organisation's assumptions as to what he should do and get and hence what he should be. Secondary adjustments represent ways in which individuals stand apart from the role and the self that were taken for granted for him by the institution. (p. 172)

The full set of an individual's secondary adjustments brings him into contact with others and a social structure grows around them: this is the *underlife* of the institution. Goffman originally draws attention away from the implications of these adjustments for the individual and towards the unofficial social structure that they generate:

An individual's use of a secondary adjustment is inevitably a social-psychological matter, affording him gratifications he might not otherwise obtain. But precisely what an individual 'gets out of' a practice is perhaps not the sociologist's first concern. From a sociological point of view, the initial question to be asked of a secondary adjustment is...the character of the social relations that its acquisition and maintenance require. (p. 181)

He goes on to look at the secondary adjustments that he discovered in the mental hospital in terms of the facilities available for their development, and to classify the relationships that arise in the course of carrying them out. In his conclusion, however, he comes back to the problem of the nature of the self and makes several suggestions about the implications of the existence of secondary adjustments. These are worth quoting in full:

The simplest sociological view of the individual and his self is that he is to himself what his place in an organisation defines him to be. When pressed, a sociologist modifies this model by granting certain complications: the self may not yet be formed or may exhibit conflicting dedications. Perhaps we should further complicate the construct by elevating these qualifications to a central place, initially defining the individual, for sociological purposes, as a stance-taking entity, a something that takes up a position somewhere between identification with an organisation and opposition to it, and is ready at the slightest pressure to regain its balance by shifting its involvement in either direction. It is thus *against something* that the self can emerge...

Our sense of being a person can come from being drawn into a wider social unit; our sense of selfhood can arise through the little ways in which we resist the pull...(p. 280)

It is here, presumably, that we come to what Goffman has previously subsumed, at least in part, under the heading of 'psychological processes'. It is suggested that the self is built by the individual in part against the institutional definition of himself; an area of independence and autonomy is constructed within the framework set by the institution. The problem however is that this argument is as general as that in which he discussed the institutional definition of the self. It still tells us nothing about why one line of action should be adopted in preference to another, why one 'self-image' should be preferred to another and it gives us no means of comprehending what might be the *individual* meanings of the same activity to different persons. In other words, it offers no way of understanding what people *do* in concrete terms; it subsumes all sorts of activity under headings that are so general that any action can be included under them. Also – and importantly – it does not let us see the 'social structure' of secondary adjustments as *created* by the individuals concerned; it is abstracted (deliberately and in the name of sociology) from the individuals who produce it and thus we cannot understand in what way it may change over time, from where the changes may come, or what it means to the individual involved. We are left with the assumption that if the sources of and facilities for secondary adjustments do not change then the social structure created around them remains stable. Yet given the 'underground' nature of that structure this would appear to be unlikely.

The problem of the level of generalisation at which Goffman works becomes apparent when we look at some of the specific secondary adjustments he mentions. For example, the practice of mental hospital patients of shamelessly 'bumming' a cigarette from visitors can be considered in any one of three ways. It could indicate a 'sophistication', an insulating of the self from the ups and downs of institutional life. It could equally well be an indication of 'demoralisation', of the way in which the institution has worked upon the self of the patient concerned to destroy it. Lastly it could be an incident in one of the secondary adjustment processes, in which cigarettes are used as a form of currency, and indicate an affirmation of the self against the institutional definition. The same goes for the 'marriage moratorium' already mentioned: any one of the three explanations could be appropriate.

Although there was no *a priori* contradiction in Goffman's conceptions of the self, and no reason why they should not be used together, it seems that, in practice, the way in which they are used is so general that they do not allow us to understand the complexity of the activities we are faced with and they cannot be used together. If either conception can supply an explanation for, or an understanding of a specific action, then the one employed must be a matter of what argument is being pursued at the time. If they are used in conjunction, then one will be obviously redundant. Although Goffman has tried to keep his conception of the self 'sociological', he has only done so at the cost of its adequacy.

We can now attempt, on the basis of these criticisms, to develop a conception of the self which can cover the variety of activities that we meet whilst maintaining its relevance for any study of social structures.

iv. The pursuit of the self

It was argued earlier that Goffman regards the self as some sort of entity, it can be 'mortified', 'demoralised', or constructed by the individual against the institutional definition. When it comes to the elements that go to make up this entity we get very little firm information and this would indicate that perhaps the 'self' is not something that can be described as if it were a possession or a construction. On occasions Goffman does talk about some *feeling* of identity, a sense of 'what a person ought to be' and a useful starting point is to distinguish these two ideas between which Goffman does not differentiate, treating the latter as dependent on the former: if one has a self then one has a feeling of identity and vice versa.

A sense of identity implies something more than the substantive traits that we can list in answer to the question 'Who am I?'[1] I possess a number of physical characteristics, a number of institutional roles – I am a husband, a student, etc. – a number of attitudes to the world and other people, certain fairly consistent ways of acting towards the world and others, but none of these carry a *feeling* of identity: all could belong to *anybody*; if for no other reason than they are expressed in words that belong to everybody and are therefore applicable to everybody. The characteristics that most separate me from other people – my particular address, the specific title of my institutional role – are precisely the ones that are most anonymous. My National Insurance number, for example, is unique. On the other hand, my most intimate characteristics, my loves and my hates can only be expressed in terms that give them an anonymity, in words that do not point directly to me.[2] The *feeling* of identity, then, does not lie in what comes after the 'I am . . .'. It does, however, involve stating 'I am', and it is at this statement that we must look more closely.

When one says 'I', one gives a unity to one's actions, feelings, ideas, etc., to everything that 'comes out' of one, independently of how it may have 'got in'. All the characteristics that I may list to define myself find their unity in the 'I'. Further the 'I' distinguishes itself from everything that surrounds it: statements such as 'I am angry', 'I am a machine' separate the 'I' from the anger and the machine. Anger is an emotion, a relationship to the world or a part of it, that finds its source in the 'I' but which *is not* the 'I'. Otherwise the simple statement 'Angry' would be sufficient.[3] The point comes over even more clearly in the second example. 'I am a machine' designates two separate beings; if it did not either it would be tautological ('I am I'), or impossible (machines don't talk

[1] On this topic, see in particular Bennet Berger's essay (1971): 'The Myth of Identity'.
[2] Poetry can be defined as the attempt to overcome this, see in particular Sartre (1972c).
[3] The statement 'Angry' would in fact capture the pre-reflective relationship; the separation of consciousness from the world is implicit and 'lived' at this level; the ego appears on reflection. It is, significantly, the sort of statement a young child might make.

– at least not spontaneously: to do so, they have to be programmed). Of course, this also indicates the separation of an individual from his illusions or hallucinations and his complicity in maintaining them.[1]

The 'I' then provides the unity of the characteristics in the list that follows the 'I am . . .' but is separate from and more than each component on that list or their sum. The distinction between the self-image expressed as substantive characteristics and the feeling of identity, then, indicates that the latter is the ability to say 'I', to separate oneself from the rest of the world and from one's own possessions. This is a more radical separation than that implied by Goffman's suggestion that the self is defined both in compliance with and against the institutional definition; it is a separation that is prior to any identification with or opposition to a definition presented by others. However much I may identify with the institutional definition of myself, I still separate myself from it by saying ' I '.

The 'I' seen in this way, then, cannot be identified with any substantive characteristics and therefore it is not something that we can reveal by means of empirical research. We can underline some of the dangers in the notion of the substantive self which ignores the 'I am': Gouldner (1971) has pointed out a relationship between Goffman's work on self-presentation and a consumer-orientated society with its emphasis on presenting goods in the most favourable light, on public images and manipulative politics. In *Asylums*, the picture that Goffman suggests in the 'underlife' essay, of the individual who, as it were, 'by nature' requires some private possessions and an area of autonomy and 'freedom' of movement and activity, is perhaps more in accordance with classical liberalism. The point is that if one seeks empirically the nature of the 'I', there is a tendency to reproduce current ideological assumptions about human nature: it involves the adoption of categories developed through impure refection as it was defined in the last chapter. In Goffman's case this tendency is augmented by starting with the institutional definition of the self: the individual can either accept or reject this definition (or do both, to a certain extent); if he accepts it, then we have the 'consumer society' view, if he rejects it, then we have the 'classical liberal' view. There is no alternative beyond some combination of these two.[2]

[1] See in particular Sartre (1949b). Much of Laing's work assumes this point.
[2] Daniel C. Foss (1972) offers a highly original view of Goffman's 'dramaturgy' which sees it as a criticism of itself. He does so in the

If we see the feeling of identity as the ability to say 'I', then the self can no longer be a quality or a substantive entity belonging to the individual since whenever he tries to describe it, he separates himself from it. The distance expressed in the 'I' is the distance Goffman regularly discerns behind individual behaviour: the activities that he cannot handle with the institutional definition of the self, and which he accounts for either in terms of 'psychological processes', or the tendency of the self to construct itself against the institutional definition, or, on one occasion, by the individual's ability to form 'affective' relationships; all these activities refer us eventually to the 'I'. It was argued earlier that the institutional definition of the self is too generalised to explain actual activity; this does not, however, imply that the institution does not present its members with a 'self'; to accept that it does – and we will see shortly that it can be of some help to us – does not imply that the individual must accept or reject the self as if it were an *entity*, like an item of clothing that can be worn, left off, or used for more than one purpose. If we are to discover the way in which we may use the concept of the institutionally defined self, we must first explore more fully the nature of the 'I'.

Goffman notes on two occasions that a number of activities become redefined over a period of time and in the light of later events. Thus a pre-patient career only becomes a pre-patient career when the individual becomes an in-patient (pp. 134–5); similarly the psychiatric ideology may provide the ex-patient with a view of his stay in the hospital which defines it as a period of time during which he was able to overcome serious defects in his relationships with others, whereas during the stay he had not experienced it in any such way at all (p. 334). It is important to distinguish such redefinition from what is usually called 'rationalisation'. The latter involves explaining an act or event in an essentially false way (although the false explanation may have real consequences) either because the 'true' explanation is unknown or because it is in some way unpalatable, or both. In the above example, however, it is the *future event* – admission to the hospital in the first case, discharge from it in the second – that causes an original explanation to be redefined.

In the statement 'I was . . .' we can discover the same 'distance' between subject and predicate that we found in the 'I am . . ', only

(*n 2 continued*)
course of a difficult argument but one which would seem to be making some of the points made here; his central point seems to be that man is both 'producer' and 'consumer' at the same time, and to learn about him we must study ourselves as 'producers', in this case of selves.

this time it is more evident. 'I was . . .' immediately reveals the possibility of 'I am no longer . . .', i.e. that there has been change. The change, however, has not altered the *past*, rather it has altered its *meaning*. Thus the actions of the 'pre-patient' remain the same actions whether or not he becomes an in-patient; it is his becoming an in-patient that leads to these actions receiving the title 'pre-patient career' rather than some other meaning. Similarly, the actions of the in-patient remain the same actions whether he is discharged or not; if he remains in the hospital, they remain symptoms of his illness, if he is discharged, they become associated with his recovery.

What this feature of 'I was . . .' means for 'I am . . .' is that the predicate is always to some extent 'in suspense', it depends on the future. If the statement 'I am . . .' goes beyond a simple statement of physical characteristics, spatial position etc. then it is always saying, to some extent 'This is what I hope the future activities of myself and others will have shown me to be.' Thus the 'I am' not only expresses a distance from something but an intention towards something: the 'I' is an 'empty' unity which is attempting to become identical with the predicate; in this sense the self is not what I possess but what I am pursuing.

It should now be clear that we have worked back to the concept of the project, in this context seen as the pursuit of a 'self'; we can now return to *Asylums* to discover how we can use this concept in conjunction with the concept of the institutionally defined self in order to achieve a better understanding of the activities that Goffman observed.

v. Conclusion: Asylums

We have seen that there is no hierarchy of projects; each act is involved in a set of complex relationships to each other act and each finds its meaning in those relationships and in relationship to the 'ultimate possible', the fundamental project. The project has to be chosen within the social organisation in which the individual finds himself and which offers him both a number of possibilities and a number of ways of living these possibilities.

Entrance into a total institution involves a severe restriction on the number and variety of possibilities open to the individual, at least in comparison with outside society. The fundamental project, expressed as a relationship to Being which lies in the future, is a free choice which cannot be changed by others; what others can do is change the means available to pursue this project. It is here that we find the radical difference between the total institution and the outside world, not in a redefinition of the self as Goffman suggests. In fact this limitation, this cutting off of possibilities, is implied in the idea of the mortification of the self, insofar as the latter involves strict control over activities, but this remains in the background in Goffman's discussion. We can, as a by-product, also make an important distinction between different sorts of total institutions: those which the individual enters in the course of a freely chosen project and those into which he is put by others. Goffman recognises this distinction but does not seem to think that it is as important as the similarities that he notes. It is likely, in the former case, that the structure of secondary adjustments and the initial reactions on entrance would be very different from those that Goffman discovers in the mental hospital, if they are to be found at all. Monks are unlikely – at least at the novice stage of their monastic career – to trade with each other in cigarettes, an army volunteer is unlikely to feel betrayed and withdraw from interaction. In these cases the institution will have a very different meaning for the individual who enters it and a different internal social structure.

It was argued that the institutionally defined self is not radically different from the definitions that the individual is presented with outside society, rather that it is only intensified, made more obvious. This can now be seen as a feature of the limitation of possibilities: there are fewer options open and there are less materials available for the pursuit of the self. If the institutionally defined self is seen as making up a part of the 'material' which the individual uses in his project, then we must be clear in what way it is used. The implication in Goffman's work is that it is 'internalised', in some way taken 'inside' the individual. We have seen, in the previous chapter, that consciousness is not an empty container that can be filled up; rather than 'internalise' all or part of the institutionally defined self, it *assumes* it as a means of going beyond its situation (see below, Chapter 6). This means that there is no inevitability in the use made of the material and that its meaning is different in different projects.

We discover the project in a multitude of ways; we find it in the individual's relationships with others in general, in his relationships with a set of particular others, and in his relationship to the society in which he lives. This latter is expressed through his choice of career, through the way in which he lives the work prescribed for him (or the lack of it), in his 'lifestyle', his 'worldly ambitions' (and his other-worldly ambitions). All of these contribute to an understanding of, and are understood in the context of, the fundamental project.

Forcible entrance into a total institution cuts short a large number of the ways in which the individual relates to his society, it removes him from those others with whom his closest relationships had been formed, and it provides him with a totally new situation from which he has to pursue those relationships which continue. It is in this context that we can understand two of Goffman's observations. Firstly, we mentioned that he sees the mental hospital as creating similar characters out of the varied selection of individuals who enter it. We can now see this not in terms of similar characters but in terms of different 'characters' making use of very limited materials and engaged in a very limited number of activities. The similarity lies in the instruments, not in what they are being used for. Secondly, we can also understand why the period of time spent in the institution should be regarded by many as wasted or destroyed; as something to be tolerated and passed as pleasantly as possible (p. 67). In terms of the achievement of the possibles they had chosen in outside society, the period inside is wasted. This also enables us to understand the dominant tactic of 'playing it cool' which, we noted above, Goffman was unable to explain in his own terms.

In conjunction with Sartre's description of Being-for-Others, we can also look at the reaction of withdrawal on entrance into the institution. To be betrayed requires that I should first posit myself as a valued object in the eyes of the betrayer only to find myself treated as a degraded object, with no priority over any other object in his world; if the betrayer acts with some third to whom I am no more than anybody else, the betrayal is emphasised. In this situation, withdrawal from contact with others may represent one of several courses of action: it may be a continuation of the attempt to make myself a valued object in the eyes of the betrayer, to trap his freedom, this time through forcing him to recognise and regret his betrayal;[1] in this case, the hospital is secondary – the definition it presents to the patient is used in the relationship to the outside other. The withdrawal may also be a reaction to the failure to become a valued object for the betrayer and a rejection of the type of object that I am for the institution. In this light, the 'buddy relationship' described by Goffman (pp. 242ff.) in which one patient, usually considered fairly sick by the staff, chooses another, usually even sicker, with whom he creates a special relationship, may be seen as a renewed attempt by one or both to become a valued object for another whilst maintaining the original rejections.

---

[1] This is a development of Nietzsche's idea of 'ressentiment'. Sartre uses it extensively in *L'Idiot de la famille* in connection with the fundamental project.

The withdrawal may be seen as an attempt by the patient to adopt all the features of the object which the betrayer and the hospital have defined him as; worthless in the eyes of the betrayer and powerless in the eyes of the hospital he simply tries to make himself what he appears to be. Finally, if the patient's fundamental relationship to others is one of indifference, then withdrawal may simply be the revelation of this relationship brought about by the stripping away of other projects such as commitment to a career, which, in the outside society, may hide it.

This use of the concept of the project enables us to understand any line of activity adopted by the patient and does not confine us to the broad categories used by Goffman. Changes in 'tack' can be understood in terms of the dialectic of interpersonal relations and the eventual failure of any one relationship to the Other. By regarding the self as something 'aimed at' through the hospital's definition of its patients, we can handle contradictory activities with the same set of concepts; Goffman's classification of possible reactions to the mortification process may be regarded as the basis for an eventual classification of projects. In addition to understanding what happens in the mental hospitals in a more adequate way, the concept of the project enables us to look at social structure in a new light. Part of the situation with which the patient is confronted on his entrance to the hospital is a set of deprivations concerning various personal belongings, money, access to goods and services, movement, etc. One of the ways in which the situation is lived – and changed for future patients – is through increasing access to various goods. In the course of his project, an individual relates to other people and to objects; he also relates to objects by means of other objects and through other people and to other people through objects and other-other people. Trade in these circumstances may be a means of enslaving another, being enslaved by him or maintaining a distance from him; it may involve using or being used by another in order to gain access to goods; each of these alternatives is a manifestation of a more fundamental relationship to Others and to Being. Goffman distinguishes the relationships that arise in terms of personal coercion, economic reciprocity and social reciprocity, the latter being subdivided into 'buddy' relationships, cliques, sexual relationships and patron relationships (pp. 232ff.). As it stands, this is a fairly loose classification (almost too loose to deserve the name of a social structure) but he goes on to point out that they overlap each other on several occasions.

We can find the central reason for the looseness and overlapping in the fact that each category tries to combine an element of the situation – the restrictions on individual activity and the ways in which these restrictions are overcome – with the project, the particular use of these restrictions and avoidances by the individual. The economic relationships are already there on entry, at least to some extent; the social relationships must appear after entry. The former may be taken up as a means to the latter or vice versa, and no clear division into Goffman's categories is possible.

From this argument we gain a conception of structure as the 'situation' in the sense in which the term was used in the last chapter (although not including all the elements that were outlined there). It includes the institutional definition of the self, the organisational structure of the mental hospital – the ward system etc. – its routines and activities (in other words what Goffman describes as the sources of secondary adjustments), its rules and restrictions and the network of economic relationships that are built around the secondary adjustments and which, in one sense, comprise the secondary adjustments. These latter are basically the ways of obtaining money and goods in the institution and distributing them. The social relationships that are formed within this structure are formed in the course of the projects of the inmates and staff, and in the case of the structure of secondary adjustments, it seems reasonable to suggest that the structure in its detail is likely to vary and change over time; it is closely bound up with the sort of social relationships that appear.

Given the 'situation' facing the new patient on entrance to the hospital, it should be possible to understand his individual project as it develops and from this to arrive at a general classification of projects such as we attempted above when we were looking at the 'tack' of withdrawal. This would, of course, require abandoning some of the individuality of meaning that we have accused Goffman of ignoring, but we would be working at a more specific level than Goffman and would be able to recognise the existence of even more individual 'layers' of meaning. In this way we should be able to understand the 'underlife' as both a structure and as fluid at the same time: we can understand the way in which individual activity can change the structure – something Goffman does not take into account. When we come to the more formal structure of the organisation, it should again be possible to understand the way in which individual activities may change that, and – which is more likely – the way in which individual projects are alienated by that formal structure; again this is something left untouched by Goffman who cannot deal with it because he appears to lack any conception of the project, of something which is there to be alienated. An example of such alienation would be the patient who is attempting to identify himself with the institution and who finds that the contact with staff members necessary to express that identification and to have it recognised is denied him for reasons of organisational efficiency. In a similar way the patient who is attempting to develop a sexual relationship in the course of his project may find himself confined to the ward all day, his desire or attempt to get out being interpreted as further reasons to keep him in. In both examples, the individual's project is taken away from him by others, diverted as it were, either into a dead end or back against him.

On a superficial reading, there would appear to be distinct similarities between Goffman and Sartre, yet by now it should be evident that there are any number of conceptual inadequacies in Goffman's work – inadequacies we have begun to overcome with the help of Sartre. This alone should be sufficient to reveal the relevance of the latter to any sociology which explicitly or implicitly works with a conception of 'self' (and that, inevitably, must cover most sociology). To establish his general relevance, however, is still only a first step. In the next chapter, we will attempt to demonstrate the more specific relevance of the style and detail of his philosophy.

4
Language and the world

1. Introduction

The structure of this chapter will be similar to that of the previous one: beginning this time with a criticism of the three examples presented by Garfinkel in the essay 'What is Ethnomethodology' (1967), we will try to work back to the descriptions of Chapter 2, drawing out Garfinkel's general assumptions about the nature of consciousness and the world and showing the way in which they effect his empirical studies. There will then be an attempt to draw together the arguments of these two chapters and to delineate clearly the relationship between Sartre's phenomenological investigation and sociological research; this will involve a deepening of the concept of understanding and an extension of the relationship between the sociologist and those he studies.

Garfinkel's examples are more complete and self-contained than Goffman's and therefore open to a more thorough re-analysis; there is also a relationship – however unsystematised it might be – between Garfinkel's work and phenomenology, and this makes it easier to draw out his underlying assumptions;[1] in the course of doing so we will also examine the work of Alfred Schutz, whose attempt to construct a phenomenological sociology is very systematic and whose work certainly appears to have influenced Garfinkel. We will also refer to the latter's more sophisticated theoretical position developed in a paper written with Harvey Sachs: 'On Formal Structures and Practical Actions' (in McKinney and Tiryakian, 1970).

[1] That Garfinkel has been influenced by phenomenology is established by his references to Schutz, Farber and Husserl. However the former writings have both been criticised for modifying Husserl's work (see Hindess 1972; Ames 1955). The extent to which Garfinkel's work can be called phenomenological at all will be a major theme of this chapter; Bauman (1973) makes, in very general terms, some of the points that will be made in a more detailed way here.

II. Deciding cause of death

In his first example, Garfinkel looks at the way in which workers at the Los Angeles Suicide Prevention Centre (SPC), in conjunction with the local coroner's office, set about determining whether or not a particular death is a suicide. He starts by listing the factors which those involved recognised as conditions of their work and as matters they take into account when assessing its adequacy. These are worth quoting in full:

(1) An abiding concern on the part of all parties for the temporal concerting of activities; (2) a concern on the inquirer's part to give evidence of his grasp of 'What Anyone Knows' about how the settings work in which he had to accomplish his enquiries, and his concern to do so in the actual occasions in which the decisions were to be made by his exhibitable conduct in choosing; (3) a concern for the practical question *par excellence* 'What to do next?'; (4) matters which at the level of talk might be spoken of as 'production programmes', 'laws of conduct', 'rules of rational decision making', 'causes', 'conditions', 'hypothesis testing', 'models', 'rules of deductive and inductive inference' in the actual situation were taken for granted and were depended upon to consist of recipes, proverbs, slogans and partially formulated plans of action; (5) inquirers were required to know and be skilled in dealing with situations of the sort for which 'rules of rational decision making', and the rest were intended in order to 'see' or by what they did to insure the objective, effective, consistent, completely empirically adequate, i.e. rational character of recipes, proverbs, prophecies, partial descriptions in an actual occasion of the use of rules; (6) for the practical decider the 'actual occasion' as a phenomenon in its own right exercised overwhelming priority of relevance to which 'decision rules' or theories of decision making were without exception subordinated in order to assess their rational features rather than vice versa; (7) finally, and perhaps most characteristically, all of the foregoing features, together with the inquirer's 'system' of alternatives, his 'decision' methods, his information, his choices and the rationality of his accounts and actions were constituent parts of the same practical circumstances in which inquirers did the work of inquiry – a feature that inquirers if they were to claim and recognise the practicality of their efforts knew of, required, counted on, took for granted, used and glossed. (1967: 12–13)

The essential point of this description seems to be that the workers' activities are best understood in terms of the 'practical circumstances' of their work rather than in terms of some formal and/or informal rules of procedure. The ways in which they come to their conclusions (decisions, choices) are contained within these

practical circumstances and are implicit and assumed. More importantly – and this is perhaps the most significant point that Garfinkel
is continually making – the ways in which the workers reach their
decisions and the ways in which they describe how they reach them
at the same time involve a description of their practical circumstances and constitute their practical circumstances. To describe a
setting is at the same time to constitute it. This is what Garfinkel
calls 'reflexivity': ' . . . the activities whereby members produce and
manage settings of organised everyday affairs are identical with
members' procedures for making these settings "accountable"'
(p. 1).[1]

To make an action rationally account-able seems to be to make
it be understood by others as rational and reproducible; to do this
is to constitute that action, order it in a specific way. This ordering
of activities makes use of indexical expressions – expressions which
cannot be understood in isolation but require reference to 'What
Anybody Knows' about the situation they describe and constitute.

In deciding which label to attach to a death, in deciding what
'really happened', the workers at the SPC were not only constrained
by the practical circumstances listed above, but had to make constant
reference to the future, to the use that could be made of the final
categorisation by the relations of the dead person, and in the
political processes centred on the coroner's office. Their work had
to satisfy anybody who could have access to their reports that it was
as scientific, as thorough, etc. as could be expected 'in the circumstances'. The procedures they used to come to their decisions were
on the one hand designed to eliminate doubt as to 'what really
happened', but on the other hand actually invited doubt both in
the process of reaching the decision and after it had been reached.
The act of writing the decision on the relevant file announces that
a decision has been reached and is therefore an invitation to
question it:

It is not that the investigator, having a list of titles, performed an
inquiry that proceeded step-wise to establish the grounds for electing
among them . . . Instead titles were continually postdicted and foretold.
An inquiry was apt to be heavily guided by the inquirer's use of
imagined settings in which the title will have been 'used' by one or
another interested party, including the deceased, and this was done by
the inquirers in order to decide, using whatever 'datum' might have
been searched out, that *that* 'datum' could be used to mask if masking
needed to be done, or to equivocate, or gloss, or lead, or exemplify, if

---

[1] The term 'members' is not defined in this essay, but in the essay
written with Sachs it is defined as 'natural language users'.

they were needed . . . When assessed by a member, i.e. viewed with
respect to actual practices for making it happen, a routine inquiry is not
one that is accomplished by rule, or according to rules. It seemed much
more to consist of an inquiry that is openly recognised to have fallen
short, but in the same ways it falls short its adequacy is acknowledged
and for which no one is offering or calling particularly for explanation.
(pp. 14–15)

Throughout Garfinkel's description the emphasis is on the assumed
and implicit ways of working in contrast to what the workers are
explicitly 'supposed' to be doing. Thus they are not deciding 'facts'
in a way that may be reproduced by following rational rules of
procedure existing outside of their work. Rather the way in which
they arrive at the 'final' decision is via a set of implicit assumptions
and 'rules' which not only describe their ways of working but also
constitute the situation in which they work and the 'reasonableness',
'adequacy' etc. of their decisions. In each case the contingent
situation in which they find themselves takes priority not only over
formal rules of procedure but also over the informal, or taken-
for-granted rules.

To understand this description properly, it needs to be placed
in the wider theoretical approach that motivates it. Garfinkel's
treatment of the SPC finds its justification in his development of
a sociology which studies the ways in which people understand one
another, the way in which they produce 'rationality' and thus the
setting in which they operate. Rationality cannot be assumed and
is not simply 'there': it is a constant work carried out by individuals
in all their activities. Thus, although the emphasis of this particular
example is superficially that of what Douglas (1971) calls 'situational
ethnomethodology', i.e. it is initially concerned with the practical
circumstances in which the SPC workers carry out their activities,
the underlying concern is not with what these practical circumstances *are* but with showing that included within them and constituting them, are ways in which activities are made 'rationally
account-able'. The concern is not, as has often been assumed (e.g.
Gouldner, 1971), with *substantive* taken-for-granted assumptions
upon which activities are based, but with the taken-for-granted ways
in which rationality is constructed.

The relationship of this approach to a more conventional study
of the SPC, looking at the activities in terms, for example, of formal
and informal groups and rules, is not discussed in the essay.
Elsewhere it is dealt with as 'ethnomethodological indifference'
(McKinney and Tiryakian, 1970) and we will examine its theoretical
justification later. In the SPC study Garfinkel simply ignores any

relationship that there might be between what a conventional sociological study might discover and the ways in which activities are made rationally accountable, and we can question this neglect on an empirical basis.

As we have seen, the example is intended to show the existence of an area of study which is available exclusively to ethnomethodology. *The existence of this area, however, is shown by means of a conventional (what Garfinkel calls 'practical') sociological reasoning.* The factors which are listed at the beginning such as the temporal co-ordination of activities, a concern with what to do next, the taken-for-granted assumption of the ways in which decisions are reached, the consideration of the possible uses of the final decision by others, etc., none of these factors are unavailable to practical sociological reasoning. All of them can, on principle, be discovered by any observer. The argument that rationality is a constant work and accomplishment is an insight built upon these observations, but it is not an insight that is necessarily derived from them in a tight logical argument from initial premises; nor is it immediately self-evident in the descriptions of the workers' activities. That description comes from conventional sociological activities: observation, questioning and interpretation. The insight of rational accountability as a constant work is an act of interpretation: there is nothing in the way in which it was derived that justifies a concentration on this feature of human activity as separate from and unconnected to other activities. The insight is an undetermined act of consciousness, it has no necessity.[1] There is no empirical justification of 'ethno-methodological indifference' here.

Neither the SPC nor the Coroner's Office exist in isolation nor were they created by the people who work in them. The task of constructing or reconstructing a death, together with the labels and the formal rules by which it is decided which label is appropriate are not the sole constructions of the people who work there, and the activities that Garfinkel describes are dependent on these pre-constructed elements. The very existence of the agencies and their specific investigations are pre-existed by, and limited by, the possible labels that may be attached to a death, the decision that the relevant label that is attached to it should be publicly investigated and made known, and the decision that 'suicide' is something that should be prevented. However vague the definitions of 'suicide', 'homicide', 'death from natural causes', however vague and

---

[1] It will be argued in Chapter 5 that all 'logical' arguments require such a free act of consciousness. See also Ricoeur's comments in a discussion with Lévi-Strauss (Lévi-Strauss 1970).

abstract the formal rules that outline the procedures to be followed and however abstract their rationality, and whatever happens when these rules are ostensibly followed and these labels applied, they all pre-exist and provide the framework for the activities studied by Garfinkel. They are not created in the work situation, but rather provide the 'raw material' upon which the workers observed were working.

The considerations listed above as taken into account by the workers in their everyday activities provide a structuring of the situation on one level only: they take the already existing structure of meanings, rationality and procedures and reconstruct them in a particular way according to the everyday exigencies of the situation. This is not to dispute Garfinkel's insight that the rational accountability of activities is an ongoing accomplishment, but to point out that his 'reflexivity' involves the construction of a setting within a setting. The wider setting is chronologically and logically prior to the setting the construction of which Garfinkel describes; the former is not the result of the latter, nor unconnected to it. It is the absence of any exploration of the relationships between the two that is empirically unjustified.

There are, in fact, two elements involved in this discussion: on the one hand, there is the problem of *how* people understand each other – and this seems to be the eventual focus of ethnomethodology – and on the other there is the problem of *what* they understand. The two are obviously connected and our argument implies that the meaning (the 'what') of, for example 'suicide' is contained on one level in the formal procedures of the SPC and on another, more specific, situational level, in the everyday practices of the workers.[1] The relationship between levels and forms (the 'how') of rationality remains to be explored and it will be argued later that Garfinkel eventually subsumes what is understood into how it is understood. For the moment, we can make some further observations on the basis of the above argument: if it is the case that the activities of the SPC workers give a specific form to rationalities and meanings which already have a general form, then their activities are to an extent 'rationally accountable' before they are carried out and part of the ongoing work of 'members' is to maintain, as much as to create, rational accountability. Garfinkel studies this specific maintenance and creation but there are several possible relationships between such activity and the more general levels: firstly the ways in which settings are created as rationally accountable may already

[1] For a discussion of 'levels' of meaning Jack Douglas 1970a, 1970c, Michael Young 1972.

be contained *in toto* in the general forms of rationality that make up formal rules and which are studied by practical sociological reasoning – this would take us in the direction of Durkheim and socially created categories of thought. It is however unlikely that this would be the case: the inherently indexical nature of language should always leave some necessity for creation on the specific level. Secondly, there might be a multiplicity of possible combinations of ways of constructing settings and meanings, some of which might contradict the more general rationalities, some of which might comply with them. In either case, the specific ethnomethodological study would be part of a wider more inclusive study.

A further general observation can be made before moving on. We are dealing with a radically different approach to Goffman's and with a writer who would, presumably, express indifference to theories of the self and to studies of relationships between people that take into account features other than the construction of rational accountability. Until we have established that this indifference lacks any theoretical, as well as empirical, justification, it would be wrong to accuse him of ignoring some of the features that Goffman deals with so ably on occasions, such as the body and its use,[1] or other features of activities such as emotions. We can however note that 'Garfinkel man' would appear at first glance to be essentially a constructor of rationality by the use of *words*. We will come back to this point later.

III. Following coding instructions

The second example concerns a study carried out at the UCLA outpatient's clinic which aimed initially at determining the criteria by which those who came into contact with the clinic were selected for treatment. (It is written up more fully in a later paper in the same book.) Correlations were sought between characteristics of patients, clinic personnel and types of patient career. It was thought necessary to code the relevant information and the problems met in the process of coding provide the basis of the examples:

To no one's surprise, preliminary work showed that in order to accomplish the coding, coders were assuming knowledge of the very organised ways of the clinic that their coding procedures were intended to provide descriptions of. More interestingly, such presupposed knowledge seemed necessary and was most deliberately consulted

---

[1] It seems that the body is, in a limited way, open to ethnomethodological description: see D. Sudnow's paper in Sudnow 1972.

whenever, and for whatever reasons, the coders needed to be satisfied that they had coded 'what really happened'. (p. 20)

Reference was made to this presupposed knowledge however clear the coding instructions and however clear or dubious the information to be coded. Further study revealed that the coders used 'ad hoc' procedures[1] in recognising the relevance of the instructions to the information to be coded and in coding the information (the information being supplied by the clinic workers in the course of their activities):

Ad hocing occurs (without, I believe any possibility of remedy) whenever the coder assumes the position of a socially competent member of the arrangement that he seeks to assemble an account of, and when from this 'position' he treats actual folder contents as standing in a relationship of trusted significance to the 'system' in the clinic activities. Because the coder assumes the 'position' of a competent member to the arrangement he seeks to give an account of, he can 'see the system' in the actual content of the folder. (p. 22)

The coder treats what he has to code (the folder contents) as 'sign-functions' for the order of the clinic activities. The central consequences of this is seen as follows:

If the work of ad hocing is required to make such claims (of disinterested description) intelligible, it can always be argued – and so far I do not see a defensible reply – that the coded results consist of a persuasive version of the socially organised character of the clinic's operations, regardless of what the actual order is, perhaps independently of what the actual order is and even without the investigator having detected the actual order. Instead of our study of patient's clinic careers . . . having described the order of the clinic's operations, the account may be argued to consist of a socially invented, persuasive and proper way of talking about the clinic as an orderly enterprise, since 'after all' the account was produced by 'scientific' procedures. The account would be itself part of the actual order of the clinic's operations, in much the same way that one might treat a person's report on his own activities as a feature of his activities. *The actual order would remain to be described.* (pp. 23–4)

Thus:

Coding instructions ought to be read instead as consisting of a grammar of rhetoric; they furnish a 'social science' way of talking so as to persuade consensus and action within the practical circumstances of the clinic's organised daily activities, a grasp of which members are expected to have as a matter of course . . . It furnishes an impersonal

[1] The procedures are listed as: '"et cetera", "unless", "let it pass" and "factum valet" (i.e. an action that is otherwise prohibited by a rule is counted correct once it is done)'. (pp. 20-1)

way of characterising their affairs without the members relinquishing
important organisationally determined interests in what the account, in
their eyes, is 'after all' about . . . (p. 24)

The heart of this example seems to be the relationship between
language and whatever it is that lies outside language. Garfinkel
talks about the 'actual order' of activities in the clinic as if they had
an existence outside what was said about them, an existence which
is fixed and discoverable. Yet it has already been pointed out that
these examples are in the context of an approach which defines the
area of study not as 'what really happens' but as how whatever it
is that really happens is organised and recognised as 'rationally
accountable'.

Most of the argument quoted above is again not the specific
province of ethnomethodology: it is very similar to arguments about
the ideological and political use and content of allegedly 'scientific'
arguments (for example Bendix, 1956). 'Practical sociological
reasoning' it appears is always open to the accusation that it is 'a
socially invented, persuasive and proper' way of talking about things
and the implication is that what should be studied is not the
substantive content of accounts but the way in which those accounts
are constructed.[1] We have seen, however, that Garfinkel establishes
ethnomethodology's subject matter by means of 'practical sociological reasoning', that his insight is open to any observer or participant who looks at a situation in a certain way. In this sense, too,
his argument is open to the same accusation: that it represents a
'socially invented, persuasive and proper' way of talking about
things, in this case the social group in which it would be a persuasive
and proper way of talking about things being sociologists or, more
specifically, ethnomethodologists. The significance of this will
become apparent later.

We can progress further in our analysis of this example by
looking more closely at one of the 'ad hocing' procedures: 'et
cetera'. Cicourel (in Douglas, 1971) defines 'et cetera' as the actor's
treating a given lexical item, category or phrase as an index of larger
networks of meaning. This activity is taken for granted in every
interaction and it would be impossible to understand statements
without it; it seems to rest on the ability to collect words, phrases
and categories together and to be referred to the collection by the
mention of one item.[2] The coding rules referred coders to a set

---

[1] This comes out very clearly in Alan F. Blum's: 'The Corpus of
Knowledge as a Normative Order' in McKinney and Tiryakian (1970).
See also the articles by Blum and McHugh in Douglas (1971).
[2] For a useful example of 'etcetera', see Lindsey Churchill 1971.

of meanings that comprised 'reasonable circumstances', 'for all practical purposes' according to which it was decided whether or not a specific rule applied. Thus the information was coded, according to Garfinkel, by reference to assumed rationalities constructed by the clinic workers in the process of and as comprising their activities; these were adopted by the coders. Here we find no reference to anything that happened outside of the clinic workers' accounts, no 'actual order', the idea of which Garfinkel appears to drop in favour of locating the actual order in the accounts given by the workers and assumed by the coders not in their substantive content but in the way in which they are constructed.

The use of 'et-cetera' shows that self-reported activity cannot be translated directly and without fear of inaccuracy into categories they do not originally contain, and that any rationality about practices lies in those practices themselves or in the way in which they are described by the practitioner rather than in categories established in some other 'scientific' context. As a criticism of a sociology which regards activity as governed by rules and easily translatable from the actor's terms into the sociologist's terms, this is fair enough. It must be remembered however that we started off with three aspects of the problem: what the clinic workers do, what they say they do, and how the coders classify what the clinic workers say they do. By concentrating on the process of coding, Garfinkel surreptitiously slips what the clinic workers do into what they say they do. The 'actual order' of activities in the clinic is initially posited as having an existence independent of how it is described by the workers, an existence available to the sociological observer. It is used in the critique of 'practical sociological reasoning'. It is then dropped as an item of analysis either because it is unavailable to the observer or because it is contained within the description; the latter is implied and attention is focussed on the coding operation rather than the problems of 'getting at' the actual order. In this way, 'reality' is merged into what is said about it.

Garfinkel also points out that the coder, in order to effect a 'successful coding' takes the position of the clinic worker whose statements he is coding; this in itself would open the way for a reference to the 'actual order', rather than statements about it, in the coding process but again this feature of coding is only mentioned in the critique of practical sociological reasoning. It will be argued later that this 'taking the position of' the other is a necessary precondition of any understanding – whether the intention is to talk about *what* the other says or about *how* he says it. Garfinkel, however, by implication of treating it as a factor in practical sociological reasoning which produces 'a socially invented, persuasive and proper' way of talking about their activities, seems to suggest that it can be avoided.[1] Before we can discuss this properly, however, we must look at the third example.

iv. Common understandings

Garfinkel begins by pointing out that sociologists usually distinguish the 'product' meanings of common understandings from the 'process' meanings – shared agreement on substantive matters from the ways whereby what is said is recognised to accord with a rule. He claims to show that both consist of 'an inner-temporal course of interpretive work'.

Students were asked to write an actual conversation on one side of a sheet of paper and on the other side what each partner understood themselves to be talking about. One example is reported:

HUSBAND:
Dana succeeded in putting a penny in a parking meter today without being picked up.

This afternoon as I was bringing Dana, our four year-old son, home from the nursery school, he succeeded in reaching high enough to put a penny in a parking meter when we parked in a meter zone, whereas before he had always had to be picked up to reach that high.

WIFE:
Did you take him to the record store?

Since he put a penny in a meter, that means that you stopped while he was with you. I know that you stopped at the record store either on the way to get him or on the way back. Was it on the way back, so that he was with you, or did you stop there on the way to get him and somewhere else on the way back?

HUSBAND:
No, to the shoe-repair shop.

No, I stopped at the record store on the way to get him and stopped at the shoe-repair shop on the way home when he was with me.

---

[1] The phrase 'taking the position of the Other' here should not be confused with Mead's use of the idea, which he sees only on the reflective level. This will become clearer later on in the chapter.

WIFE:
What for?

I know of one reason why you might have stopped at the shoe-repair shop. Why did you in fact?

HUSBAND:
I got some new shoe laces for my shoes.

As you will remember, I broke a shoe lace on one of my brown oxfords the other day so I stopped to get some new laces.

WIFE:
Your loafers need new heels badly.

Something else you could have gotten that I was thinking of. You could have taken in your black loafers which need heels badly. You'd better get them taken care of pretty soon.

Referring to the right hand column Garfinkel writes:

As I progressively imposed accuracy, clarity and distinctness, the task became increasingly laborious. Finally, when I required that they assume I would know what they had actually talked about only from reading literally what they wrote literally, they gave up with the complaint that the task was impossible. (pp. 25–6)

Garfinkel claims that the task was impossible, not because he could pedantically insist on the right hand side being exhaustive but because the writing on the right hand side of the page actually expanded the conversation – each version provided more and more to be explained. In short, indexical statements or phrases could not be avoided.

If a common understanding required agreement on substantive matters, Garfinkel argues, the students' task would have been the same as that which professional sociologists normally attempt. It would have involved a distinction between what was said and what was talked about and because of the sketchiness of the former, they would need to look elsewhere for its corresponding contents (i.e. for what was talked about) and find the grounds to argue for the correctness of the correspondence; these grounds would be found in the beliefs or intentions of the conversationalists and these would be confirmed by citing observed actions:

all of which is to say that students would invoke their knowledge of the community of understandings and their knowledge of shared agreements to recommend the adequacy of their accounts of what the parties had been talking about, i.e. what the parties understood in common. Then, for anything the students wrote, they could assume that I, as a competent co-member of the same community . . . should be able to see the correspondance and its grounds. (pp. 27–8)

This description of the task, based on the idea that common understanding consists of shared agreement on substantive matters would explain the increasing difficulty of the task and the students' complaints, but it would not account for the eventual impossibility and the recognition of this by the students, nor does it account for the fact that the way of accomplishing the task multiplied its features, i.e. it does not account for the unavoidability of indexical statements. Garfinkel continues – and this is particularly important in the light of what was said earlier about the relationship between descriptions and 'the actual order':

An alternative conception of the task may do better. Although it may appear at first strange to do so, suppose we drop the assumption that in order to describe a usage as a feature of a community of understandings we must at the outset know what the substantive common understandings consist of. With it, drop the assumption's accompanying theory of signs, according to which a 'sign' and a 'referent' are respectively properties of something said and something talked about, and which in this fashion proposes sign and referent to be related as corresponding contents. By dropping such a theory of signs we drop as well thereby the possibility that an invoked shared agreement on substantive matters explains a usage.
If these notions are dropped, then what the parties talked about could not be distinguished from *how* the parties were speaking . . . (p. 28)

The right hand column, then, is a mistaken attempt to show how the parties were speaking by describing what they were saying.

'Shared agreement' refers to various social methods for accomplishing the members' recognition that something was said according-to-a-rule and not the demonstrable matching of substantive matters. The appropriate image of a common understanding is therefore an operation rather than a common intersection of overlapping sets. (p. 30)

On the face of it, this argument would appear to be the empirical justification that was missing in the first example, and it contains explicitly the absorption of what 'really happens' into what is said about 'what really happens', or, rather, how it is said. It is necessary, however, to look at the example more closely.
There are in fact two instances of interaction: that between husband and wife, and that between Garfinkel and his student (we are informed elsewhere that husband and student are the same person).[1] We will concentrate, for the moment, on the latter

---

[1] See 'Studies in the Routine Grounds of Everyday Activities' in the same book; interestingly, in this earlier paper, Garfinkel seems more concerned with the substantive assumptions behind the conversation.

interaction. In the course of his argument Garfinkel likens the task that he set the student to that normally undertaken by the professional sociologist in the course of reporting his observations, and he finds that the usual conception of the latter fails to explain the impossibility of the former. This is not surprising because they are *two very different tasks*: the 'normal' sociological task, as he points out, assumes a shared agreement on substantive matters; this is precisely what he forbids his students to do.

If the task set the student and task usually faced by the sociologist are different from the outset then it is self-evident that the 'normal' conception of the latter cannot help us to explain the difficulties of the former. The assumptions that Garfinkel drops to explain the impossibility of the task that he sets the student were implicitly dropped *in the setting of the task* and not logically derived from his description of the 'normal' sociological task at all. If he shows that the 'normal' conception of the 'normal' sociological task is inadequate, then it is because he has made it inadequate from the outset by implying that it has an aim that in reality it has not got at all: to explain observations exhaustively by the use of words, so there can be no doubt as to their meaning. In fact, if we retain the assumptions that Garfinkel drops – the sign/referent (or signifier/signified) conception of language, then we can understand the impossibility of the task that he sets the students very well. To confine the student to the level of the signifier is to place him in the middle of a set of mirrors that constantly reflect only each other and then ask him to describe what is outside.

v. Language

The three examples that we have studied can be seen as an ongoing argument climaxing in the definition of the field of study of ethnomethodology as comprising the ongoing construction of rationality, language use to convey meaning, and the separation of the study of this process from any other sort of study. Our criticisms have centred on this separation, arguing that it is at least empirically unjustified.

It is now possible, drawing in particular on the last example, to develop a view of 'common understanding' different from both Garfinkel's description of the 'normal' sociological task and his own description, but which includes elements of both.[1] From this it will

---

[1] This description will be based on the signifier/signified distinction that Garfinkel drops. The terminology 'signifier/signified' belongs to structural linguistics (see in particular Roland Barthes 1968) although it is used by Sartre in a different sense (see Jean-Pierre Faye 1966). It is

be possible to draw out some of Garfinkel's most fundamental
assumptions and move the discussion on to a more general level.

(i) It will be remembered that Garfinkel drops the assumption
that there are substantive common understandings and with it the
signifier/signified conception of language. However, if the words
are not signifiers, if they did not 'point' to anything, then the
conversation as reported would not have been possible. The reason
for this is fundamental and lies in the nature of consciousness.

We have seen that consciousness is always consciousness *of*
something, and to be aware of something is, then, to be aware of
it in relation to myself, to be aware of it as *not-me*; consciousness
is a relationship. This means that whatever I am conscious of points
towards my consciousness, it signifies me, it 'means' me.[1] If
nothing else it signifies my spatial relationship to it. In this sense,
everything is meaningful, I can not be conscious of something that
is meaningless, that does not point anywhere. As we have seen, the
specific meaning of a phenomenon is understood in terms of the
project of the For-itself that reveals it. Garfinkel does not eliminate
the signifying function of the words he looks at, he only gives them
a different signification. Rather than signifying something outside
of themselves, he sees them as signifying their own 'hidden'
qualities – qualities that are discovered when he drops the assumptions that he does drop. What the words as reported by the student
signify to Garfinkel is the way in which they are spoken, and the
terms in which he expresses this are as much 'outside' the words
as any substantive agreement that the speakers may or may not
assume. The 'dropping of assumptions' makes the way in which the
words are spoken the most important signification whereas in fact
it is one amongst many.[2]

In the reported conversation, there are two 'levels' of shared
substantive agreement. Firstly there is the pre-reflective recognition
and agreement that 'there is Being' and that Being is neither of
the participants and that therefore they are in relationship to it and

being used here for its implication that language is *also* a structure as
described in Chapter 2. For the structuralists, the word is a sign
comprising both signifier and signified. In Sartre's use, which is being
followed here, the 'signified' is something outside the word.

[1] In *Saint Genet* (pp. 276–310) Sartre distinguishes signification, or the
substitution of one object for another, from meaning, where one object
points towards another. There is, however, self evidently an element of
meaning in any signification.

[2] Using Barthes' definition, this may be regarded as a 'mythical'
interpretation of language: the original sign (signifier/signified)
becomes a signifier in a new sign – the new signified in this case being
the way in which the words are spoken. See Roland Barthes (1972).

the pre-reflective recognition by each that the other is an Other (otherwise one or both parties would believe that he was talking to himself). Secondly there is a shared agreement on the more complex meanings conveyed by naming the various objects and relationships mentioned in the conversation. For the conversation to take place at all, both parties must have had some idea of what pennies, parking meters, record stores, shoe-repair shops etc. 'are', and they must have some idea of the movements involved in 'putting', 'picking up', 'taking' etc. These substantive shared agreements might be 'typifications', and each party may assume that each word means the same to the other party as it does to himself at least for all practical purposes, but in each case the word refers both speaker and listener to a substantive entity or to a relationship to that entity which is 'objective' in the sense that it has an existence recognised by both and thus belonging to neither. In some cases the shared agreement on the meaning of a word might be built into the object itself, for example, the meaning of the record store is built into the way in which the objects are arranged inside it, but without these shared agreements the reported conversation would have been broken up by statements, comments and questions such as 'What's that?', 'What do you mean?', 'Never heard of it', 'Where's that?' etc. In other words, it could not have taken place as reported.

It is difficult to conceive of a conversation that would not assume a shared agreement on at least the first of these levels. Elsewhere (McKinney and Tiryakian, 1970) Garfinkel gives an example of a 'gloss' way of talking about something that cannot be said in so many words, which might appear on a superficial level to involve no shared substantive agreement. On close inspection, however, we can find such an agreement. A speaker makes a comment or in some way gives an indication that appears to refer to 'something' although he has no particular 'something' in mind. He waits to find out from his conversationalist what he is talking about. In such a situation, both parties must agree that 'there is something' about which it is possible to talk. Furthermore, the initiator does not, in Garfinkel's terms 'find out what he is talking about' but rather he finds out what his companion thinks he is talking about, which is rather different. Eventually the conversation, already based on the shared agreement that there is 'something' to talk about, could not continue without in some way elaborating this basic agreement.

(ii) We can turn now to the problem of the ends or 'intentions' of the speakers. Garfinkel recognises that these play a part in his description of the 'normal' sociological task, but he includes no reference to them in the description of a common understanding that he develops. If we look more closely, however, we find that the ends of the speaker are very relevant to the way in which the works are spoken.

Hypothetically, we could suggest several ends that the speakers were aiming at. The reported conversation may suggest an intention on the part of the husband to convey information about their son's growing ability to do various things, and an intention at a later stage on the part of the wife to discover if the husband's shoes still require repairing, or simply where their son had exercised his new found ability. The student's explication would indicate several intentions of this kind, each aiming at a future state of knowledge in the light of which future action may be taken, which, in turn, will confer a new meaning on the reported exchange. If, for the moment, we ignore the student's explication, we can suggest various other interpretations. For example, the wife might be attempting to discover if her husband has been in contact with a suspected mistress during his afternoon absence; or the husband might be attacking the wife for her neglect of wifely duties – he had to go to the shoe repair shop himself – and the wife might be retaliating by pointing out that since she knew that his loafers needed repairing and he had done nothing about it, she knew much better than he what his material interests were. They might both have been trying to find inconsequential comments to make until they could turn the tape-recorder off.

We can see from these suggestions that the ends or intentions of the speakers are implicit in the student's explications. If he were honestly reporting the conversation, and the intentions of the speakers had, for example, been similar to those outlined in the previous paragraph, then the student's explication would have been different to what it is. If we are to decide between different interpretations of intentions, then Garfinkel is correct to argue that it is *how* the words are spoken that matters; but how the words are spoken is implicitly a matter of indicating the ends of the speakers.

(iii) From these arguments we have developed three qualifications to Garfinkel's own model of a common understanding which lead us back towards the conception he rejects without abandoning his position completely. *How* the words are spoken is still important, but not all-important. The first qualification is that we are referred outside of the words to substantive entities and to a shared agreement on the nature of those entities: it must be emphasised again that these render the conversation as reported possible and that although the relationship between the 'how' and the 'what' may be reflexive in that the 'what' is indicated in the 'how' and although the shared agreement on the 'what' may be built up in the course of the 'how' the relationship between the two is never completely self-contained; there must always be a shared agreement of some sort on the existence of a Being outside the words and towards which the words point. It is this that explains the impossibility of the task that Garfinkel sets his students: it tried to avoid a reference to this transcendent Being.

The second qualification is that the 'how' itself refers us beyond the words spoken to the ends of the speaker ignored by Garfinkel. We do not understand a sentence only by listening to how it is spoken; how it is spoken serves as an indication of, and as something to be understood in terms of, the situation and the project (i.e. the ends, the intentions) of the speaker.

The third qualification is based on the second and on the pre-reflective recognition of the existence of the Other: if the husband is to understand the wife and vice versa, and if Garfinkel is to understand his student's explication, then each must operate a pre-reflective *identification* with the other, he must recognise the other as sharing the same 'human reality'. It is this identification, in its reflective form, that Garfinkel noted in his discussion of the coding operation, and the reflective form is based on the inevitable pre-reflective form.

From this we can offer a description of a common understanding that involves three elements:

1. The objects and relationships to objects about which the words are spoken; beyond the simple recognition that there are objects and relationships, these are invested to some degree with meanings that are shared by the conversationalists. In the first example that we discussed, these included the official structure of the SPC and the Coroner's office, the pre-defined ways of dying and so on, everything that we argued Garfinkel assumed without discussing. In the second example, they include the 'real order' of events in the clinic, which Garfinkel merges with what was said about the 'real order'. In the third example, they include the objects and actions referred to by husband and wife.

2. The words spoken; through their structure and the way in which they are spoken, these words confer a *specific* order on the first element. It is here that we find what Garfinkel calls reflexivity, where the participants to some extent create situations by describing them.

3. The situation and projects of the speakers and the observer; each, to understand what is being said, must refer or be referred to both situation and project of the other. This adds two new dimensions to reflexivity as it is described by Garfinkel: the words spoken not only create and describe a present setting, but also, to a degree, describe and create a past setting and posit in some way a future setting into

which the speaker wishes the participants to move. Both past and future settings, as well as the present settings, contain and refer to the first elements by means of the second.

We have tried to show that Garfinkel's 'indifference' to the first and third elements is unjustified empirically, and, furthermore, that it is unsuccessful in that his descriptions have assumed or implied the existence of these elements. Garfinkel argues that:

An analysis of students' experiences in reporting commonplace conversation suggests that for either case, for 'product' or 'process' a common understanding consists of an inner-temporal course of interpretive work

and that:

'Shared agreement' refers to various social methods for accomplishing the member's recognition that something was said according-to-a-rule and not the demonstrable matching of substantive matters. The appropriate image of a common understanding is therefore an operation rather than a common intersection of overlapping sets. (p. 25)

This analysis has suggested firstly that a common understanding or shared agreement is *both* a matter of a 'demonstrable matching of substantive matters' *and* an 'inner-temporal course of interpretive work' involving the accomplishment of 'the recognition that something was said-according-to-a-rule', and that an understanding cannot take place unless both of these features are present; and secondly that the temporal interpretation of the conversation by the parties involved takes place within an infinitely longer temporal span than that imagined by Garfinkel and covers a very wide area of substantive matters and intentions.

We can now look at two of Garfinkel's points in terms of our description of a common understanding. Firstly, it will be remembered that he argues that sociologists are creating their own settings by means of glosses and other taken-for-granted ways that do not necessarily tell us anything about the setting they are studying, i.e. that they produce only another 'socially invented, persuasive and proper' way of talking about things. This argument is only possible on the assumption of the existence of certain specific objects, relationships and other people, i.e. on the existence of an 'actual order'. If this assumption were not there, or rather if what were assumed were not there, then no form of communication would be possible.[1] Secondly, we can locate glossing not only as a feature of

---

[1] For example, Sach's paper 'An initial investigation of the usability of conversational data for doing sociology' (in Sudnow 1972) seems to be centred on the assumption of mutual expectations held by those being

language use but as a feature of all activity. To the extent that all my activities are open to a future re-interpretation, to the extent that I may confer a different meaning on them by my future activities, then I never *know* what I am doing: 'not knowing what I am talking about' is one manifestation of this opening toward the future that is present in all activity.

The view of language that is becoming increasingly explicit in these criticisms is that of language as a tool which is used not only to make activities rationally accountable (and in that sense to constitute them) but to do this as a means of defining and changing relationships between objects and persons that have an existence outside of words. Neither of these uses may be understood in isolation. This view is based on an ontology, a view of the relationship of consciousness to the world and of the nature of both. Garfinkel's conception of language also implies an ontology, and in attempting to discover what this ontology might be we can turn to the two aims of this chapter which have so far remained in the background: the establishment of the relevance of what Sartre is talking about to sociological research and the exploration of the relationship between philosophy and sociology that is implicit in Sartre's work.

VI. Philosophy and sociology

We can now examine Garfinkel's 'ethnomethodological indifference' and compare it to the phenomenological reduction, and, through an examination of Schutz's work, we can try to 'situate' Garfinkel in relation to phenomenology to draw out his ontological assumptions. A fairly extensive analysis of Garfinkel's assumptions is possible because of the comparative closeness of his work to phenomenology. It is, however, in principle, possible to discover such assumptions in the work of all writers, even if we cannot explore them in such depth.[1]

Any view of language as a tool presupposes a user: it puts language outside of consciousness. It is apparent that Garfinkel does treat language as a tool, albeit for a limited purpose, the creation of rationality, and he sees the subject matter for ethnomethodology

(n 1 continued)
studied about the roles played by kin. In other words a study of language use has to be based outside language.

[1] Thus, for example, it would have been possible to extend our analysis of Goffman to include an identification of consciousness with mind in the physical sense. The consequent inability to understand the origin and nature of negation (since the physical mind is pure positivity) could be seen to be at the root of his reliance on the institutionally defined self and his inability to handle individual activities in anything but very broad categories. The identification of mind and consciousness is apparent in Mead (1938) and also in Van Meter Ames (1956).

as being language *use*. On the other hand, the nature of the 'user' is unimportant to him, he pays it no attention. It is this lack, together with his 'indifference' to practical sociological reasoning that implies a second, contradictory, assumption about the relationship of consciousness to the world which co-exists with the first and is at the root of the inadequacies we have tried to illustrate.

i

Garfinkel appears to present no satisfactory empirical justification for 'indifference', and when he discusses it explicitly, it receives very little theoretical justification; it is, simply stated as a matter of policy:

We call attention to the phenomenon that formal structures are available in the accounts of professional sociology where they are recognised by professionals and claimed by them as professional sociology's singular achievement. These accounts of formal structures are done via sociology's mastery of natural language and require that mastery as the sine qua non of adequate professional readership. This assures to professional sociologists' accounts of formal structures its character as a phenomenon for ethnomethodology's interest, not different from any other member's phenomenon where mastery of natural language is similarly involved. Ethnomethodological studies of formal structures are directed to the study of such phenomena, seeking to describe members' accounts of formal structures wherever and by whomever they are done, while abstaining from all judgements of their adequacy, value, importance, necessity, practicality, success or consequentiality. We refer to this procedural policy as 'ethnomethodological indifference'.

. . .our work then, does not stand in any modifying, elaborating, contributing, detailing, subdividing, explicating, foundation-building, relationship to professional sociological reasoning, nor is our 'indifference' to those orders of task. Rather our indifference is to the whole of sociological reasoning and *that* reasoning involves for us, in whatever form of development, with whatever error or inadequacy, in whatever forms, inseparably and unavoidably, the mastery of natural language . . . (McKinney and Tiryakian, 1970; 345–6)

'Indifference', then, expresses the intention to look at sociology as an ongoing practical activity, as a way of making a setting rationally accountable, without referring to its substantive content; sociology is treated as another example of language use. We can see here a similar assumption to that noted in the SPC example; there is no mention of the possibility of a connection between the substantive content of sociology and 'doing sociology' as a practical achievement, or of studying the latter in terms of the former or vice versa.

'Indifference', then, has no empirical justification and no elaborate theoretical justification: it is simply assumed that language
use, in Garfinkel's sense, can be studied independently of wider
considerations. Nevertheless, in some respects it bears a striking
resemblance to the phenomenological reduction. What is bracketing
if not an expression of 'indifference'?; the resemblance is certainly
suggested by Garfinkel's admitted antecedents, and the two have at
least a superficially similar purpose: the phenomenological reduction enables us to study the constitution of the world by consciousness, 'ethnomethodological indifference' enables us to study the
constitution of rationality of language. By comparing the two more
closely, we can begin to bring out the nature of the phenomenological enterprises and hence of Sartre's philosophy insofar as it uses
the phenomenological method.

The aim of phenomenology, unlike that of ethnomethodology,
is very much one of foundation-building; we have seen that Husserl
was seeking the foundations of the sciences. The phenomenological
reduction seeks to make the foundations of knowledge apparent:
it is a tool which enables the philosopher to ask 'How is knowledge
possible?'. Natanson (1970, 9) writes:

Placing our believing in the world in suspension means, most
importantly, becoming explicitly aware of the character of that
believing (in the existence of the world). Two elements are important:
first the believing is focussed on, reflected on, made an explicit theme of
analysis; second, the scope of that believing must be comprehended,
for its range includes all perceptual experience . . .[1]

In contrast, ethnomethodological indifference is not an indifference to the whole of perceptual experience but presupposes a
degree of that experience. The use of language, the 'mastery of
natural language', practical activity in any setting, presupposes that
members (in Garfinkel's sense) have already constituted[2] a world
and, more importantly, that they have constituted a psychological
ego by means of which they are able to co-ordinate their experience
in a particular way, and that they have constituted language. Only
some of our beliefs in the world are placed in brackets and the
investigation therefore goes only half-way to the roots of our
experience. Garfinkel, however, seems to believe that he has gone
the whole way, otherwise why would he ignore the pre-constructed
settings of the SPC workers?

---

[1] On the reduction, see also Hindess 1972, Bauman 1973, Neisser 1959.
[2] 'Constituting' is used here in its phenomenological sense; in its
      Sartrean sense it would have a rather different meaning, expressing the
      nihilation and revelation of Being by consciousness; the difference
      between the two uses stems from the ontological proof.

The phenomenological reduction enables the philosopher to trace the development of meaning, the constitution of the world, including the constitution of language. Paul Ricoeur writes (in Lee and Mandelbaum, 1967; 213)

We have elaborated in this way a model of analysis which may be called a genesis, but not a genesis in the chronological sense; it is a genesis of meaning, a sense genesis, which consists in unfolding the layers of constitution deposited as sediments on a presupposed raw, mute, experience.

The constitution that Garfinkel studies is not the constitution of meaning as such but the constitution of rationality within which meaning is contained, developed, conveyed etc.; we have seen that meaning is originally created in a relationship of consciousness to Being. Garfinkel studies only one layer in the sediment, or one aspect of several or all layers. We have argued that language use presupposes a user, but Garfinkel does not refer to a user (consciousness) and indifference is, thus, not justified as part of a wider philosophical investigation; at the same time his indifference is to the meaning constituted in the framework of rationality, i.e. it is to practical sociological reasoning, and he does not justify this empirically. The result is an implicit identification of language with consciousness on the one hand and with the world on the other – everything is telescoped into language. 'Man' becomes 'language' and nothing more. It is this implicit identification, alongside the equally implicit presupposition of a 'user' that is the central contradiction in Garfinkel's work.

Another vital difference between the phenomenological reduction and ethnomethodological indifference lies in Ricoeur's statement that it is not a *chronological* but a *theoretical* genesis that is constructed; the latter can neither be discovered nor reproduced empirically. In this sense, then, Garfinkel's indifference as an empirical operation *has* to be justified empirically if it is not simply a matter of ignoring inconvenient aspects of what is being studied. To achieve this justification would require a complete discussion of all possible relationships between what is being studied and what is covered by the indifference in order to show that the latter can be safely ignored without affecting the adequacy of the study of the former, and it would also require it to be shown that the indifference is positively productive, i.e. that it enables a study which would otherwise not have been possible. Garfinkel does not appear to tackle either of these tasks.

ii

We have already discovered one of Garfinkel's ontological assumptions in his identification of consciousness with language. We can extend our understanding of this, and discover other assumptions by looking at his work in the light of Schutz's writings. Garfinkel does not appear to derive his ideas from Schutz in any direct way, but Schutz is an acknowledged predecessor and we can find implicitly assumed in Garfinkel's work many of Schutz's arguments.

An emphasis on rationality is something that is particularly prominent in Schutz – most clearly if we compare his conception of the project with that of Sartre (Schutz, 1962a): there is no room in Schutz for the original 'irrationality' of the choice of project, or the possibility of apparently contradictory actions being understood in terms of one project. A similar emphasis appears in his analysis of relationships with others, and at the moment it is this which is of greater concern to us. The usual phenomenological proof of the existence of others starts with the perception of the Other's body from within the epoché and then argues by analogy. Sartre has shown (1957a: 233–52) that this argument still leaves us in the realm of probability: it is only likely that the Other exists as a consciousness similar to mine. As we have seen, nobody seriously doubts the existence of the Other and the eventual proof of this existence is to be found in my experience of myself as an object in the organised world of the Other, and it is from this position that the dialectic of the relationship with the Other begins.

Schutz (1962a) accepts Sartre's critique of Husserl, but argues that in Sartre's work there is no place for co-operation with the Other, for joint action. He finds the provision for co-operation originally in the 'life-world': individual consciousnesses are united through sharing the same typifications of the world and their experiences in it, and these typifications make up the 'life-world', they comprise the 'common-sense' knowledge with which everybody operates and out of which scientific knowledge is formed. It is the investigation of the 'life-world' that seems to be the main aim of Schutz's sociology and he sees contained within it various 'types' of rationality which Garfinkel, on occasion, takes up; the latter, however, modifies Schutz insofar as he sees rationality as constantly created rather than as possessing a substantive existence. It can be seen that the existence of the life-world, whether or not it 'contains' rationality in a substantive form, provides a way of uniting separate consciousnesses which avoids the changing and essentially non-rational (in the usual scientific sense of the word) dialectic of

Sartre's analysis of interpersonal relationships; at the same time, it is easier to handle and fits more readily into conventional sociological analysis (as well as providing a view closer to the 'normal' view of the world and of individuals' relationships to each other).[1]

The life-world occupies an intermediate position: on the one hand, it is, presumably, constituted by the transcendental ego, and on the other Schutz sees it as the source, the root of scientific knowledge.[2] By concentrating his analyses on the life-world to the exclusion of consciousness, Schutz tends to portray one world – that of scientific knowledge – as constituted by the other, the life-world. Effectively consciousness is merged with the life-world; it loses any transcendental character and becomes a collection of individual consciousnesses with the same content (typifications). Any sort of project is then understood in terms of typifications, forms of rationality, and the points at which the taken-for-granted life-world comes into question.[3] The concept of an intentional conciousness disappears.

We find here exactly the same features that we discovered in our discussion of ethnomethodological indifference: the 'bracketing' stops half-way, in Schutz's case at the life-world, and whatever is left unbracketed is identified with consciousness and seen as what constitutes the world. Garfinkel goes further than Schutz in that he sees the life-world as *only* language: thus consciousness is language and the world is created out of language.[4] In our earlier arguments we also made the point that Garfinkel was assuming agreement on substantive matters, assuming the preconstruction of settings and ignoring the fundamental importance of understanding the Other by grasping his situation and project; we can now see these assumptions and inadequacies as the assumption of Schutz's view of the life-world: each consciousness is 'filled' with the same typifications out of which rationality is constructed and the existence of the other is not a problem because a shared life-world presupposes that

---

[1] 'Normal' means of course, in this context, normal to one group or class in society. An analysis of Schutz's work which relates it to his personal career has not yet appeared, although there appears to be plenty of scope for a treatment similar to that of Parsons by Gouldner in *The Coming Crisis*; Hindess (1972) makes some passing comments.

[2] To reach the life-world, scientific knowledge has to be bracketed. Hindess points out the difficulty of distinguishing a life-world which has not incorporated the assumptions and findings of science.

[3] This conception is similar to that of G. H. Mead; see in particular *The Philosophy of the Act* (1938).

[4] In this light the increasing attention paid by ethnomethodology to Wittgenstein – rather than Husserl – becomes a logical next step. See in particular, Coulter 1973, Ryle 1971, Sinka 1963.

existence; understanding becomes a matter of grasping the Other's organisation of typifications and nothing more. The identification of consciousness with the life-world or language destroys the possibility of a critical sociology: we are confined to the description of an already existing life-world or the use of an already existing language structure; the source of possible change, a consciousness transcendent to the life-world or to language, has disappeared.

The basis for these criticisms is a conception of consciousness as outside both the life-world and language; consciousness assumes language and the life-world (thus assuming a specific language) in the first case making itself human, in the second making itself a member of a specific human collectivity. These assumptions are made in the wider context of the relationship between consciousness and Being and between consciousnesses embedded in facticity. Language and the life-world, including the practices by which activity is made rationally accountable in terms of 'What Everybody Knows' become tools or material in a wider project, and not, as happens with Garfinkel, the only conceivable project. The reflexivity by which a setting is created in its description becomes part of a deeper reflexivity of a consciousness creating itself by going beyond itself. We will see in Chapter 6 that this leaves room for a different conception of unity between consciousnesses, based on ways in which I grasp the Other in the subject/object dialectic.

iii

It would be difficult to dispute the importance for sociology of the problems that Garfinkel tackles: the problem of what we mean by 'understanding', the use or otherwise of verbal reports for 'doing sociology', the status of our conclusions as 'scientific' or a 'socially invented, persuasive and proper' way of talking about things, and so on. We have tried to show that these problems directly or indirectly imply other problems which belong to phenomenology and ontology, i.e. to a branch of philosophy superficially some distance from sociology, and that any empirical study directly or indirectly raises these problems and makes what may very well be self-contradictory assumptions about their solution.

We have also tried to establish that the problem of consciousness and Being is not open to an empirical solution: it should now be becoming increasingly clear that an empirical study by its very nature assumes the existence of objects, a certain manner of their existence, the existence of consciousness, and certain relationships between these existences. Goffman's studies make these assumptions in a fairly straightforward way; Garfinkel tries to eliminate

them but, as we have seen, fails. Without them no empirical
investigation would be possible simply because we would not know
whether there was anything there to investigate.

We have further tried to establish that the tools and concepts of
the theoretical[1] analysis cannot be applied empirically or in a
piecemeal manner. If 'indifference' is to be maintained, it cannot
be introduced from nowhere or 'lifted' from phenomenology in
isolation; it only becomes justified and productive in the context of
the general phenomenological project. It is interesting to note in
this respect that what distinguishes Garfinkel from those sociologists
– such as Schutz, Natanson, Berger and Luckmann – who are also
classed as 'phenomenological' is his concentration on empirical
studies; the others do not attempt to derive their positions empirically, rather they manufacture examples in the course of the
theoretical arguments.[2]

Finally we have tried to establish that if sociology is to learn from
philosophy, then the latter must be clearly understood, the concepts
used must be clear in their relationships to each other. The
confusion of egos and the confusion of consciousness and the
life-world apparent in Schutz's work[3] and assumed by Garfinkel
involve a number of distortions that are reproduced in empirical
studies.

VII. Philosophical sociology

Given that the ontological proof – the separation of consciousness and Being – the relationship of one to the other, and the
relationship between different consciousnesses present problems
that are important for sociology and bear on the adequacy of its
empirical descriptions, we can turn to the way in which the conclusions of the theoretical argument are to be employed by sociologists.
At least some of the answers should now be apparent.

To begin with, we have shown that it is possible to argue back
from empirical descriptions to the conclusions of the theoretical
argument, but this is simply a repeat of the theoretical argument
and not in itself a sociological enterprise. We can now explore more
thoroughly the differences between the two types of argument. This
study is an attempt to explore the relationship between philosophy

---

[1] 'Theoretical' will from now on be used to indicate the
phenomenological description of consciousness and Being, as part of
an attempt to distinguish philosophy and sociology in a different way to
that involved in the conventional boundaries between disciplines.

[2] See Natanson 1970, Schutz 1962a, b, c; Berger and Luckmann 1966.

[3] Hindess (1972) outlines several confusions in Schutz that have not been
explored here.

and sociology through the work of one specific philosopher, not to provide a criticism of that philosopher as such. Such a criticism would be an exercise in theoretical argument, an exercise that would involve a more inclusive description of consciousness and Being, excluding Sartre's description as a possibility within it, or incorporating and extending Sartre's description in such a way that there were no internal contradictions, or only insoluble contradictions – contradictions that accurately reflect contradictions in experience.

A sociological analysis or description cannot prove or disprove the theoretical argument. The former inevitably makes assumptions that the latter is investigating. The starting point of the theoretical analysis is myself; my own consciousness is the only one to which I have direct access and my awareness of other consciousnesses assumes my own consciousness of myself-as-object organised into their world and of the Other-as-object organised into my world. The arguments back from the empirical studies in the last two chapters have not moved in a direct line: they have moved from a particular problem in a study, the nature of the self or the nature of language, to the implications for consciousness of a particular view of the self or language; although it is likely to have been obscured because the discussion to an extent assumed its own starting point and because it was frequently carried out in impersonal terms, 'consciousness' has always been *my* consciousness. The activities of those observed, their use of language, their self-image, have been implicitly treated as if they were *my* activities, or rather the activities of the impersonal consciousness to which the *my* is attached in reflection. There has been a gap between the studies discussed and the conclusions of the theoretical argument insofar as the latter cannot be derived from the former without the intervention of the one consciousness to which I have direct access – and which I question prior to any empirical investigation.

We can suggest three ways in which the theoretical argument bears on sociology: in the first place it tells us what we are looking at, it provides an *a priori* description of the objects of study and on the basis of that description it traces the limits of their relationships; secondly, it directs our attention to particular matters, it tells us what we are looking for insofar as our task is to give specific content to the categories that it has developed; thirdly, it enables a reflexive understanding by which the sociologist, those he studies, and the relationship between the sociologist and those he studies can all be grasped in the same movement.

The theoretical description tells us that we are looking at relationships between consciousness and the world and consciousness and consciousness; it tells us that consciousness is a nothingness in the midst of Being which aims at a constant possession of Being. We are looking at a consciousness which is in situation, and which defines that situation by moving beyond it to possess Being. All substantive features of the situation are outside of consciousness, including language and the self. It tells us that we are looking for the project of consciousness towards Being, the way in which and means by which a consciousness is attempting to achieve its union with Being and the precise form of this union.

By examining these statements more closely, we can explore the reflexivity that they imply. To an extent, the situation of the sociologist and those he studies is the same in that (usually) a 'life-world' is, to a degree, shared; language, and often *a* language is common to both and both are presented with meanings that have already been determined by others and that surround the individual consciousness. These include and are included in language and are describable by both the sociologist and those he studies, and it is possible, to a degree, to describe the situation in general or abstract terms at the level of meanings which neither create. Thus it is possible to describe the situation of the mental-hospital patient as a structure of relationships of varying degrees of permanence, as a physical structure and as a collection of meanings attached to particular objects by particular people, all of which will define and include the patient on entry. It is also possible to describe language and types of rationality etc. in terms of structures and methods which are not created either by the sociologist or those he studies but which are 'possessed' by both.

The project of the mental hospital patient is not understood in terms of his 'definition of the situation' (which, so far, could very well be that of the sociologist) but through his action in the situation and what he says about his action in the situation. *His* situation – i.e. the specific meaning that he gives to the structures that we have described – and his project – the act by which he confers these meanings – are grasped and understood at the same time. Thus if we understand the project of the mental hospital patient as aiming at a particular form of self, then we understand the specific meanings that he gives to his situation: understanding that a patient is seeking to avoid the responsibility for his own action by making himself into a mechanically malfunctioning physical object and seeking to have this view of himself confirmed by others is *at the same time* to understand that he accepts the hospital regime, obeys its rules, and expresses respect and gratitude towards it. The conferring of meaning on the situation, the defining of the situation *is* the project, the action, and at the same time it is one manifestation of it, insofar as *this* project finds its full meaning in the ultimate possibility, the fundamental project. Similarly, to understand the way in which a statement is an attempt to change, as well as create and describe, a setting is to understand both what is said and how it is said.

Any one situation may be lived in a variety of ways. In the case of the mental hospital, it was argued that the closed nature of the structure meant that comparatively few materials were available for the project of the patient and this should enable the discernment of general categories of ways of living the situation, of projects which whilst sacrificing some elements of individuality enable us to grasp a greater complexity of meaning than do Goffman's concepts. In the case of language on the other hand, the much greater complexity of the structure[1] is likely to allow a greater multiplicity of ways of living it: Garfinkel suggests that there are probably as many types of glosses as there are people, but ways of living language are open to classification as well – styles of literature and poetry and different codes of varying degrees of extension and restriction are discernible, and the relationship between a way of living language and a way of living a wider situation may allow an 'indifference' between various ways of living the former in the context of the latter. Again, however, the general classification loses some degree of the original uniqueness of the project.

It is through the understanding of the Other's project and situation that we move on to reflexivity. It was argued earlier that what makes any action in principle understandable is that a situation and a project are common to all individual consciousnesses, they are a common 'human reality'. The act of understanding involves a movement back to the situation and forward to the projected change in the situation and each is grasped in the same movement. Each act of understanding, however, takes place in the course of a project of the one who understands, and it is itself a project aiming at a state of having understood as a precondition for further action.[2] As we have seen it involves a 'subjective identification' with the actor to the extent that it involves the recognition of situation and project

[1] There is a degree of arbitrariness in defining a situation as being of greater or lesser complexity. The structure of language is part of the situation of the mental hospital patient but a study of the former would make a study of the latter almost impossible without unlimited facilities. The situation of the mental hospital patient is of course only 'less complex' when compared with situations in the outside world.

[2] Again a similar idea may be found in G. H. Mead (1938), but again it appears only at the reflective level.

as common to both, as a common human reality. This identification is provided for in the recognition of the Other as the one-who-looks and myself-as-object-in-his-world, it is a precondition and a source of all human interaction and as such cannot be avoided, whether the sociologist analyses the actions of the other in terms of categories worked out in his own project or whether, in Douglas' terms (1971) he 'maintains the integrity of the phenomena'. Indeed, 'maintaining the integrity of the phenomena' is part of the sociologist's project, not an abstention from imposing his categories but a specific imposition, since for the actor, the phenomena have their integrity and the problem of maintaining it does not arise. Even loss of integrity has its own integrity insofar as it is directly experienced by the one who loses it.

Although there is a basic identification between observer and observed, it is not a complete identification. Consciousnesses cannot merge, each is trapped in its facticity, each is its own project towards Being, and the identification may only take place from the standpoint of each consciousness in the course of its unique project. However close this identification might succeed in becoming, a total identification is never achieved and thus *any* understanding of the Other involves a loss of intensity, a loss of the immediacy of the Other's experience of and relationship to the world, and their incorporation into my own project. This loss is a common feature of any act of understanding whether or not the aim is to categorise the ways of living a situation, and identification with the Other is also a common feature of any act of understanding, whether or not it is intended to grant 'the integrity of the phenomena'. At the same time, then, that these concepts enable us to understand the interaction of others, they enable us to understand the relationship between the sociologist and those he studies.

Weber's concept of 'Verstehen' has been deepened in the following ways: understanding action as subjectively meaningful is a precondition for any human interaction, including sociology; it is not confined to rational action, 'irrational' actions being understood as well, even if only (and wrongly) as being irrational for the actor; empathy and common-sense shared meanings and taken-for-granted ways of making action rationally accountable – ways in which Verstehen has been interpreted[1] – are only secondary in the process of understanding, made possible by the primary movement and unintelligible without it. The act of understanding can, how-

---

[1] For a discussion of the various interpretations of 'verstehen', see Leat 1972, Rickman 1960. In the latter's terms, this argument may be seen as an 'epistemological revision' of the concept.

ever, never capture the immediacacy of lived experience, the Other must always remain to some extent an object. Thus deepened, the concept is able to be, as it were 'applied to itself': the 'sociology of understanding' looks at those observed as subjects organising their own worlds but only within limits imposed by the sociologist. They are subject-objects (or object-subjects) the degree to which they are dependent on the sociologist's project. They may be Schutz's simple rational puppets (object-subjects) or Sartre's complex and 'irrational' Genet (a subject-object) but the element of 'objectness' cannot be removed. Sartre can never become Genet, only interpretively understand him.

The type of objects that those observed became for the sociologist, whether it be the type of object that possesses and presents a self that Goffman describes, or the type of object described by Garfinkel, who is a subject to the extent that he uses language, is understood in terms of the project of the sociologist. We have already looked at the 'sociological project' in general terms and we can now extend that discussion by outlining some features of the project to possess the world through knowledge that are discovered in sociology. To begin with, the sociologist's project is usually conceived of as being in some way a 'scientific' project. 'Scientific' will have specific connotations for each writer and the conception of science held by the sociologist, whether it is held unaltered from the start or whether it is constructed or changed in the course of the study, will determine the type of object-subject or subject-object he is looking at. In the course of his scientific project he endows those he studies and/or their actions with qualities and meanings which can be summed up in the phrase: 'objects that are open to scientific study (in my sense of "scientific")'. In this respect Sartre makes the minimum definition of those studied as 'objects whose actions are capable of being understood in terms of consciousness and being'.

Secondly, insofar as he is concerned with one aspect of action, he endows those he studies with specific limited qualities: Goffman gives them a self, Garfinkel gives them language. Again it is possible that this attribute may be changed in the course of the study, but in some substantive areas of sociology, such as the sociology of religion or the sociology of the family, they are in advance defined as objects who behave religiously or take part in family life. In these cases those studied are defined in a way determined by the growth and development of sociology as a discipline and this leads us on to the third point which in some respects is one of the determinations of the point we have just discussed.

Together with science as a project, there is the project of being a sociologist, the project of establishing oneself as a bona fide sociologist in the eyes of other sociologists. Both Goffman and Garfinkel would appear to have met this problem and it may be considered as part of their project. Goffman seems to have settled fairly happily in the no-man's land between sociology and social psychology although we saw that his emphasis on the institutionally-defined self was partly justified as being the most relevant feature of the self for the sociologist. Garfinkel appears to be having more difficulty and throughout our discussion of his examples, the attempt to justify the existence of ethnomethodology by contrast with (although not necessarily in opposition to) conventional socio-logy was noticeable. We also saw that ethnomethodology can itself be seen as creating a 'socially invented, persuasive and proper' way of talking about things, the relevant social group being ethno-methodologists, and this creation carries its own definition of the object-nature of those studied. It is in connection with this also perhaps that we can understand the particularly complex and strained terminology that he uses.[1] In both cases those studied are endowed with characteristics which are 'sociological' in nature and which mark them off from the types of objects studied by other disciplines. Goffman's selves are contained in the social structure unlike the selves of many psychologists; Garfinkel's 'members' work together to create rationality as an ongoing and empirically dis-coverable process, unlike, say, the isolated language-use studied by linguistic philosophy.

The sociological project that is contained within and suggested by Sartre's analysis is the one which would begin by defining its objects simply as beings who are in principle understandable. In the search for the projects and situations in terms of which each activity of those studied is to be understood, each action must be described in as many ways as possible, as many meanings as possible must be examined and subsumed under the project or discarded. To describe as many meanings as possible is to describe as many futures as possible: we must be involved in drawing out and exploring the future possibilities of those studied if we are to keep their 'object-ness' to the minimum. Whether or not it is possible to carry out a full existential psychoanalysis, i.e. to subsume all possible meanings under one fundamental project, or whether we are limited to classifying general projects, general ways of living situations, the aim must be the exact opposite of that of Schutz: the 'puppets' must be liberated as far as is possible, allowed as many

---

[1] For a general discussion of the role of sociological jargon see Mills 1959, Gouldner 1971, Roshier 1972.

complexities and 'irrational' ways of acting as possible. This is as much a project to possess the world and the others in it as objects as any other sociological project, but it is a project which aims at possessing those involved as free objects as opposed to possessing their freedom. This is the fundamental difference between the 'existential' sociological project and the sociological projects of Goffman and Garfinkel: they allow their objects a freedom but they, the sociologists, possess that freedom by defining its limits and its course according to what they are looking for: the presentation of the self, language-use. We should extend the forms of freedom of our objects as far as is possible, to describe all possible futures and to grasp all present meanings and situations as the free products of those studied. The aim is to possess our objects through understanding, in the way that I possess an intellectual argument by following it through from beginning to end; the alternative is to possess through simple knowledge, to learn the conclusion without grasping the arguments or the possibility of future developments in it.

To understand a fundamental project is to enable its understanding by the individual involved, to increase his awareness in such a way that his future activity is open to new forms of control and choice. To describe possible meanings, possible futures, is to describe the range of choices available to those studied. Thus although classification is part of what this study proposes, the intention is not to limit everything under a certain number of headings but to extend the range of headings as far as is possible. This opens up a new dimension of interaction between the sociologist and those he studies, a dimension open towards the future through the activities of those studied, not necessarily excluding the sociologist. These future activities will be based on the study and the understanding that it achieves. In this way, it moves the future of the study out of the sociological world, where it will be criticised, used as a basis for future study or simply forgotten, and out of the world of social administration, where it will be used to decide or justify policy, and places it firmly in the everyday world of those studied.

The second part of this study will draw on Sartre's later work to extend this rather schematic programme, elaborating on each of the points and the problems that it presents. The gaps in the earlier work are self-evident: the inability to handle social structures in anything more than a perfunctory way, and the inability to handle group activities are the most important. We will be considering these problems as far as possible without abandoning the basis we have established for understanding individual activities.

5
The absolute and the relative

1. Introduction

In the introduction it was suggested that no essential break exists between *Being and Nothingness* and the *Critique de la raison dialectique* and that it would be wrong to see Sartre as having abandoned his earlier positions. Nevertheless, there is a problem about the relationship between the two works; to describe it as a move from the ontological to the ontic and to draw a parallel between the For-itself and praxis and the In-itself and the practico-inert is insufficient. There is certainly a similarity in spirit between the two: both are concerned with freedom and the individual, both are opposed to any sort of mechanistic determinism. But at the same time there are striking differences: *Being and Nothingness* examined the nature of an atemporal absolute, a consciousness which was responsible for time and not produced by it; the *Critique* is concerned with History and its relativising effects, even to the extent of relativising his own earlier description of the absolute: '[Existentialism] is a parasitical system living on the margin of knowledge which at first it opposed, but into which today it seeks to be integrated' (1963b: 48).

If this relativisation does not represent a break with his earlier work, then what does it represent? *Being and Nothingness* asserted the absolute freedom of man, the *Critique* talks of necessity and destiny; the former was concerned with the unavoidable conflict of self and other; the latter talks about reciprocity and group activity.

A depth relationship between the two works, then, remains to be established. Rybalka and Contat (1970) point out that most commentaries either assert the complete continuity or the complete discontinuity of the two works and there is no attempt to come to grips with the complex philosophical problems that they present.[1]

[1] They suggest that the major problem is whether or not there is an epistemological break between the two works. Although we will argue that the continuity lies on the level of epistemology, this should not be confused with an argument about the 'break' which is a concept

What follows is by no means the rigorous study required, but it should be regarded as an attempt to deepen the study – a first step towards a full analysis, but one sufficient for our present purposes. The continuity of this study is self-evidently dependent on there being a continuity between Sartre's two works, and therefore the problem has to be approached. This necessity is reinforced by the fact that on another level it is concerned with a division, apparent in sociology almost since its birth, between methodological individualism and a holistic approach, and as we continue with our study of the *Critique* it should become apparent that we are cutting right across this division.

11. The dialectic

To begin with it is necessary to establish what Sartre means by the 'dialectic'. The aim of the *Critique* is to 'found' the dialectic in human activity, to show that this is not, as Engels argued, a law of nature that governs the world including man, but something that man creates in and by his own activity. Whether or not there is a 'dialectic of nature' is, for Sartre, still an open question; in any case, the problem cannot be resolved by the natural sciences which are strictly analytic and quantitative. However, if, without waiting for the answer, it can be shown that the structure and intelligibility of *human action* is dialectical, then it will be possible to establish firstly that history is man-made and secondly, in what way it is man-made, i.e. it will be possible to explore the dialectic of necessity and freedom implied by Marx when he stated that men make history but do so on the basis of previous circumstances. If it is projected into nature as a natural law, the dialectic becomes unintelligible, contingent, it just 'happens to be' the case. The *Critique* attempts to show the intelligibility of the dialectic, and consequently of History, i.e. to provide the basis for Marxism that Marxism has failed to provide for itself, and the absence of which has contributed to its 'sclerosis'.

What does Sartre mean by 'dialectical intelligibility'? Elsewhere he writes:

A dialectical thought is initially, in the same movement, the examination of a reality insofar as it is a part of a whole, insofar as it negates [*nier*] the whole, insofar as the whole comprises it, conditions

(*n continued*)
developed by Althusser, the use of which in the present context could only cause confusion. See L. Althusser (1970, 1972). The best English commentary, although it has its ommissions, is W. Desan 1966. The clearest exposition of many of the ideas of the Critique is to be found in M. Contat 1968.

and negates it; insofar as, in consequence, it is at the same time positive and negative in relation to the whole, insofar as its movement must be a destructive and a conserving movement in relation to the whole; insofar as it is in relationship with each of the parts of the ensemble of the whole, each one of which is at the same time a negation of the whole and includes the whole within itself; insofar as the ensemble or sum of these parts at a given moment negates – insofar as each contains the whole – the part that we are considering, insofar as this part negates them, insofar as the sum of the parts, again becoming the ensemble, becomes the ensemble of structured parts, i.e. the whole less this one and acting against it, insofar, finally, as all that gives, considered each time as positive and negative, a movement that moves towards the restructuration of the whole. (1972d: 76)

The very complexity of this statement (my own literal translation) is an example of what some critics have regarded as the 'unread-ability' of the *Critique,* yet it explains its own complexity, which lies in what is being described and not in the description.[1] Any simple statement about the part or the whole must at some stage be qualified by a statement of its own contradiction and of its contra-dictory relationships with other parts or with the parts that comprise it. No simple description, even of the abstract 'moments' – in the sense of analytically separated elements of a continual movement – that make up the theoretical exploration is possible. Although the nature of Sartre's dialectic in relation to that of Marx and/or Hegel would require a study in itself, it can be seen that this description includes what are treated as 'dialectical laws' by Engels: the inter-penetration of opposites, the negation of the negation becoming an affirmation, the transformation of quantity into quality etc. It is obviously a more complex conception than that usually held by sociologists in which the dialectic is often reduced to the simple co-existence of conflict and stability, or to the fact that sociologists are part of what they study.[2]

Sartre, then, sets out to show that the dialectic is the structure of human activity (or praxis) and that this structure can only be understood dialectically, the eventual criteria for intelligibility and understanding being, as we will see, self-evidence. For example, it is by no means self-evident that the negation of the negation must be an affirmation, there is no reason why the negation should not

---

[1] Although the conditions under which Sartre was writing did not help his style – see Simone de Beauvoir: 1968. There is a problem here concerning the possibility of different modes of description which will be mentioned at several points in what follows.
[2] See in particular Pierre Van der Bergh 1963, and R. Friedrichs 1972; Louis Schneider 1971 gives the subject a more complex but still very vague treatment.

co-exist in a latent affirmation (which was allowed for in Hegel's dialectic, see Lefebvre 1968). The affirmation (and indeed the original negations) only appear within a movement, and more specifically in a totalising movement which aims at a new totality beyond the original totality and its negation. The totalising movement is thus itself the negation of the negation and the new affirmation. If, therefore, the dialectic exists, and if it is to be intelligible, then it must be a totalising movement of thought and action. Each praxis must be shown to posit a field of action – a totality – and to proceed by a rigorous separation of this field into its parts (the first negation) and their re-integration (the second negation – this time of the parts) into a new totality (the affirmation). Dialectical thought must proceed in the same way and so, more importantly for the moment, must the critique of dialectical reason itself. If intelligibility is dialectical, then it must be shown to be so dialectically.

If dialectical reason is to reveal the intelligibility of praxis, then it must be shown in its superiority to any other reason, not by dismissing that reason but by taking it up into itself as one of its moments. Analytic reason, for example, breaks the field of action down into component parts and keeps it there: the parts are seen as acting causally on each other through external relationships (the 'billiard-ball' explanation, in Sartre's terms 'relationships of exteriority'). It must be shown that analytic reason is only one moment in a dialectical movement towards a new totality, new in the sense that there is something present that was not there before. Sartre's example is that of a rigorous mathematical proof, the peak of analytic reason: all the terms are strictly equivalent and enter into equivalent relationships with each other. Yet what is left after the proof has been worked through is a *new* knowledge; something that was there before, contained within the terms as a hypothesis, a possibility, is transformed into knowledge. Analytic reason provides the proof but cannot account for the transformation of possibility into knowledge, since amongst the equivalences that make up the proof, there is no room for any new element to enter. Its appearance may only be comprehended dialectically in terms of a relationship of interiority between the old state of knowledge and the new, the way in which the former, dialectically but by means of analytic reason, transforms itself into the latter by positing the result as something to be proved and thus creating the gap which will be filled by the new knowledge. There are in fact what Sartre calls two intelligibilities: the first is the intelligibility of the 'dialectical laws' in the movement of totalisation – the lucidity of the dialectic – and the second is the intelligibility of the practical moment of the dialectic through the future totalisation. As in *Being and Nothingness*, to understand the present activity we need to grasp what is being aimed at: in the former work this was expressed in terms of the possession of Being by consciousness, in the later work, concerned with the *structure* of praxis, the future state is simply a 'totality'.

If action is dialectically intelligible, then History itself must be shown to be dialectically intelligible as the product of human action and this provides a further aim of the *Critique*: to found the possibility of History as a totalisation in progress with a discoverable meaning. Conventional Marxism, argues Sartre, has assumed History, taken it for granted and has consequently been unable to understand it. By 'intelligibility' Sartre again means dialectically intelligible to the individual in the same way that his own action is intelligible. History is the totalisation of the totalisations operated by individual praxes and again the criteria of intelligibility is self-evidence.

Just as the critique of dialectical reason must be dialectical so the attempt to found the possibility of History must be historical. Sartre sees his work as one of the many attempts to rediscover and revive Marxism occasioned by the movement of 'destalinisation' and the softening of the Stalinist 'sclerosis' of Marxist thought. It is a moment of reflexivity in Marxist thought which is itself a particular moment of Marxist practice.

The ways in which this attempt may be related to *Being and Nothingness* are complex and fall on a number of levels. A 'Sartrean' study would involve an interrelation of his personal history – and the history of his time – the social and historical conjuncture that produced him and what he made out of it – and the themes and structures of his work as they appear on the surface and are revealed by a deeper analysis in the light of other factors. A very broad outline of the historical relationships was offered in Chapter 1; thematically the development of his thought may be traced through three levels of his work: the dramatic, the critical and biographical, and the political and philosophical.[1] Here we will be concerned with a deeper thematic relationship on the final level: it will be argued firstly that a fundamental 'theoretical' project unites both works, secondly that they are based, despite this unity, on different theoretical levels, or at least that they take place at different theoretical moments and thirdly that what unites these

[1] McMahon (1971) gives an excellent overall account of Sartre's development as it appears in his fictional treatment of love.

moments or levels into a unity is a semi-explicit epistemology common to both.

III. Theory and theoretical levels

As we have seen, the 'theoretical' nature of *Being and Nothingness* lies in the fact that it is an analysis of what is not available to empirical investigation. The only consciousness to which I have access in my own and, self-evidently, I cannot separate myself from it. Thus my critique of Sartre's thesis cannot be a matter of proof or disproof, it must be directed at the internal rigour of the argument, its ability to sustain its own contradictions or to be destroyed by them. Its final validity lies in its ability to illuminate the reader's experience both of himself and of others, and in its inclusiveness, the areas of experience that can or cannot be accounted for within its categories. These features are covered by the term 'self-evidence'.

If we now turn to the *Critique* the immediate difference appears to be that it does concern something which may be empirically observed: neither my actions nor my history are available only to me. In addition to the criteria listed above a fourth element is added: 'reality' in the sense of something outside of myself and open to examination by others, History, the 'concrete'. Nevertheless the reader, myself, still plays the same role as in the earlier work: although I have access to action and History outside of myself, I only have access to my own understanding, and although the understanding of others is made available to me in an objective, external form in books, speech etc., I have to make it mine before it is effective. The aim is to reveal the intelligibility of History in the same terms in which my own action is revealed as intelligible, and if my action is intelligible it must be revealed in the same way in which my consciousness is revealed to me, through my own interrogation of it. The first moment of the *Critique*, then, is a description of praxis which is very much in the style of the phenomenological description we find throughout *Being and Nothingness* and is subject to the same criteria of judgement, at least initially. This is the first qualification of the difference between the two works.

Praxis, in its elementary form, is the activity of consciousness embedded in its facticity – a facticity which has its needs for survival and on which the survival of consciousness depends. Thus there is more than a methodological connection between the last moment of *Being and Nothingness* and the first moment of the *Critique*: both deal with the situated For-itself, but whereas the former handles it in terms of the original project, the way in which the For-itself lives its facticity and its situation through its activities, the latter work. deals with the structure of those activities in relation to the material world:

> The epistemological point of departure must always be *consciousness* as the apodictic certitude (of) self and as consciousness *of* a particular object. But it is not a matter of questioning consciousness on itself; the object that it must give itself is precisely *life*, i.e. the objective being of the inquirer in the world of Others, in so far as this being has totalised itself from birth and will totalise itself until death.[1] (1960: 142. All quotations from the *Critique* are my own translation – See bibliographical note)

Thus the structure of praxis may be described objectively as external to consciousness, but it must be described as it appears to consciousness; we are again referred back to our own consciousness.

We can now make the second qualification to our statement of the immediate difference between the two works. Praxis is action on matter; in *Being and Nothingness* the In-itself was 'pure' Being, unobtainable to the For-itself in its purity since the latter is a relation to the In-itself and by that fact endows it with at least an elementary meaning – its own relationship. 'Matter' as discussed in the *Critique* has not only been invested with this elementary meaning, but has its own structure the nature of which is revealed to the organism through the latter's needs (in much the same way that the project of climbing the mountain makes it steep). Thus in addition to the description of praxis, the structure of matter and the relationship between the two have to be described, *but* this is not yet the concrete in its fulness.

The aim is to show the dialectical intelligibility of History, the concrete, as a product of human praxis. To begin with the concrete in its full complexity would be to prejudge the question; we must begin with praxis and not derive it from History. Consciousness is an integral moment of praxis as Sartre defines it and consequently praxis can no more be derived from 'reality' than can consciousness. The new reference point for the *Critique* then, is the 'abstract concrete' rather than the concrete itself. This involves, firstly, a distinction between the 'abstract' and the 'theoretical' that is not usually made. Conventionally the two are regarded as synonymous, implying an epistemology that sees thought as a parallel to and

---

[1] In this sense Howard Burkle's argument (1966) that the Critique extends the analysis of the situation and the project is correct but insufficient.

incapable of reproducing, reality in its fulness. The distinction suggested here as being implicit in Sartre's work is that the abstract is something which is taken from the totality, in the sense implied in the verb 'to abstract', whether that totality be a concrete or a theoretical totality. If the *Critique* is a theoretical totality, then any one moment of it is abstract in both senses. It can now be seen that both works are essentially theoretical in that although the concrete, the objective, is present in the *Critique* as an *eventual* reference point, it is *not yet* being used as a standard by which the theoretical work is being judged. We are not yet attempting to understand what we know about History in terms of the categories developed in the theoretical work – to do so would be an exercise in history, or anthropology or sociology. The *Critique* attempts to found these disciplines by showing their possibility. Thus we are left with the same standards by which *Being and Nothingness* was judged – the internal cohesion of the description and its relevance to the experience of the reader.

The abstract moments of the *Critique* can only be abstracted on the theoretical level, they cannot be abstracted on the level of the concrete and empirically investigated. The sort of abstraction that is possible on the level of the concrete would be the abstraction of one moment of History which would be studied by means of the totality of concepts developed on the theoretical level. Praxis, the practico-inert, the group-in-fusion etc. are theoretical abstractions; the General Strike, the French Revolution are concrete abstractions. In sum, the *Critique* describes what is open to empirical investigation but what cannot be investigated in its purity: it is in this way that it should be regarded as theoretical and should be distinguished radically from that type of social theory which sees its categories as having identifiable concrete correlates, as 'representing' reality. The aim is not to represent reality but to reveal its intelligibility. Sartre is not saying: 'This is what happens in History' but 'This is how we may understand History.'[1]

Sartre sees the *Critique* as the regressive moment of a dialectical regressive–progressive movement. It is regressive in that it starts with the abstract praxis of the individual and merges it into historical categories – his relationships with matter and with others – until History itself is attained. The progressive movement would be the application to the concrete of the dialectical method estab-

---

[1] Thus the theory again cannot be 'tested': it can only be used as a means for understanding the concrete. It fails if there are elements of the concrete that cannot be understood by it. There is a slight similarity here to what Cohen (1968) calls 'metaphysical theory'.

lished in the regressive movement in an attempt to understand it.[1] Until the end of this movement the existence of History as a meaningful unity (history with a capital 'H') can only be assumed.

Given the above arguments, the regressive movement can itself be broken down into a progressive–regressive movement on the level of theory alone. Both *Being and Nothingness* and the *Critique* start with the individual consciousness. The first work moves backward to the nature of this consciousness and the second forward to the world in which the consciousness is situated, one moves back towards the absolute, one moves forward to historical relativity. Both find their fulfilment in the study of the concrete and it is at this level that their full unity is achieved.

The theoretical unity of the relative and the absolute was already present in *Being and Nothingness*. Consciousness is an absolute nothingness, an absolute hole in the In-itself: it is in this sense that it is absolutely free. Yet in its absolute freedom, it is relative to the In-itself, it is a relation to the In-itself, embedded in its facticity. The relativity of the absolute and the absoluteness of the relative is the basis of Sartre's thought and would appear to provide the only possibility of a humanistic Marxism: an absolute *content* attributed to human nature (as opposed to Sartre's absolute nothingness) would be incompatible with Marxism because of the latter's emphasis on historical relativity. A total relativity, on the other hand, would make man only the product of his society: there would be no room for any intrinsic 'human' element, constant throughout history, to enter into the equation. This has an obvious bearing on the problem of relativity in the sociology of knowledge, since it allows both for an 'absolute' truth which is expressed as the structures of consciousness and a relative truth which is the relationship of that consciousness to the world. The dialectic of the absolute and the relative cannot be grasped by formal logic which can only dismiss it as nonsense. A dialectical thought which would give meaning to the contradiction can only show its superiority to formal logic by including the latter within it as one of its moments (cf Lefebvre, 1968). This demonstration is part of the purpose of the *Critique*. It is at this conjunction of the relative and the absolute that we find the epistemology that provides the underlying link between the two works.

It is also at this conjunction of the absolute and the relative that

---

[1] This was to be the task of the second volume of the *Critique*, which is now unlikely to appear. The study of Flaubert is intended to be the fruition of the progressive–regressive method: an attempt to understand as much as is possible of one man.

we can pinpoint what is perhaps the most important modification of Sartre's thought since his early work. What he now seems to reject of the latter is a too easy identification of absolute, ontological freedom and a relative practical freedom – an identification that he accounts for in terms of the clarity of political choice presented by the Nazi occupation of France (Sartre, 1969b). Further he modifies the availability of the absolute as it is manifested in the fundamental project to the reflective consciousness, i.e. the relative. Even a pure reflection cannot grasp itself in absolute clarity and in this sense *Being and Nothingness* presented an over-rational conception of man – a conception which goes hand in hand with the transfer of absolute freedom from the ontological to the ontic level.[1] In his later work, freedom on the ontological level is limited very strictly to ways of living determinations on the practical level rather than of overcoming these determinations through individual action. The exploration of the absolute becomes secondary to the exploration of its relativity:

The idea which I have never ceased to develop is that in the end one is always responsible for what is made of one. Even if one can do nothing besides assume this responsibility. For I believe that a man can always make something out of what is made of him. This is the limit I would today accord to freedom: the small limit that makes of a totally conditioned social being someone who does not render back completely what his conditioning has given him . . . (1969b: 45)[2]

IV. Thought and existence

The For-itself is an absolute nothingness, an absolute nihilation of Being and a positing of itself. We have seen that the relationship between the two is one of intuitive knowledge and that the only possible certain knowledge is intuitive. It is therefore an *absolute* intuition, initially that 'there is' Being and that I exist in relation to it, and later that 'there are' Others.

At the same time that this knowledge is absolute it is also relative, or, at this stage of the argument, an absolute knowledge of a relationship of existence. The For-itself, however, is not only a nihilation, it is an active nihilation, a nihilation of Being and a flight

---

[1] This has involved the development of the idea of 'lived experience', rather than a clear reflective grasp; reflection is seen as a constant totalisation in progress, thus never complete and clear. See in particular Sartre 1969b.

[2] Sartre is talking specifically about Genet but the latter's personal project has much in common with the activities of, for example, Black Power and Women's Liberation groups. The central feature is the assumption of an external definition *against* the defining group.

towards Being, a project. Thus beyond the absolute relationship of existence there is a dynamic relationship to the In-itself, but these should not be conceived of as two relationships: it is a matter of one relationship which is both absolute and relative.[1] The relativity of the relationship increases as we move from the ontological to the practical level. The For-itself is situated spatially and temporally and 'possesses' a facticity – the first source of the relativity; the second source lies in the choice of the basic project, the way in which the For-itself attempts to achieve Value, and the third source is in the selection, however limited, of the practical projects through which the original project is lived out.

'To know', then, is a pre-reflective intuitive knowledge of a relationship. To move further in the argument we must distinguish clearly between 'knowing' and 'thinking', essentially a distinction between the pre-reflective and the reflective levels of consciousness. Pre-reflective knowledge can go no further than the dynamic relationship of existence; to think is to reflectively grasp this relationship and the project that it is. The reflective consciousness is consciousness of being conscious (of) but the move from the pre-reflective to the reflective level is also a move from the ontological to the practical and within this move lies the creation of language and articulated meaning which is used as a tool by the reflective consciousness. The reflective consciousness, then, lies on the same level of analysis as praxis, but it is inseparably linked to the pre-reflective consciousness, not as a separate and parasitic consciousness but as integral structure of consciousness (1960a: 140).

Thus the reflective consciousness is still a relation and still a project. It follows that when I think, I do not think *about* the world, which would put consciousness opposite and outside of the world, whereas as we have seen, it is inescapably situated in the world. The word 'about' implies a separation rather than a nihilation. To use the verb transitively takes us further,[2] but not the whole way. 'To think the world' again implies a similar separation, with the possibility of treating the thinking and the world as governed by the same

[1] If it were a question of two relationships some form of absolute split, probably between the reflective and pre-reflective structures, would be present in consciousness and this would be inadmissible in the light of the system developed in *Being and Nothingness*.

[2] Such a use would appear to be easier in French than in English. Sartre dismisses the idea that it is easier to express synthetic ideas in one language rather than another (cf 'L'Ecrivain et sa langue', 1972d) but although they might cancel each other out, it would appear on the surface that certain ideas can be more easily expressed in French than in English and some more easily in English than in French.

laws (magically)[1] and of an idealistic distinction between the real object and the object of knowledge. This in turn would imply either a removal of the object from the world and into consciousness, which, as we have seen, is incompatible with Sartre's system, or the creation of the object in the world by thought, leading us back to an Hegelian idealism.

We have seen that thought is itself a relationship to the world. In fact, still using the verb transitively, *I think relationships* to the world, *I think my project*: my thinking is my project and my project is my thinking. Thought, then, is active, a direct manipulation of one category of matter – language – and an indirect manipulation of other categories of matter. In *Being and Nothingness* the hypostatising of this movement, the absence of an absolute lucidity of consciousness in its reflective structure, was seen as the product of impure reflection. In the *Critique*, its sources are found in serial thought and in institutional thought, which can be seen as a 'situating' of impure reflection in the world rather than, as before, only in the relationship between structures of consciousness.

Thought, then, is one 'category' of action, of praxis. It is action on man, made matter – language – and to this extent can perhaps be separated from action, on matter which has a Being totally independent from man, a Being which is simply revealed to consciousness and which does not find its origins in consciousness. The two 'categories' of action are perhaps better conceived of as two moments of praxis, each giving rise to the other.[2]

This argument is by no means explicit in the *Critique* where 'praxis' is usually used to refer to the 'non-thinking' moment. The *Critique* itself should however be regarded as the 'reflective' moment produced on the basis of and depassing[3] the previous 'acting' moment of Stalinism and the previous 'reflective' moment of Marx. The appearance of the reflective moment in any praxis is then historically conditioned[4] (1960a: 141).

[1] This would appear to be Althusser's use of the verb; for criticisms that explore these points more fully, see Norman Geras 1972 and Glucksmann 1972. The latter is particularly relevant.

[2] This is similar to the pragmatic conception, with the difference that we have already mentioned that pragmatism would identify consciousness and mind (i.e. Being) and thought would thus be determined by matter.

[3] 'To depass' is the dialectical movement which goes beyond a particular phenomenon but preserves it in the new totality.

[4] This argument moves away from Sartre's individual project to the level of History and back again, thus assuming what the *Critique* sets out to establish, i.e. the possibility of History. Given the nature of this last

Insofar as the pre-reflective would appear to have priority over reflective structure of consciousness (in that it is only at the pre-reflective level that absolute certainty exists) then the 'acting' moment of praxis would have priority over the 'reflective' moment, a priority emphasised by the necessity for language to appear before the reflective moment becomes effective. But since we are not concerned with and cannot discover any moment of history when reflection was impossible, the priority of the pre-reflective is a theoretical construct enabling us to understand the concrete, and only has a practical importance in certain situations, for example in an attempted psychoanalysis. Two further points can now be made.

Firstly, the relationship between thought and the world is something which can only be settled on the theoretical level and not empirically. If the relationship outlined above is used as a means of understanding the concrete, a central problem in the sociology of knowledge disappears: that of only being able to draw parallels between what happens in society and what happens in the world of ideas (cf. Merton, 1967, 119–216). The activity contains its own idea, and the idea contains the activity: they are two moments of the same praxis. The relationship between the two moments and the ways in which they are expressed depend on the physical and intellectual materials available and on the nature of the social relationships within which projects are thought. It is a question of specific relationships to Others and to matter which reflexively condition the way in which they are thought. These relationships affect the articulation of their own expression in words and the way in which they are lived, the articulation of their action.

The second point is that the problem of the 'autonomy' or lack of it possessed by ideas. With one provision which we will discuss shortly, a particular change may be brought about initially either on the level of thought or of action and then translated onto the other level. The level at which the solution is discovered is entirely specific to and conditioned by the nature of the case in question. The provision, however, is an important one and gives us the limits of thought: thought can only go so far as the relationships which it thinks, it is no more complex or abstract than the complexity or abstractness of the social structure it is thinking. Each structure provides a limit to the progress of thought and this cannot be broken until the structure itself has been broken. Sartre sees philosophy

project, not to assume it at certain moments in advance of its establishment would be very difficult, if not impossible. It should, however, be kept in mind that it is an assumption.

as totalising all possible thought in a given structure and the
moments of creation are rare.

Between the seventeenth century and the twentieth, I see three such
periods, which I would designate by the names of the men who
dominate them: there is the 'moment' of Descartes and Locke, that of
Kant and Hegel, finally, that of Marx. These three philosophies become,
each in its turn, the humus of every particular thought and the horizon
of all culture; there is no going beyond them as long as man has not
gone beyond the historical moment which they express. (1963b: 7)

Although we cannot go beyond Marxism, Marxism itself has
congealed in its infancy; it claims to be a totalised knowledge –
'Truth' – and not the living movement of thought which alone is
capable of understanding the modern world. It is the restoration
of this movement that is the immediate political aim of the *Critique*.

v. Conclusion

We have attempted to establish the relationship between
Sartre's earlier and later work by arguing that they are both
theoretical works starting from the same point and by arguing that
there is an epistemology – a conception of what thought 'is', of
what ideas and knowledge 'are' – that is common to both. The
second half of this work will situate the 'absolute', consciousness,
in social structures and in history, the existence of both of which
was assumed and referred to during the first part but not explored
in any depth. It may be discovered that in many cases, the absolute
freedom established in *Being and Nothingness* has no practical
importance beyond its own existence, i.e. beyond the lived experience of the individual, whose fate is written in the structures in
which he is placed, whose thought is dominated by them, but who
can still bear witness to his freedom through the particular flavour
that he gives to his destiny. It is his ability or inability to change his
destiny and the structures that map it out that will be the centre
of investigation.

The structure of the next chapter will be determined by the
nature of the theoretical argument, which, as we have seen, moves
from the abstract to the totality through a series of increasingly
complex moments; we will look at each moment as a theoretical
moment and then look at two 'concrete abstractions' which we will
abstract even further by looking at them only in the light of the mode
of intelligibility developed in the theoretical discussion. The two
concrete abstractions will be sociology itself as a discipline and a
specific sociological study and thus we will be able to pursue the two

lines of argument that were developed in the first four chapters: the development of a reflexive Sartrean sociology and a delineation of the practical differences between a sociology rooted in Sartre's philosophy and 'conventional' sociology.

Following the development of the theoretical description in this way has other advantages. The totality, whether theoretical or concrete is, as we will see, exceptionally complex and it would be difficult to handle if we start with it *in toto*; instead we will build up its complexity step by step, progressively deepening our understanding of both the theory and the concrete at each step. Further, it should have become apparent in the first four chapters that the meaning of the theoretical analysis becomes clearer when we use it to look at concrete situations and it is only in this way that we can establish its relevance to sociology: the proposed structure enables us to do this clearly and precisely.

The sociological studies that have been chosen for re-analysis are Gouldner's *Patterns of Industrial Bureaucracy* and *Wildcat Strike*; together they contain material relevant to each moment of the theoretical description and they are very much 'traditional' sociology: through them we move back towards the centre of the discipline. In comparison to these studies Goffman and Garfinkel can be said to be on the 'fringes' of the discipline, however well established they are becoming. At the same time, although Gouldner has presented the most comprehensive discussion so far of 'reflexive sociology' he has not looked at his own earlier work in its light. By taking these two studies for re-analysis, it is hoped that we will reveal that 'reflexivity' involves more than the drawing out of 'domain assumptions' and that Gouldner does not offer us the means to understand his own role in his earlier works.

6
Praxis

A. SOLITARY PRAXIS
1. Theoretical description

The abstract, theoretical starting point, then, is individual praxis taken in isolation. It must be emphasised that this is not an attempt to build a model of 'reality' starting with the individual. Solitary praxis is an abstraction both on the theoretical and on the concrete level.

The first and most elementary relationship between man and his environment is need, and it is this relationship that must first be shown to be dialectical, to contain the first totalisation, the first negation of the negation and the source of praxis. 'Praxis' as used by Sartre has a complex of meanings: most simply it is man's action on the world at any level of complexity, including both thought and physical activity as moments; it is productive work – labour in the Marxist sense; and it is action in the Weberian sense of purposeful action, but with the deepening of Weber's classification implied by Sartre's earlier work which includes emotional activity and apparently 'irrational' behaviour as action which is purposeful and therefore understandable.

Need is primarily a *lack*, and a contradiction between the organic and inorganic which threatens to reduce the former to the latter.[1] This is the first negation: the negation (and threatened extinction) of the organism in the form of a lack. The negation of the negation is the movement of the organic towards the inorganic in order to satisfy the need. This movement is totalising and depassing: the needy organism goes beyond itself, totalising the inorganic environment[2] as a unity from which the means of satisfying the need

---

[1] There is an obvious parallel here between need as a lack and consciousness as a lack. We will see that this does not involve any substitution of one for the other.

[2] Sartre uses the terms 'organic' and 'inorganic' in a highly individual way: the former indicates 'the conscious human organism', the latter covers everything else. One imagines 'organism' is employed by Sartre to indicate the new, materialist roots of his philosophy.

is to be selected, but maintaining itself within this new totality. The negation of the negation is an affirmation in that it affirms the existence of the organism and creates the new totality and we see within this fundamental *movement* (it has an urgent dynamic of its own) the intelligibility of what was for Engels a 'law'.

We also discover in this simple movement the intelligibility of another of Engels' laws: the interpenetration of opposites. In order to act upon the environment to satisfy its need, the organism, at one moment of its praxis, has to make itself inorganic. To act upon matter, it must make itself matter, and the relationship between the two is one of mechanical, exterior causality. To pluck a fruit from a tree or pull up a root, I transform myself into a physical force to overcome a resistance, I make my hand the inorganic means to grasp the inorganic (or I use an inorganic tool). We are left with a circular movement of need, satisfaction and the reappearance of need in which the organism constantly aims at renewing itself (1960a: 147). This circularity is characteristic not only of the organism but also of certain 'primitive' societies and it is broken by the contingent fact of scarcity at which we will look in the next chapter. What is important at the moment is that it is the *movement* which makes the dialectical law intelligible.

We find a second moment of the interpenetration of opposites in the maintenance of the unity of the environment. The organism projects itself on to and beyond the environment which both serves and represents its end,[1] which at this stage of circularity is the organism itself. Thus the inorganic field takes on an organic nature in that the relationships between its elements are given and maintained by the praxis of the organism and in this sense are 'links of interiority': they depend on the end of the organism rather than on any 'natural' force; in the terms of *Being and Nothingness* the For-itself is giving meaning to the In-itself in the course of its project. The organism interiorises the material environment (making itself inorganic to act upon it) and exteriorises itself in the environment, giving the latter a form of organic unity.[2] It is in this

[1] i.e. the means (to the satisfaction of the need) are in the environment and are united in and by the end.
[2] It is important to distinguish 'interiorisation' and 'exteriorisation' from 'internalisation' and 'externalisation' as they are used in psychoanalysis and some sociology (e.g. Berger & Luckmann 1966). 'Internalisation' implies taking inside something from the outside – e.g. a value – which then becomes a *part* of the individual; 'interiorisation', on the other hand, implies the assumption of something outside *in order to go beyond it*, the value becomes a tool. In the same way, 'externalisation' implies putting outside something that was inside, whereas 'exteriorisation' is the moving beyond what was interiorised (even if this movement only supports the former value). In psychoanalysis the terms imply that consciousness is an absorbent substance.

sense that the movement of the organic towards the inorganic is a depassing totalisation.

Within this totalised environment, maintained by the praxis of the organism, work is carried out on one part of it. But this separation of the part involves a contradiction and conflict.

One will see, in effect, that in the field of existence and tension determined by the whole, any particular is produced within the unity of a fundamental contradiction: it *is* the determination of the whole and, as such, it is the whole that gives it being; in a certain way, insofar as the being of the whole demands that it is present in all its parts, *it is the whole itself*; but, at the same time, as a halt, a return to itself, an enclosing, it is not the whole and it is precisely against [the whole] (and not against a being transcendent to the whole) that it is particularised; but this particularisation, in the framework of this contradiction, is produced precisely as a negation of interiority; as a particularisation *of the whole*, it is the whole opposed to itself, through a particular which it governs and which depends on it (pp. 170–1).

Work, whether direct or through the mediation of the tool, inevitably entails this contradiction. The first totalisation of the environment is immediately a negation of that totalisation as the organism separates a part of it to work on; the meaning of this will become clearer when we look at alienation in the next chapter. The negation of this negation is the retotalisation of the environment after the satisfaction of the need. It is this movement of totalisation and negation as the structure of praxis that Sartre indicates when he says that human work is '*entirely* dialectical' (p. 173).

There are three points that we can make about this description. In the first place, the superficially behaviourist terminology – organism, needs etc. – should not be allowed to lead to confusion. The description only makes sense if the organism is *conscious* and *human*; consciousness mediates between the lack and its need and the need and its satisfaction transforming each into a motive for its activity in the way which we outlined in Chapter 2; only a conscious organism can totalise and select, and the description of praxis, presupposes the description of consciousness in *Being and Nothingness*.[1]

Secondly, although Sartre has attempted to show that the action of the organism is dialectically intelligible, the *existence* of the organism remains unintelligible and has to be taken as given. Here

[1] The important point here is that the two works are on different theoretical levels. One way in which they may be shown to be contradictory is by arguing that they are on the same level, i.e. that they are about the same thing; see in particular Doubrovsky 1961.

we are referred back to the contingent and absurd fact that 'there is' being and consciousness that is described in the earlier work.

Thirdly, although people regularly attempt to express themselves in the terms of analytic reason, this does not mean, as Sartre puts it, that 'their praxis is not conscious of itself' (p.176). Whatever the terms in which it is described, praxis itself must inevitably be dialectical in its structure and take account of that structure in its operation. The mediations between praxis and the way in which it is thought will become apparent as the analysis continues.

The description of solitary praxis is fundamental to the whole of the theoretical description in two respects. Firstly, it establishes the dialectical intelligibility of praxis and the intelligibility of the dialectic. If the description is adequate, then the dialectic is intelligible in the sense that it is brought into the world by human action, in the same way that nothingness comes into the world through human consciousness. It is not a contingent natural law but the structure of intentional human action as it creates itself, and it can only be understood dialectically through the progressive–regressive movement of understanding. This is what Sartre means when he says that the dialectic is its own intelligibility, that it is self-evidently transparent to itself: it is produced in and by human action and can only be understood dialectically. This is the most intense form of the tautology implicit in any action theory and, like the relationship between the absolute and the relative, it is inaccessible to analytic reason.

Secondly, the description is fundamental in that it provides the basis for the dialectical intelligibility of History. If praxis is free in the sense that it dialectically creates its own dialectical structure, then History, if it exists, must be freely created on the basis of individual praxes: if History were the working out of certain 'laws' then praxis itself would be determined, and as we have seen, this is not the case, it creates its own laws. The other two possibilities are either that History does not exist, in which case there would simply be a vast multiplicity of individual activities, or that it is the accidental product of the random intermixing of individual activities and thus not open to any sort of understanding at all. The theoretical description will attempt to eliminate these two possibilities as it continues.

11. Sociological praxis

The first 'mode' of intelligibility, then, is that of simple praxis and we can now look at the activity of the sociologist as simple praxis. At the end of Chapter 4, we attempted a brief sketch of the 'sociological project' with the aim of discovering the intelligibility of the type of object that those studied comprise for the sociologist. It was argued that an integral part of this was the project of becoming a recognised sociologist – an impossible aim in the sense that such a 'being' can never be achieved. We can now look at this particular project as a dialectical praxis, but one which thinks itself and tries to organise itself in analytic terms, again with specific consequences for its presentation of those studied.

To the extent that the sociological project is one of becoming a sociologist, the sociological praxis has as its first totalisation 'sociology' – a complex of knowledge and theory represented in books, papers etc., a group of people called 'sociologists', more or less formulated ways of acting and ends, and appropriate values built up around those ends. To the extent that the sociological project is one of possessing the world through knowledge, sociological praxis has as its totalisation 'the world', or 'society' or the 'social system', or some part of 'the world', etc. as a set of elements organised in a more or less definite way. The actual extent of this totalisation and its degree of organisation is not important: what matters is that insofar as the choice of the topic to be studied is a *choice*, then it is selected from some wider set of elements, and it is this 'set' which comprises the initial totalisation. It is in the relationship of these two totalisations, 'sociology' and 'the world' (whether or not the 'world' covers the whole of the world) that we can discover one of the reasons why sociology should think and organise itself analytically.

To help us do this, we can look at a form of everyday praxis, for example a divorce, which also has as its initial totalisation 'the world' (this time in the sense of the immediate relationships of the individual to those around him, friends, relations etc.). The 'need' to which this praxis would respond can take an infinite number of practical forms but common to all of them would be a lack or insufficiency experienced by the individual in his relationships with others, a 'physical' lack, or a 'spiritual' lack, the precise form does not matter. The end of the praxis would be to re-arrange the initial totalisation of relationships in such a way that the insufficiency would be removed. This would require a practical re-organisation of one or more relationships within the initial totalisation, which would proceed dialectically in the way outlined in the theoretical description: the breaking down of the first totalisation into its elements, the 'carving out' of one of its components (the relationship with the wife), its alteration and its re-integration back into the initial totality which would now be a new totality. The act of

'working' on the 'part' – divorcing the wife – introduces change
and conflict into the initial totalisation: friends may take sides and
no longer remain friends, an area of social contact, such as in-laws
may disappear, the way in which the man is seen by others changes,
he becomes, for example, a bastard for ditching his wife and kids
and going off with a girl half his age, or a friend who is having
problems and needs sympathy and help etc. The new totalisation,
then, is more than simply the initial one minus the wife.

We can compare this with sociological praxis: both share a
similar initial totalisation, 'the world' – a set of social relationships
but each has a different end in view. The sociological end, in
respect to the initial totalisation, is to know, the practical end for
the husband is to change in a certain way. The sociological end may
be to know in order to change, but the important point here is that
in the vast majority, if not in all cases, the agent of change will not
be the sociologist himself. Similarly the lay individual may need to
know in order to change, but knowing is a secondary end, subordinated to change. In the case of sociological praxis, the projected
agent of change may vary, the sociologist may be acting as the agent
of an official social administration, a teacher of or informant for a
social worker or a theorist for the proletariat or 'the people' in
general, but the immediacy of change is not present for him. In this
respect sociological praxis is one moment, precisely the analytic
moment, of a praxis that includes it but goes beyond it. This is not
to say sociological praxis is not dialectical in structure but its
purpose is analytic and it is likely to conceive of itself in analytical
terms. This likelihood is further established when change plays no
part in the sociological praxis at all, even as something to be
implemented by a distant other, when 'to know' becomes the only
end. The man who divorces his wife cannot help but include
himself in his initial totalisation, simply because he is the end of this
totalisation: what he does will effect him immediately and personally. In this respect, it becomes impossible for him to remain at
the analytic stage: the breaking down of his relationships and his
direct action on one or more of them has immediate repercussions
on all the others which immediately concern him. If the absence
of immediate practical change by the sociologist makes possible the
analytic sociological study as a moment of wider praxis, then the
absence of any prospect of change whatever separates the sociologist
in any immediate personal sense from what he studies and confirms
this possibility, since in no way can the study react back on him and
force him to include himself in the initial totalisation, except in
those cases where this separation is short circuited by those being

studied.[1] The 'interpenetration of opposites' – in the theoretical description the inclusion by the organism of itself in its totalisation of the inorganic environment – does not take place: the world becomes something entirely 'out there', 'to be known'.

We have seen that to possess the world through knowledge involves an 'objectification' of those in the world, and we can now elaborate on this. To possess through knowing implies that what is possessed is stable and defined. This is so for two reasons: if what is possessed changes, then it is no longer known; to 'possess' and to 'know' implies that what is possessed and known is outside of oneself. Here, then, 'to know' as the end of sociological praxis implies in several ways the analytic breaking down of what is studied and the exclusion of the sociologist.

The comparison of the structure of sociological praxis with that of an individual's direct praxis has, then, established the possibility of sociology being an analytic description of the world to the extent that: (a) it is the analytic moment of a wider praxis and (b) the sociologist is personally excluded – or excludes himself – from what he studies and his project is simply to know the world.

We can now return to the relationship between the two totalisations, of 'sociology' and 'the world', that we distinguished at the beginning of this section. There is no *a priori* reason why either of these should not take precedence over the other: the sociologist may be attracted to a particular social problem or even a problem which relates to him personally, in which case the former would be subordinated to the latter;[2] or he might choose a particular problem from sociological theory or from a previous study, or he might simply choose a study that would readily achieve publication (cf. Berger, 1963), in which case the position would be reversed. He might simply have his research topic set by whoever employs him, in which case either relationship would be possible.

To see them, however, as two separate totalisations is to be too schematic: they merge into each other, one becomes a way of seeing the other. Perhaps we can speak, in this context, of a 'sociological unconscious' in the sense that Bordieu speaks of a 'cultural unconscious'[3] but with the reservation that 'unconscious' is misleading,

---

[1] It may happen when those studied reject the sociologist or it may possibly happen 'accidentally' that an event causes the sociologist to situate himself in what we have called the 'initial totalisation'. See e.g. Morgan 1972.

[2] The selection of e.g. race relations might fall into this category. For a more personal example, see the appendix to Whyte 1955.

[3] Bordieu (1966) seems to offer a basis for a synthesis between a more conventional structural approach and Sartre's conception of the project or, in terms of American sociology, between what is being argued here and Friedrichs' (1970) attempt to apply Kuhn to sociology.

it is rather the case of an interiorised framework from within which the world is seen. The sociological totalisation, whilst remaining an end in the sense that it is sociology as a body of knowledge to which the researcher is contributing, also becomes the filter through which he makes his totalisation of the world. Occasionally, of course, the position may be reversed: the totalisation of the world becomes a means of assessing sociology. The important point here is that the greater the importance of the sociological totalisation, as an end and as an 'unconscious', the more radical the separation of the sociologist from those he studies, the more radically different his ends from the ends of those studied. The project of knowing the world merges into that of becoming a sociologist and the latter becomes dominant.

The 'sociological totalisation' is complex but we can consider one of its components: sociological theory. The importance of theory in an empirical study, the exact nature of the role it plays, is problematic, so what follows should not be regarded as applicable to all sociological studies. There are, nonetheless, a large number of studies that are derived from and contribute to a theory, the name of the theory in this context being unimportant, and it is instructive to look at this use of theory in comparison to the conception of theory that we have been developing in this study. Insofar as theory comprises an element of the sociological totalisation that intervenes between the sociologist and those he studies to determine subjects for empirical research and at the same time to set itself up as an end, to be modified or supported by the research, then it must be *analytic*, both a result of and a mechanism in the sociologist's exclusion from what he studies.

Dialectical theory, as we saw in the last chapter, aims to *totalise*. Analytic theory, derived from or applicable to empirical material aims to *generalise*. Generalisation involves the reduction of aspects of the concrete to the lowest common denominator (usually, admittedly, as high a one as possible); it selects what is common to a number of examples of a particular occurrence and posits its conclusion, a series of hypotheses as common to all examples, and open to further proof or disproof in other studies. Dialectical theory, on the contrary, aims to keep every possible and ascertainable aspect of the concrete, but to unite it into a whole in such a way that each particular aspect is intelligible in terms of the others. Because it seeks what is common, analytic theory aims at being logical, there must be no contradictions within it since contradictory aspects of phenomena cannot be common to all (unless the contradiction itself is common to all examples, in which case it becomes one aspect in terms of the theory). Dialectical theory, on the other hand, sees contradictions in and between phenomena as essential to their intelligibility. Given that no contradiction results, aspects of analytic theory can be changed with no effect on other aspects, certain hypotheses can be removed or altered without changing the others. No component of dialectical theory can be changed without all other components being altered. All these differences are secondary in comparison to the central distinction: dialectical theory is precisely *the investigation of what is not available to empirical research* in the usual sense of the latter. It should be emphasised again, however, that analytic theory is by no means the only sort of theory existing in sociology, although it tends, or has tended to be, fairly common. The exact status of a particular theory would have to be established through a fairly exhaustive study.

We have attempted to show, in this section, that sociology, whilst remaining dialectical in structure, can – and very likely will be – analytic in content. It is important to emphasise, however, that this is not *necessarily* the case. The dialectical structure – the initial totalisation, the selection of an area or topic for study (the first negation), the study and the retotalisation (the negation of the negation) – can as it were be 'filled out' by the inclusion of the sociologist in the original totalisation. What we have called the 'interpenetration of opposites' involves my recognition of my Being-for-Others and the other's Being-for-Themselves and vice versa and neither of these two dimensions can be completely eliminated. The extent to which the sociologist is aware of them and can take them into account however varies considerably, by no means the least important factor being the reaction of those studied. It could also be the case that some specific areas of study question the sociologist, about his ethics or his very profession, more than others independently of the behaviour of those he studies. The recent developments in the sociology of deviance would indicate that this might be one example. The important point, however, is that a precondition for analytic sociology is that the sociologist excludes himself as completely as possible and, in terms of the structure of sociological praxis, this exclusion is effected through the dominance of the 'sociological totalisation'.

III. Gouldner's self-exclusion

The aim of the re-analysis of the Gouldner studies will be a reconstruction of the material that he presents into a dialectical unity, the precise meaning of which should become clearer as the study progresses. As we saw in the previous chapter, it will move in the opposite direction to the re-analyses of Goffman and Gar-finkel, towards the full complexity of the concrete rather than towards a basic ontology. The aim is to show the material as a whole rather than a sum of parts and a whole that is intelligible as created or maintained by the free dialectical praxis of those involved, even if that praxis is alienated from its moment of completion. Here, we will only attempt to establish the analytic nature of what is to be restructured.

The first point to make is that what we have called the 'sociological totalisation' dominates both studies, and this domination must be explored. Primarily it appears through the medium of sociological theory: *Patterns of Industrial Bureaucracy* begins with an outline of Weber's theory of bureaucracy and some suggested criticisms (pp. 15–30); it is argued that the extent of bureaucracy, rather than a result of an inexorable process, is mediated through certain indivi-duals and groups whose interests it serves or threatens. This is what is then established by the study, which ends with systematic general-isations about types of bureaucracy and the factors that influence the development of each type. Here we have the initial totalisation and the eventual retotalisation, in which the use of theory is analytic in the sense described above: it is built up in relation to an empirical study and can be taken apart, subtracted from and added to without necessarily changing every element. Thus certain fea-tures of Weber's work are selected for criticism and modification, yet the overall 'ideal type' would appear to remain unchanged; Gouldner implicitly reduces 'bureaucracy' to the simple existence of rules, both in his theoretical discussion and in the study itself, and the nature of these rules as 'bureaucratic' is not changed in any way by the means by which they are established. 'What bureaucracy is' and 'how bureaucracy appears' would seem to be unconnected.

In *Wildcat Strike* the analytic nature of the theory is more self-evident in that the 'Theory of Group Tensions' (Ch. 9) is built up directly out of the empirical study through the explicit process of generalisation; each hypothesis is by no means necessarily depen-dent on the others and can be dropped without affecting them, and each hypothesis corresponds to some element in the concrete. The dominance of the sociological totalisation appears through the very exercise of theory building in a particular way and, marginally, through a gesture to Parsons as a source of the first hypothesis.[1]

---

[1] This seems to be a particularly easy target in that, as a rule, sociological theory tends to be arrived at through a more complex process; in fact Gouldner's attempt does not seem to have been followed up anywhere. It does contain, however, in exaggerated form, features common to much sociological theory-building.

The domination of 'sociology' as an end, then, is an exclusion of Gouldner from what he studies, but it would be an over-simplification to leave the argument here: the exclusion is not complete. The *sociological totalisation* can, of course, include the sociologist, even if he excludes himself from what he studies. He will, thus, feature indirectly in the study, and since here the central feature of the sociological totalisation is sociological theory, the important question is the extent to which that theory includes the sociologist as an element to be taken into consideration. Gouldner would seem to be operating with an implicit combination of Weber's action theory and structural functionalism and from this we can make some general comments. The latter school, on the whole, would tend to exclude the sociologist from its way of operating but Weber did on various occasions take account of his place, principally his role in choosing what is to be studied, which must be a value-laden choice although values can be eliminated in the course of the study; the role of the scientist of course has its own values. Gouldner has elsewhere (1964) discussed this last point and emphasised the connection between the practice of sociology and wider human values. This approach recognises that the sociologist and those he studies share at least a common humanity in that they both have ends and values, but it is recognised as part of the sociological totalisation and on the level of generalised theory, and in the particular studies we are looking at it is manifested in the form of an endorsement of generalised cultural values and a generalised humanism. Thus:

... the sociologist will eschew the role of a mortician, prematurely eager to bury men's hopes, but will, instead, assume responsibilities as a social clinician, striving to further democratic potentialities without arbitrarily setting limits on these in advance (1954a: 245)

and again,

We could only say, finally, that we believed in our work and that we intended and hoped that it would help people; or, more properly, it would provide them with the knowledge so that they could help themselves in their human predicaments. (p. 268)

But these are statements of intent rather than integral parts of the study: they leave the 'scientific' method and conclusions untouched, and, in fact, the content is dealt with analytically. Policy-making and action is left for others and the sociologist's inclusion remains on a generalised and theoretical level.

Patterns of Industrial Bureaucracy is analytic in that it investigates a number of features or events – the succession and its consequences, the indulgency pattern, its causes and consequences, organisation on the surface and in the mine, market forces (minimally) etc. – which are interrelated but which are not portrayed as comprising a whole; rather they are seen as separate factors which somehow coincide and reinforce or reject each other; they are seen as reacting on each other externally rather than being integrated into a complex unity which can be structured to give priority to some factors rather than others. The central conclusion of the study, the classification of bureaucratic types is inherently analytic, involving as it does separation and opposition through a process of generalisation. Similarly *Wildcat Strike* lists the factors which somehow coincide at the point of the strike without examining the full complexity and structuring of their relationships. Both studies are analytic in method to the extent that they break down the object studied into component parts and then re-assemble them more or less as a sum rather than a totality. In the first study, for example, the parts are deliberately physically isolated from each other before being added back together:

Since the informants were to be talking about their jobs and co-workers, it was necessary that the interviews be conducted away from their immediate place of work. (p. 257)

The views were added together and classified into aggregates: 'market' or 'traditional' men, miners and surface workers, workers and management etc.

The exact analytic nature of this approach will become increasingly apparent as the restructuring progresses. Here we have attempted to show that the Gouldner studies, whilst being dialectical in structure, are analytical in content and method on the lines suggested in the previous section with one or two modifications, principally the inclusion of the sociologist into the dominant sociological totalisation. Before we can begin the restructuring, we must move on to the second moment of the theoretical description.

B. HUMAN RELATIONSHIPS
1. Theoretical description

The next problem for the theoretical description is the way in which each individual praxis is related to others. The orthodox Marxist answer would be that relationships are determined by History, or, more specifically, the nature of the society in which those relationships are situated. (See e.g. Marx and Engels, 1968.) If this were the case, however, then praxis itself would be deter-

mined in the same way, man would be made by, not make, History.
Sartre argues that while the *content* of human relationships may be
seen as being determined in such a way, the fundamental structure
of the relationship is not; there is a basic human relationship which
provides for the possibility of all historically present actual relationships, and this basic relationship is created by praxis. The purpose
of the theoretical description is to arrive at and describe this
fundamental form which, by itself, is not available to empirical
analysis, but which is available to the phenomenological description
of immediate experience.

The example that Sartre uses here is that of a 'petit-bourgeois
intellectual' (one of his favourite characters, almost invariably
referring to himself) on holiday in the country. He is watching, from
his window, two mutually unaware rural workers, separated from
each-other by a wall. The first act of the observer is a negation, he
separates himself from the workers he is watching, he is of a
different class, follows a different life-style, is on holiday while they
are working etc. But this understanding is only possible on the basis
of a commonly understood set of relationships, he has to understand
not only his own situation and ends but theirs as well. This
understanding involves a reference to a particular society, a particular division of labour, a particular distribution of wealth etc.
(1960a: 182)[1]

Further, he sees the two as organising the material world around
themselves, and what is unavailable to him is the way in which they
organise this world, the particular meanings that they give it. This
constitutes them as *other* than him. In a description reminiscent of
Being and Nothingness, the consciousness of each of these workers
is a 'perspective of flight, a plughole in reality' (p. 183) whilst their
bodies are objects in the observer's perceptual field. At the same
time as they are other than the observer, they are united to him
by the fact that each of the three organises the same material world
around them. The observer can thus establish a relationship of
mutual reciprocity between the two workers: despite their ignorance
of each other they share the same world. Their mutual ignorance
is not something which appears *to* the observer, but *through him*; it
could not exist if there were nobody there to recognise it (again,
in much the same way that the mountain is only steep if somebody
wants to climb it). Each one is producing himself through his praxis
as a specific individual in a specific place carrying out a specific task

---

[1] Sartre's description here is reminiscent of Schutz with its emphasis on
shared knowledge; but the former sees it as a 'tool' depassed in the
project, whereas the latter sees it as a 'sediment'.

in the world that is unified by his praxis. By so doing, he is giving himself the possibility of discovering the other both as an object in his world and as a source of flight.

The possibility of a relationship between the two workers is, then, provided for by the nature of their praxis, and their separation and ignorance is, therefore, contingent. Each *can* be totalised into the field of praxis of the other, and their reciprocal ignorance thus becomes a special case of their reciprocal awareness. Having established this, we can move on from this particular example.

Seeing the other as object is a link of exteriority between him and myself; seeing him as a source of flight is a link of interiority; it involves my grasp of him as another consciousness, another acting organism and my grasp of myself as an object for him. This is the fundamental relationship of reciprocity which must exist so long as there are more than two individuals in the world. If there is an Other, it is impossible not to grasp both him and myself as both subject and object at the same time.[1]

In isolation, however, the dyad does not establish reciprocity: I simply totalise the Other through my praxis as an object and as a source of flight. The reciprocal relationship between us appears only through an observer – the Third – and each individual is a Third at the same time that he is an Other and himself.[2] The pure comprehension of one Other in my field of praxis is thus never possible: in some situation I have already been a Third and through that I can recognise the reciprocity existing between myself and the Other. Since, at the present stage of the description, each is capable of being the Third in turn, there is no totalisation of the dyad or the triad, but rather a plurality of totalisations, the reciprocity of any two being established by a third.

As the fundamental human relationship, reciprocity is always present as a concrete, not an abstract link, since to live in a world without other men is unimaginable and my praxis must always totalise *these* specific men into my world as they must totalise me into theirs. All other relationships are based on this fundamental

---

[1] This refers back to the description in *Being and Nothingness* of which no modification is implied. From the base of reciprocity, the dialectic of conflict of the earlier work is certainly a possibility. The concentration on conflict in that work, whilst possibly one of the 'ideological' manifestations of Sartre's own history, may also be seen as the description of a situation which, as we shall see in the next chapter, is historically (but not ontologically) dominant.

[2] Thus the reciprocity of, for example, kinship systems, only appears as such to a Third – either the anthropologist (Sartre uses Lévi-Strauss as an example) or to the society which they comprise – i.e. the society itself is Third to its members.

reciprocity and must recognise it. The relationship of exploitation, for example – treating man as an object – is based on a free contract which recognises the freedom of both parties at the same time that it alienates and mystifies the freedom of one. Similarly slavery – treating man as an animal – first requires recognition of him as a man: the slave owner is permanently on guard against his slaves revolting as men.[1] The full implications of reciprocity are as follows:

(1) That the Other be a means to the same extent that I am a means myself, i.e. that he be a means to a transcendent end but not *my* means; (2) that I recognise the Other as praxis, i.e. as a totalisation in progress at the same time as I integrate him as an object into my own totalising project; (3) that I recognise his movement towards his own ends in the same movement in which I project myself towards mine; (4) that I discover myself as the object and instrument of his ends in the same act which constitutes him as an objective instrument for my ends. (Sartre 1960a: 192)[2]

Such reciprocity may be positive or negative, the former towards common or individual ends. Negative reciprocity involves my using my objectness for the Other in order to trick him with my subjectivity. This refers us to scarcity with which we will deal in the next chapter.

The triad, then, presents us with a plurality of totalisations; each individual can in turn be the Third through whom reciprocity as such appears. The possibility of there being only one totalisation is indicated, however, through the mediation of objects and through the presence of a Third to a joint praxis. The example that Sartre uses here is that of two workers working together on the production of one object; the first hint of unity comes through the object produced which combines the work of both in an anonymous form, but this unity comes only after the work has been completed. For the workers themselves, while they are working, the work is co-operative and increasingly intimate, but it is not a synthetic unity. I recognise my own project in that of the Other but as *over there* and each of his actions refers me to his consciousness which is only signified and which I cannot totalise into my field. My totalisation of my field poses itself as essential and at the same time recognises the essentiality of that of the Other, and vice versa (p. 194).

---

[1] The worker's freedom is mystified in that he apparently freely surrenders his freedom when in fact his only alternative is starvation; on slavery, Sartre elaborates this idea at length in his introduction to Fannon 1968.

[2] Homan's exchange theory (and that of Mauss) could possibly be seen as a reification of this fundamental relationship.

Because each of us has at some time been a Third, and because our work finds its unity in its object, we recognise our unity as a possibility, but it remains only that, a phantom unity experienced as a lack, an 'insufficiency' of being. As with reciprocity, unity can only appear through a Third; it then becomes possible to interiorise the unity we thus receive in an attempt to make up that insufficiency.[1]

The Third, in Sartre's example, is a time-and-motion study man. He grasps the unity of the two workers in the light of his own ends, to which they become the means; his ends are imposed on them as an imperative:

Objectively, and *through* the Third, the independence of the end
transforms the reciprocity into conjunction of movement . . . it
metamorphosises double action into a single event which subordinates
the two workers as secondary structures whose particular relations
depend on global relations and who communicate to each other through
the mediation of the whole. (p. 196)

Whereas up to now the subjectivity of the two workers has been seen as essential in that it is precisely what has prohibited unity, it now becomes inessential through the ends of the Third. As a Third pursuing my own ends, I see the subjectivity of each worker as simply the interiorisation of their ends; they are, for me, men-who-are-doing-a-certain-job and nothing else and each is equivalent to and interchangeable with the Other.

The relationship of the Third to the two workers is one of interiority since at the same time he modifies them, subordinating their subjectivity, and modifies himself through totalising them into his field of praxis. It is not, however, a reciprocal relationship, since he does not let himself be totalised into their fields of praxis. In this respect it represents an embryonic hierarchy. At the present stage of the theoretical description (and leaving the example) we have not provided any justification for regarding it as a permanent hierarchy: each member of our theoretical Triad can become Third in turn. Whether or not and in what way a hierarchy may develop depends upon historical circumstances.

On the basis, then, of the dialectical intelligibility of praxis, we have discovered the intelligibility of the fundamental human relationship which, quite simply, is the relationship of one praxis to another. It has its origin in simple plurality: the fact that there is more than one acting individual, and this is a contingent fact which

---

[1] Although, as we will see, an ontological unity is never achieved. This
description may be seen as an elaboration of the 'Us-object' mentioned
in *Being and Nothingness*.

conditions, without determining, the relationship (p. 198). We have seen that there is a possible totalisation of human relationships through the Third, but at the moment, each is a possible Third; for a totalisation proper to be achieved the mediation of matter is necessary. However, we can, from this description, understand certain individual human relationships even if we have not yet discovered the tools for understanding the existence of groups. In the following analyses the existence of groups must, to some extent, be assumed.

II. The sociologist as Third

To describe the sociologist as a Third, subordinating the subjectivity of the Other is simply to restate a point made regularly throughout the study. It does, however, allow us to see the subordination of the Other's subjectivity as more than a simple act of consciousness.

It follows from our description of sociology as praxis that the greater the domination of the 'sociological totalisation', the more radical the difference between the ends of the sociologist and those he studies, the more completely he establishes himself as a Third. Reciprocity is ruptured but not, at the moment, interiority. Reciprocity vanishes because the more the sociologist establishes himself as Third, the less he allows himself to become an object in the field of praxis of those he studies.[1] Interiority remains because the activities of those being studied obviously modify the practice of sociology at the same time as the sociologist modifies those he studies through the subordination of their subjectivity. The reverse side of this interiority – that those being studied may modify their own activity to the extent that they take account of the activity of the sociologist, is a constant bugbear for the latter.

We can, in fact, see the subordination of the Other's subjectivity as involving two steps, becoming more complete as the dominance of the sociological totalisation becomes greater, and eventually breaking the relationship of interiority as well as that of reciprocity. The treatment of Spiedman in *Wildcat Strike* provides us with a good example. His 'subjectivity' is, for Spiedman, a totalisation of the world in the light of a particular project, a selection of ends from that totalisation, the pursuit of those ends and a retotalisation in an ongoing movement which embraces much more than his everyday tasks in the plant. Initially in the study, it becomes much less than this, merely a means to his success or lack of success in his task

[1] See e.g. Gouldner's research team's refusal to act as informant for top management (1954a: 254–5).

of introducing new machinery. He is seen as possessing a personality with particular traits and qualities which hinders his performance to the extent that it leads to conflicts with others[1]; his 'subjectivity' becomes an inefficient means to the achievement of his ends, and therefore an inadequate interiorisation of those ends. This is the first subordination. The second is more radical: in the construction of the theory of group tensions, Spiedman's subjectivity is simply an anonymous and subordinate element leading to an increase in tension between Ego and Alter; it vanishes almost completely, it becomes a contingent factor that might or might not exacerbate structural tensions. At this stage interiority has disappeared as well. Whatever his 'personality', the network of structural tensions portrayed in the theory will not be changed.

At this stage, we have filled out rather than gone beyond our previous descriptions. In the next chapter we will be able to begin looking at sociology as a structure as well as a project and as praxis.

III. Status and solidarity

We can take the first steps towards restructuring the Gouldner studies by looking at each individual in the plant as being at some time and in some way a Third. Each is a Third to the extent that he has an end which is *different* to that of the others, independently of whether this end complements or conflicts with theirs. In its most simple form, this end is determined by the division of labour in the plant, at its most complex it will include such features as the desired pace of work, life style, etc., all the elements that make up what Gouldner calls the indulgency pattern. At the moment, we are concerned with it in its most simple form, simply as the task which the individual is set to gain his wages.

The totalisation that each makes of those others whose immediate tasks are different to his will be made in the light of his task, and will involve the immediate subordination of the subjectivity of those others. Independently of any other hierarchy of ends in the plant, the end of each individual, in his immediate perception of it, takes priority over other ends. In his totalisation of the Others, he manifests certain expectations of them (for example, and very simply, that they will work in such a way as to make his task easy) and these expectations are intelligible in terms of the immediate hierarchy of ends established by the individual in carrying out his

---

[1] To the extent that others, as well as Spiedman, are seen as possessing various personality traits as 'qualities' the study is open to an analysis leading back to consciousness and Being, to Gouldner's ontological assumptions.

task. What puts each worker (or group of workers) in the position
of Third is the fact that their ends are dependent on each other
to the extent that everybody in the plant is involved in one overall
end: the production of gypsum board and its by-products. In such
a situation, the completion of my end depends upon the completion
of the Other's ends, and thus the Other as object and myself as
subject is the dominant relationship; whilst not making for a total
break in reciprocity it makes it more difficult to achieve.

Given this, we can begin to render Gouldner's analysis of 'status'
intelligible in terms of the relationship of one praxis to another.
'Status' is defined by Gouldner as a specific position in an organisation, to which he adds the element of 'power': the ability of any
holder of a status position to satisfy expectations in the face of
resistance (1954b, 129–31). We have not yet developed the theoretical tools to deal with 'power' but we can look at 'status'. A 'specific
position in an organisation' will have its own end and we have seen
how expectations are attached to each position in the light of the
ends of the other positions, i.e. as a feature of the relationships of
one praxis in the plant to all the others. This description of status
and status expectations also provides for the status imbalances out
of which Gouldner develops his theory of group tensions – such
features as lack of clarity, lack of fulfilment, change, integration,
legitimacy, etc. If expectations are no longer seen as qualities
belonging to people, and are instead viewed as the expression of
particular relationships between one praxis and another, in which
one praxis tries to subordinate the others on which it is dependent,
then we can see that an imbalance in expectations is built into the
organisation. Each praxis will have different expectations attached
to it by each other praxis and each expectation will define the status
holder simply as somebody-there-to-do-a-particular-job-in-a-
particular-way, when, as we have seen, his being for himself is
infinitely more complex. This view is different from the simple
action theory of organisations which would also see expectations as
attached to ends, in that whereas for action theory conflict would
appear through conflicting ends (Silverman, 1970), here conflict is
seen as a permanent possibility provided for by the existence of ends
that are merely different and dependent.

The subordination of subjectivity appears more clearly when
groups are considered as Thirds and when ends are conflicting as
well as different, but for the moment we are unable to render such
phenomena intelligible. We can, however, point out the form of
subordination that takes place: principally it appears as a moral
and/or practical condemnation of the Other's subjectivity when the

latter becomes apparent as a source of flight in the field of praxis of the Third. Thus, for example, workers are seen as lazy or workshy, management as unnecessarily authoritarian or personally unpleasant; miners are seen as wild and unreliable, surface workers as tame and manipulable. Of course, in all these cases, many other factors are at work and these will become apparent as the restructuring proceeds.

In the light of the theoretical analysis, we can look at the miners insofar as they are engaged in a joint praxis: as a group, they can be seen as a 'collective Third' in relation to the other workers in the plant but it is the internal structure of the group which is important here. The miners comprise a 'world apart' from the other workers, and display very different relationships to each other, not the least important feature of which is a greater informal solidarity (1954a: 129). We have seen that unity comes to those engaged in a joint praxis through a Third and that it must be interiorised by those whom the Third unites before they experience themselves as a group. To make the miners' solidarity intelligible, then, we must look at the unity that they would receive through a Third, and compare it to the unity that the surface workers would receive in the same way.

The first and perhaps the most important point is that the surface workers are united through a spatial and temporal disunity: they carry out different operations at different times and in different places. The division of labour amongst the miners, on the other hand, is minimal, the main distinction appearing to be between the man who puts the supports into place and the others (1954a: 120–2). The second point, connected with the first, is that the miners are united more completely through their product; the first hint of unity comes through the common product and of course the totalising Third will include the product into the totalisation that unites the group. A sheet of completed gypsum board has a number of features that refer to specific operations: its edges refer to the cutting, its thickness to the rollers, its texture to the mixing etc., and these in turn refer to the workers who carried out the operations. It does not, of course, refer to them personally – the knife could have been operated by anybody – but it refers to them as a specific, if anonymous, praxis, situated at a certain point in the division of labour. A load of gypsum rock, on the other hand, refers the observer to no particular activity beyond the general one of mining carried out by the whole group; no miner can look at a chunk of rock and point out the feature that depended on his praxis; the miners are drawn into their product in a completely undifferentiated way, the homogeneity of the product reflects the minimal division of labour and through the Third they achieve a unity that is qualitatively different from that achieved by the surface workers. It is, moreover, a unity that is intelligible in terms of the relationships between one praxis and another rather than as something 'caused' externally, by, for example, the dangers of the work or general cultural considerations. The unity achieved through the Third is presented to them as part of a situation to be interiorised as a means of going beyond it. Of course, we have not yet reached the full intelligibility of the different internal structures of groups, and the intelligibility will be deepened as the theoretical description gives us the tools to do so, but we have made a first step.

We can also now understand the consequences of the separation of the individual worker from his workmates in order to interview him; it establishes him firmly as a Third. To the extent that each worker is engaged in a solitary praxis, that each group of workers engaged in a joint praxis is in some way a 'collective Third', and that each worker in the plant is a Third when he is not working, this separation for the interview does not introduce any radically new status for him. What it does, however, is confirm as primary one of several relationships that he has in the plant and it does so without justification. The relationship of isolation, of the Third, becomes that on which the information about expectations, views, etc. is based, and the other relationships are ignored or deliberately dismantled. When the worker who is engaged in a joint praxis is taken away, then his immediate comprehension of his work is changed. In fact, in the most important area of joint praxis – the mine – the separation would appear, from the research report, to have been more difficult, and this might be connected with the research team's opinion that the best interview material came from the mine (1954a: 259), although this point would have to be argued more fully in the light of more complete information if it were to be established.

7
The practico-inert

A. SCARCITY

We have seen that by his praxis, man unifies the material
world around him and maintains that unity, and that matter,
through the unity that it receives from man, serves to unite men
initially in relationships of reciprocity. Matter, however – not the
pure In-itself but matter as it is revealed to science – is governed
by laws of mechanical exteriority which can turn it back against
praxis: matter can threaten man. The first threat it presents is
scarcity: the material environment may not offer the organism
what is necessary to satisfy its need and keep it in existence.

1. Theoretical description

Scarcity plays a fundamental but ambiguous role in Sartre's
system. There is no simple deterministic relationship between
scarcity and human action: it is, rather, the framework within which
human action takes place, an entirely contingent framework in no
way implied by the structure of praxis.[1] Scarcity is at the foundation
of the possibility of an intelligible History but it is not *necessary* for
there to be a History – other societies with other histories not based
on scarcity are conceivable – nor is it a *sufficient* condition for there
to be a History – various 'primitive' societies in our world appear
to have no history or to have a history which has become a simple
repetition.[2] Scarcity is simply the contingent foundation and condition of *our* history – 'our' history increasingly coming to mean the
history of the planet. History is only intelligible as a history made
in conditions of scarcity.

Man experiences scarcity through his first totalisation of matter

---

[1] Granted that we have achieved an adequate description of praxis,
anything that is entailed by praxis (such as reciprocity) becomes
necessary, as opposed to the existence of the world and of the organism
itself, which is *contingent*.

[2] It is on the problem of the place of History in 'primitive' societies that
Sartre's dispute with Levi-Strauss took place. See Levi-Strauss 1966,
Chapter 9.

as a *possibility*: the possibility of not being able to satisfy his needs, the possibility of the destruction of all men by matter and the possibility of his own destruction by matter as the result of the praxis of another. The second possibility provides for the further possibility of the unity of all in the face of scarcity, but, we will see that this needs more than simple scarcity. It is the last possibility that is immediately important.

However ignorant an individual may be of the existence of others, they represent a threat to him. They are revealed to him as the possibility that the materials of which he has need may be consumed by others. Scarcity defines a group of men in terms of the impossibility of their co-existence and it defines each member of the group as possibly an excess member; it divides the group by defining each member as Other than the Others. The individual's own praxis, on the elementary level at which it seeks to satisfy a need, is turned against him in that the satisfaction of his need becomes a threat to the Others and consequently they become a threat to him (1960a: 206).

As long as scarcity exists it is interiorised as the negation of man by matter, and becomes an 'inert structure' in man. Every man appears as a potential threat, a potential anti-man even if this potentiality is not immediately realised. Insofar as this relationship to Others has its origin in matter it is, unlike the relationship of reciprocity, one of exteriority, an exteriority which eats into reciprocity. In a relationship of reciprocity I recognise the Other as the same insofar as I recognise his ends and means at the same time as I recognise my own. In reciprocity eaten away by scarcity I still recognise him as the same, he possesses my characteristics, but they appear as my characteristics in another alien species (p. 208).[1]

It is at this level that violence becomes a basic structure of human activity. It is, of course, *always* counter-violence: the Other's very existence is a violent threat. In violence:

it is man insofar as he is man, i.e. insofar as he is the free praxis of an organised being, that I attack; it is man and nothing else that I hate in the enemy, i.e. myself insofar as I am Other, and it is myself whom I wish to destroy in him in order to stop him really physically destroying me. But these relationships of exteriority in reciprocity are complicated by the development of praxis itself which re-establishes reciprocity in

[1] It is at this point, Sartre argues, that ethics has its origin in the form of manicheism – the view that the world is divided into good and evil and that we do good by eliminating evil. This represents a considerable break with the role usually accorded values by sociology, i.e. holding a society together. In Sartre's system, they are, at origin a weapon of conflict and they only take on their full meaning in conflict.

the negative form of antagonism, from which moment a real struggle develops. From the concrete necessities of strategy and tactics, one is bound to lose if one does not recognise the adversary as another human group capable of inventing traps, avoiding them, letting themselves fall into them. (p. 209)

Conflict moves between the straightforward desire to annihilate (the complete domination of man by interiorised matter) and the carefully worked out strategy and tactics of negative reciprocity, each moment depassing the other.

Beyond this fundamental division between men, scarcity unites in that the unity of the material field becomes a tool for each conflicting group, and provides them with a unity within which they fight. This unity is basic to the development of the theoretical argument: 'we are united by the fact of inhabiting together a world defined by scarcity' (p. 211).

The role of scarcity in Sartre's theoretical description may appear fairly simple, if not naive, at first glance,[1] but it is the source of several complexities. It is more than the simple fact of scarcity acknowledged by conventional economic theory, from which it is distinguished by the emphasis on interiorisation, necessary before it can become a factor of intelligibility, and by the fact that it is seen not as determining but as conditioning praxis through a complex of mediations. It is not necessarily a straightforward scarcity of the material goods necessary for life: as each attempt to overcome scarcity results in a developing structure of needs and satisfactions, it is transformed. From a simple scarcity of food, for example, we may be led to a scarcity of men (a labour shortage, overproduction) or a scarcity of machines (unemployment), even attempts to create scarcity of various goods, each as a result of the way in which groups interiorise the original scarcity. The complex we have just outlined is dependent on the interiorisation of scarcity into a class system of exploitation, and within such a system, beyond a certain level of development, particular scarcities are revealed in the light of particular projects rather than through famine or drought (although these still have their effects). Each society or group defines itself by the nature of its scarcity and by defining its excess population in relation to that scarcity. In a very real way, each society chooses its own dead: through its deployment of medical facilities and social service benefits in advanced industrial countries, through more simple means in other societies.

---

[1] Friedrichs, for example, accuses Sartre of being exceptionally naive to assume that conflict will end with the reign of plenty. In fact, Friedrichs would appear to have a naive view of the ease with which scarcity can be overcome. See Friedrichs 1970 and Sartre 1963b, p. 34.

Perhaps the most important role of scarcity in the present context, however, is its contribution to intelligibility. It renders conflict intelligible not as a result of some contingent quality of human nature or the nature of some particular human group, nor as the inevitable result of the structure of consciousness itself (which is the impression that might have been gained from *Being and Nothingness*) but as the intelligible and rational interiorisation by praxis of an external contingency. The simple Marxist handling of class conflict obtains, in this context, an added transparency, and, more importantly for the intelligibility of Marxism as a whole, the central role of the mode of production in social structure receives its intelligibility, since it is precisely at this level that a society faces the problem of scarcity.

II. Sociology and scarcity

Beyond the general conditioning of human relationships in which the sociologist is situated, scarcity refers us directly to the position of sociology in the wider social structure. It does so through raising the problem of the degree of wealth that a particular society (or groups within that society) must possess before it devotes some part of it to the maintenance and expansion of sociology (and before that to universities and education in general); and the problem of what ends have to be chosen in relationship to what particular scarcities in order that sociology should be established (perhaps as an attempt to investigate and overcome some types of scarcity). In other words, we are referred to the historical development of sociology and its relationship to the development of the society in which it appears. This is not a move towards economic determinism: the contingent fact of scarcity is always mediated through an indefinite number of structures, not least in a case like this by what is usually called 'ideology' and/or 'culture', together with the existing educational institutions within which sociology has to establish itself. We are only suggesting that the appearance of sociology as a separate discipline only becomes fully intelligible when it can be placed in the context of a particular society's organisation of itself in conditions of scarcity.

Such a study is beyond the scope of this work; there are, however, more immediate manifestations of scarcity at which we can look: these include the scarcity of research funds, of teaching and research posts, of staff in relationship to students and vice versa, the adequacy of salaries etc. This more immediate scarcity conditions sociological praxis as it was described in the last chapter through a series of structured mediations, a network of institutions

and organisations which act within and make up a society operating
on the more general conditions of scarcity. One form of this
conditioning, and one of its results is to be found in what we called
the 'sociological totalisation': an overall scarcity of research funds,
for example, coupled with their comparatively greater availability
for some topics rather than others, effects the content of the
sociological totalisation; it influences the problems that are studied,
the ways in which they are studied and channels sociological
activities in certain directions.[1] In the competition for funds and
posts there is a permanent pressure on the individual to establish
himself as an acceptable sociologist, concerned with the issues that
are recognised by others to be central to sociology. In such a
situation, the sociological totalisation is more likely to dominate his
praxis at the expense of his own individual totalisation of the world.
Further, through competition, there are likely to be other effects
on what comprises the body of sociological knowledge: there will
be attempts, perhaps working in the opposite direction to the effects
we have just outlined, to open up new areas of research and to
establish their sociological respectability, and research in established
fields will be seeking 'originality.' It may be surmised that competition between individual sociologists (usually in the form of
antagonistic reciprocity although perhaps tending towards a
respectable form of manicheism)[2] will produce similar effects on
the sociological totalisation. The content of and dominance of this
totalisation is, then, to some extent intelligible as the interiorisation
of specific forms of scarcity, as well as the mediated interiorisation
of a more fundamental scarcity.

III. The intelligibility of conflict

In the previous chapter, it was argued that the possibility
of 'imbalances' in expectations and consequent conflict was built in
to the organisation of the gypsum plant through the division of
labour and the position of each as Third. Scarcity adds a new
dimension to the intelligibility of conflict in that it is on the basis
of interiorised scarcity that the subordination of the Other's subjectivity takes place, and the possibility is transformed into a probability
insofar as scarcity is an 'inert structure' in our perception of the

---

[1] See, for example, Friedrichs' (1970) comments about the availability of
    research funds for American sociology during the 1950s.
[2] It could be argued that the reaction to some unorthodox schools of
    sociology (such as ethnomethodology) tends towards the manicheistic
    moment. It is perhaps in deciding between what is new sociology and
    what is not sociology at all that the 'sociological totalisation' becomes at
    the same time most important and least well-defined.

Other. We are not, however, dealing with the conjunction of two external forces – scarcity and the division of labour – which act to reinforce each other; the relationship between the two is one of reciprocal mediation and it is in following through these mediations that we can begin to understand what is meant by a 'dialectical sociology' in comparison to an analytic approach which would only see the conjunction of forces.

We have already seen how scarcity mediates the division of labour: it transforms the possibility of conflict provided for in that division into a probability if not a certainty. However, further mediations will be necessary before we can grasp the precise nature of this conflict. In the reciprocal mediation, the division of labour *situates* scarcity as an inert structure of human relationships, as the permanent possibility of seeing the other as a threat; it is a determination of who is likely to see who as a threat. The third mediation which synthesises the first two is that exercised by praxis itself, insofar as it interiorises at the same time scarcity as its permanent condition and the ends given by the division of labour and exteriorises them as action against the Other.[1] It is in the everyday activities of the workers in the plant that the two achieve their fullest unity and the reciprocal mediations are realised.

On the more direct level scarcity refers to the wider society in which the gypsum plant is situated and to more immediate manifestations of scarcity, and it provides us with the first element of unity. Everybody in the plant, including the research team, receive an abstract, formal unity in that they are all operating in a society which is attempting to handle the problem of scarcity through a particular mode of production and they are directly conditioned in their praxis by the immediate scarcity of customers for gypsum board (with the 'tightening up' of the post-war market) and scarcity of jobs (following demobilisation). At the moment however this remains a formal unity, exercised by matter, and as we will see, its interiorisation is by no means straightforward.

B. UNITY AND CONFLICT
I. Theoretical description
The absolute lucidity of individual praxis to itself, as it was described in Chapter 6, is only one moment in constructing the possibility of an intelligible history, and we have now reached the point at which that lucidity becomes obscured and is stolen by the

[1] Or mistrust, or indifference, or friendship towards some against others.

material world. We have seen that men receive a formal unity through working in the same material world, conditioned by scarcity, but this is on a very general level; the next moment is of a more immediate nature and can best be understood by looking at the *tool*, in which man and matter are most intimately linked.

The tool is a crystallised praxis, a past praxis which has imprinted itself on inert matter and given it a human signification. It is one of the means by which the organism makes itself inert in order to act upon inert matter, but because it is itself inert matter, it enters into relationships with the rest of the material world. These are relationships of mechanical exteriority, different to those envisaged by the praxis of the organism (1960a: 231–2). What is true of the tool is true of any matter upon which man acts: what he produces enters into relationships with what he did not produce and these relationships may in turn re-act back upon man. For this to happen, the material world must have its own 'structure' of external relationships which may be revealed to man in the light of his project and which may be set in motion by and 'steal' human praxis. In this movement, matter acts as a more immediate unifying 'mechanism' because the praxis of each individual is stolen and united by the same material world and because insofar as the material world acts back on man, it acts on all those who have acted on it.

Sartre uses the example of Chinese peasants who individually extended their arable land by cutting their way through forests in the northern part of the country, thus removing a natural flood barrier and laying themselves open to inundation; there are plenty of examples in the modern world, for example, the creation of the 'dust bowl' in the mid-west of the United States during the first half of this century. The praxis of the individual farmer, aiming at a maximum productivity and a maximum profit in a given state of knowledge and technology and given market conditions, was initially separate from and in competition with the praxis of all other farmers. It was united with those praxes through the material world – it was the whole area that was laid waste, each section in turn affecting others – and finally turned back against all of them equally insofar as the desolation that each had separately (but jointly) created eventually drove them from the land. This Sartre calls a 'counter-finality': human praxis gives the exterior relationships of the material world a quasi-human quality which acts against the ends posited by that praxis. He is not arguing by analogy, treating the material world *as if* it had this quasi-human quality. The quality is really there and is put there by human praxis. One manifestation of this is the systematic destruction carried out by worked matter (the 'practico-inert'). 'Natural destruction' is a matter of chance in that it is to a greater or lesser degree unpredictable, both in its occurrence and in its effects: there are, for example, occasional droughts or occasional floods, the effects of which vary from area to area and may in all probability be overcome the following year. The 'dust bowl' however spread systematically over a wide area and its effects lasted for decades; it was a product of the material world ('natural laws' if you like) as is the occasional drought, but it manifested an organised, systematic nature that was put there by human praxis. It is at this point that we discover the intelligibility of what Marxists call an 'objective contradiction': a contradiction between the ends of praxis and the external relationships of matter, a contradiction inscribed in matter by praxis, independently of how that praxis is thought. Such a contradiction is in many cases objective also in the sense that it is immediately tangible and observable: the desolated land and poverty stricken farmers are there for whoever looks.

In our example, the practico-inert presents the individuals concerned with a common and therefore social threat and future. The 'passive action' of the material world appears as the threatening praxis of some 'Other' and it is interiorised into the everyday social organisation and activity of those threatened to the extent that they attempt to counter the threat or to use it, perhaps as a weapon in some already existing conflict. It is in relation to the passive action of matter that we can begin to talk of groups and their intelligibility, but more importantly at the moment, taken in conjunction with scarcity it renders intelligible the breakdown of the simple need–satisfaction circularity of the description of solitary praxis.

Thus worked matter, by the contradiction that it carries within itself becomes *for* and *by* man the fundamental motor of history: in it the actions of all are united and take on a meaning, i.e. it constitutes for all the unity of a common future; but *at the same time* it escapes everyone and breaks the cycle of repetition because this future – always projected in the framework of scarcity – is inhuman; its finality in the inert milieu of dispersion is changed into counter-finality, or produces, whilst remaining itself, a counter-finality for everyone or for some. It thus creates, *by itself*, and as the synthetic résumé of all actions...the necessity for change. (1960a: 250)

This is the first immediate experience of alienation, beyond that given by scarcity. My praxis is taken away and turned against me by the material world, by means of the power I have given it. But alienation assumes the existence of free, lucid individual praxis, it can only occur if there is something to alienate and thus it must occur on the completion of praxis not at its inception. Otherwise praxis itself would be determined, and there would be no possibility of conceiving of alienation. There is nothing metaphysical about alienation, it is an immediate experience and an identifiable and traceable occurrence.

Here we find the merging of man and matter and the domination of the latter over the former – a situation encapsulated in everyday language: we do indeed talk about nature as if it possessed some human capability of purposeful action, and we talk about human individuals and groups as if they could be understood in the same way as the material world; at least some of the social sciences try to base themselves on this assumption. Most frequently, however, we talk of units comprised of both men and matter as if they were merged into one whole: the 'nation', the 'factory', the 'university', the 'organisation' etc. This represents a fundamental mystification of which sociologists are perhaps more guilty than others, insofar as these 'units' are precisely what they study. It is mystifying in that it presents us with an entity by no means 'natural' or 'material' whilst at the same time not entirely 'human' either: it is simply not clear what it is. In one sense it conveys accurately the man/matter relationship, as we will see when we look at the 'gypsum plant'; the point is that as it stands and with no elucidation it is not intelligible. We have begun to render it intelligible in our description of the way in which the practico-inert begins to dominate human activity, and we can continue the argument by reverting to our description of the tool, or more specifically now, of the machine.

The machine, as a tool, is the crystallised, anonymous praxis of Others and enters into relationships with the rest of the material world. The praxis of the man who operates the machine is dictated to him by the machine (and through the machine by Others). Although the structure of the praxis is still dialectical and lucid, it is no longer immediately based on need but on the demands of an inanimate object; the whole history of technological development intervenes between need and praxis. The machine, as an anonymous Other, addresses the worker as an anonymous Other, in his generality as a form of more or less skilled labour power, the skill being available to anyone. The demands that it makes of him govern the expectation that the other workers in the plant have of him and in this sense it interposes itself between him and his workmates (p. 252).[1]

The demands of the machine are conveyed through humans,

[1] For Marx's own similar but more generalised description see Marx 1972.

most directly through those in immediate supervision of the work process who, as it were, give the machine a voice and limbs and the powers to reward or punish. Less directly, they take on a human form in the inventor, who makes himself the simple, inessential mediator between two essential states of matter: a previous stage of technology which is demanding certain changes and the future stage which is being demanded (p. 257).

Here we discover the intelligibility of what is usually called *interest*, my being-outside-of-myself-in-a-thing. This possibility was provided for in the description of solitary praxis insofar as the organism finds the means for its survival in the surrounding environment: it has its being-outside-of-itself but in a very general way. The present historical form of interest is private property although this is by no means the only possible one; although a historical analysis of the development of private property has no place in the theoretical description, we can take it as the 'given' form of interest and examine its intelligibility. The central point is that one's being-outside-of-oneself-in-a-thing, like any element of worked matter, enters into relationships with the rest of the material world. Insofar as I identify myself with an external material object, I am led through this object to others: one result is that the means–ends distinction becomes blurred; is profit, for example, a means or an end? Interest also manifests a particular form of domination of man by matter and of unity:

[The individual's] being-outside-of-himself has become essential and to the extent that the latter recovers its truth at the heart of the practico-inert totality, this being-outside-of-himself dissolves in itself the character of psuedo-interiority that the appropriation had given it. Thus the individual finds his reality in a material object, grasped initially as an interiorising totality and which functions, in fact, as an integral part of an exteriorised totality; the more he tries to conserve and accumulate this object which is himself, the more this object becomes Other insofar as it is dependent on all the Others, and the more the individual as the practical reality is determined as inessential in molecular solitude . . . the relation of *interest* carries thus – at the level of individual interest – the massification of individuals as such and their practical communication through the antagonisms and conformities of the matter that represents them. (p. 263)

To the extent that individuals are united in matter, my object-interest appears as also that of the Other, and therefore to be denied to him.

With interest we find the first foundation of class. The interest of one man or group becomes the *destiny* of another, it maps out his life and his fate. The machine may be seen as one element of the employer's being-outside-of-himself, but whereas the employer objectifies himself in the machine, it is the machine that, as it were, objectifies itself in the worker and not vice versa. We have seen how it dictates his praxis, but this is not all: it determines, through a series of mediations, his living standard and his life style according to the time and energy that it requires. It reduces him to an anonymous Other and on the basis of this anonymity, his personal relationships are formed; it maps out his destiny in the same way that the dust-bowl mapped out the destiny of the mid-west farmer. The worker's interest in fact lies in the future, in his ability to unite with the rest of his class to transform his destiny into interest. For the moment, however, it is only the employer who has an immediate interest and it is this very interest that prevents the unity of the bourgeoisie: we have seen how my interest must be denied to others. Only an abstract and formal unity is available to this class, one which takes as its reference the practico-inert as a whole, the accumulated object-beings of each. In this respect they are united in that each contributes to the wealth of all. As with the worker, the employer's personal relationships are built up on the basis of his domination by the practico-inert but with the difference that they are not designated in their generality but in terms of his being outside-of-himself in its specificity. The individual employer will be involved with other employers of the same type, or with those who buy his product or sell him his raw materials (pp. 238ff.).

We have moved from a self-evident and lucid individual praxis to a strange world of men-machines and machine-men, but although immediate lucidity has been lost, intelligibility has not. The passive action of the practico-inert is still intelligible, as the product of dialectical praxis and as a psuedo-dialectical praxis itself: through relationships of exteriority, it totalises and acts on men as men totalise and act on matter, but it does so only with an indirect purposefulness, given to it by men. It presents us with the first experience of necessity in that I cannot avoid there being unforeseen results from my praxis, independently of whether or not I achieve my desired ends. But these unforeseen results are still intelligible as an anti-dialectical (since matter works through its own relationships of exteriority) transformation of my praxis. Sartre is claiming here to have rendered intelligible the moment of material or technological determinism which sometimes passes for the whole of Marxism.

II. The sociological totality

The discussion of the 'sociological totalisation' and sociological praxis has so far been carried out as if the former were
dependent on the latter. The theoretical description of the practico-
inert enables us to reverse this approach and to see sociological
praxis as conditioned and demanded by the sociological *totality* in
a way roughly but by no means systematically analogous to that in
which the worker's praxis is conditioned and demanded by the
machine. Before we can go into these differences, however, we must
distinguish between 'totalisation' and 'totality'.

The totalisation is produced and maintained by a living praxis
which endows the parts with relationships of interiority to each
other and to the whole. Once produced, if it is not being reproduced
in a praxis, it falls back into the In-itself; it still remains more than
the sum of its parts but the life that it receives from praxis has gone,
it is inert. Life may be breathed back into it by a present praxis,
but this then loses its purely creative nature, it becomes a praxis
demanded by the totality. The totality is grasped by consciousness
through an act of imagination in which its parts act as analogues
for the whole, in the way in which a symphony is grasped through
its individual notes (pp. 138ff.).[1]

The sociological totality, then, is the practico-inert collection of
material elements that have been produced by previous praxis and
are sustained by the current praxis that it demands. The material
manifestation of this totality is in the books and papers produced
by sociologists, including those which set down professional ethics
and research methods; any one of its elements implicitly refers to
the others. The first demand that it presents is, in fact, for its own
dominance insofar as each element sets out problems for future
research, outlines the way in which this research might or might
not be carried out and invites – simply by being there – comments,
criticisms and modifications. Insofar as it has an internal structure
of parts dealing with the same or similar problems categorised by
previous praxis then it sets the structure of teaching, the courses
and topics through which its dominance will be conveyed to new
entrants to the discipline. By its existence as a more or less distinct
'body of knowledge' – 'sociology', the 'literature' etc. – around
which praxis – teaching and research – is organised, it sets any
individual the fundamental choice of whether to become a sociologist or not. To decide to become a sociologist is to accept at least

---

[1] This refers back to Sartre's earlier work, in particular *The Psychology of
the Imagination* (1949b).

to an extent the sociological totality and its subdivisions and limits
as a condition of future activities.

The sociological totality then sets its demands even if not in such
an authoritative manner as the machine; it is a material, practico-inert
entity and the next problem is whether or not it can be seen as
alienating sociological praxis. Perhaps the most important alienation of the sociologist's work occurs through Others, the meanings
that it is given and the uses it is put to in the hands of its readers,
but there is, nonetheless, an element of 'practico-inert alienation'
involved beyond the simple dominance of the totality.

The first alienation is an extension of that implicit in language,
itself a practico-inert totality created by past praxis. We have seen
that language belongs to everybody as common property, but it is
also that in which each has to express his own unique relationship
to the world; the simple expression of experience involves, to some
extent, its generalisation and its theft by others before it has been
read or heard by them. This becomes more acute for sociologists
the more the totality demands that they express their experience
(including their experience of others' experience) in a technical
language which further generalises and 'steals' the original raw
material. Whereas the aims of sociology, its claims to be a science,
or at least 'objective', demand a rigorous attempt to overcome this
linguistic alienation, the means it offers – a technical, conceptual
language – in some ways increases it. That such a language be used
is one of the demands of the totality, a means by which recognition
as a sociologist may be achieved.[1]

The second form of practico-inert alienation results from the way
in which the totality demands its own dominance: implicit in this
demand is a demand for its own continued growth, for further
research, criticism etc., for material contributions in the form of
books and papers. This demand is institutionalised (and added to)
by the professional organisation of teaching and career advancement. Yet the more the demand is met, the less significant the

---

[1] This is not intended to be a blanket judgement although many areas of
sociology do have their own language. Again there is the problem of
the linguistic techniques by which it is possible to capture what is being
described and some 'jargon' might do this more effectively than
everyday language.

Sartre's technique tends to be an analytic statement followed by a
series of qualifications (see the quotation on dialectical thought above);
R. D. Laing (1967, 1971) has on occasions employed a form of verse and
a 'spontaneous' style which has its origin in surrealism and Burrough's
'collage' effect. There is no *a priori* reason why such styles should not
be available to the sociologist and used by him at some point in his
study.

publication becomes: it merges with an ever-increasing quantity of similar studies where its chances of being read or of providing the basis for further research become less and less. The individual's praxis is rendered insignificant by the practico-inert even in terms of his own advancement as well as in terms of his contribution to sociology as a whole: the more applicants for a job who can list publications, the less weight each carries.

Perhaps the most important idea to emerge from this stage of the theoretical description, however, is that of 'interest'. The sociologist objectifies himself in his work: the book or article becomes the crystallised, material form of his time and energy, his intellectual development and his insights. He finds his being-outside-of-himself in a form not only accessible to possession by others, but one in which it may be challenged or attacked. If it is not stolen and rendered insignificant by the practico-inert, then in the future he cannot avoid taking up some position in regard to it, he must defend it, criticise or modify or try to excuse it. To this extent his future is dominated and conditioned by his past praxis and an understanding of his interest becomes essential to the understanding of the sociologist.[1] This in turn involves tracing the alienation of his work by others, the particular meanings they attach to it, the meanings attached to it by the author, and their reciprocal conditionings.[2]

III. The gypsum plant

a. *The general unity*

The problem of moving from the theoretical to the concrete is manifested here by the fact that we have, to a large extent, to take the existence of the plant studied by Gouldner as given, and then look at it as a practico-inert totality largely in isolation, as demanding what has so far been described as free praxis. Its existence and its unity, i.e. what makes it meaningful to speak of it as 'a plant', as more than a series of externally connected elements, come to it from the outside in the form of the historical development of the economy, which is beyond the scope of this study.

It is the development of the 'economy', itself a practico-inert

---

[1] Sartre develops this idea (mentioned in the *Critique*) to explain the problems of the 'traditional' or established intellectuals in adjusting to the new relationship between intellectuals and workers demanded by some groups after the May '68 events in France. See *L'Ami du peuple* 1972c.

[2] Bordieu 1966 makes a brief attempt at such a study of the development of Robbe-Grillet. The sociology of sociology might have a lot to learn from some forms of literary criticism in this respect.

totality, a set of structured elements created by praxis, that has demanded the existence of 'gypsum plants' as some of these elements, supplying the needs of other elements. This demand has been met on the basis of the contingent ('natural') distribution of gypsum. The fact that in this case the ore is processed at the same point at which it is mined is intelligible as a response to more specific developments in the 'economy' and its arrangement in a 'market'. It has thus been designated as a part in a relation to a larger whole and as a whole in relation to its own parts, prior to the study which simply adopts this designation. The most simple and basic unity of the parts of this whole is geographical: men, machines, buildings are clearly contained within a defined space. All other forms of unity are enclosed within this one.

The development of the 'economy' has also demanded – and still demands – the machines and techniques used and these in turn confer more specific forms of unity on the groups in the plant. The demands of the 'economy' are again mediated by the 'market', but the existence of the plant is a specific manifestation of a more general process, in this case that of the move from an agricultural to an industrial economy. The latter is the destiny of those who live in the area of the plant: the plant demands specifically, as the economy demands generally, that the individual works there if he is going to live at more than a comparatively low material standard (1954a: 242ff.).

Apart from this very general situating of the plant as a part of a greater whole – which we will be able to make more specific later – we must now consider it as an established whole by itself and we are faced with the problem of the internal organisation of its parts in relation to each other and to the whole. The parts – the mine, the surface, the management, the workers, and the individuals who make up these two groups – will be studied insofar as they are united by and into the practico-inert totality called the 'gypsum plant' and we will look at some of the ways in which, and mediations through which, this unity is interiorised.

b. The mine

We have seen that the miners are engaged in a joint praxis, the comparatively slight division of labour amongst them reflected in the amorphous nature of their product, and that this contributes to the intelligibility of their informal solidarity. We may now look at both as demanded by the practico-inert on which they work, primarily by the nature of the matter and secondarily by the tools that they use.

The demands made of the miners come directly through the material on which they work and its geological structure. The gypsum, embedded in its surrounding rock, presents itself as to-be-mined through the past praxis of others and through the demands of the 'economy' that this past praxis has created, and it presents itself as to-be-mined in a certain way, by means of certain tools. The ore is different from the rock in which it is embedded in its internal, material structure and in its spatial position, i.e. it is below some layers of soil and different rock and it is above others. Given the demands of the economy, it is this differentiation which demands that it be mined (otherwise everything would be gypsum rock, or it would be a matter of walking around and picking it up). The demands of the economy are mediated by geological structure. As we have seen the ore itself is undifferentiated, it has only to be mined and broken down into chunks and thus it calls for perhaps the most anonymous form of labour: muscle power – anonymous in the sense that everybody – literally – possesses it to some extent, although the demand is specific insofar as it is for a certain degree of physical strength. The practico-inert thus demands the division of the labour force into miners and non-miners and stipulates the criteria by which this division is to be made; once it has been made little more subdivision is required.

The distinction between the prop-man and the other miners is demanded by the one 'pure' example of counter-finality that we come across in the study. The praxis that mines the rock sets up a mechanical chain-reaction within the surrounding rock which threatens to cave in: a potential passive action by matter which has received the power to act from human praxis. This danger Gouldner talks about at length (1954a: Chap. 7): the threat designates not only the worker who protects against it as somebody of importance, but at the same time it designates the whole of the group in an even more fundamental generality, each member sees himself in the face of the danger simply as a vulnerable organism.

The blasting of the rock, from Gouldner's rather sketchy description of it (p. 32), seems to have required little skill, and the mechanical tools used – 'joy-loaders', 'shuttle-buggies', and the trains for transporting the rock through the mine – all have in common the fact that they appear to be simple substitutes for human praxis, for muscle-power, doubtless more efficient but nonetheless straightforward substitutes. Thus they are very different from the machines on the surface which not only substitute for human praxis but carry out work more complex than that which could be carried out by human beings. It is highly unlikely, for example, that a group of men working without machines would be able to achieve the consistency in thickness achieved by the rollers, even if they were able to produce board at all. Even if it were possible, it seems safe to say that the superiority of the machine in terms of speed and efficiency would be infinitely greater than the superiority of the machines in the mine. In this sense, then, the latter remain subordinate to human praxis whereas the surface machines dominate it through their superiority.

It is the practico-inert, the danger it threatens, the praxis it demands and its designations of the people who work it that is interiorised in the activities of the miners, their in-work solidarity and their informal relationships and their out of work social activities. Their activities are not 'caused' in some external way by the nature of their work, but are intelligible as a way of living a relationship of praxis to matter in which matter has come to dominate (p. 120ff.).[1] However, the fact that matter dominates directly rather than through the machine, that it is unworked rather than worked matter and that it designates the group as a group, allows the miners a form of internal freedom in their organisation and power over their joint praxis. It is this 'room for manoeuvre' that is interiorised in the group's organisation of itself,[2] its militancy in the face of supervision; it also renders intelligible the miners' reluctance to accept even machines that would remain subordinate to them, since in comparison to the matter on which they regularly work any machine threatens to become a restriction by its very function of replacing and modifying human praxis. It is in this connection that the importance and meaning of 'intelligibility' becomes evident since it is the miners' faith in the prop-man and their reluctance to accept machinery that forces Gouldner back on to comments about 'traditional' and 'magical' attitudes and comparisons between the miners and 'primitive peoples' (p. 120). Each of these factors – suggested as explanations – is essentially contingent, in the last analysis the miners 'are just like that', they possess these attitudes as qualities; any idea of intentionality is eliminated and replaced by the 'irrational' and therefore the unintelligible.

[1] Gouldner nowhere discusses the conception of 'causality' that he employs but it is implicitly one of exterior causality in many cases, assumed seemingly as a matter of 'common sense'.

[2] It must be remembered that at various points we are still having to assume the existence of some group structures.

c. The surface

We have also looked at the surface workers from the point of view of free praxis, from their position as Thirds in the division of labour. We can now make this division intelligible as meeting the demand of the practico-inert, more specifically of the machines used on the surface. The machines break down the overall task into a number of smaller tasks, separated spatially and temporally, making each dependent on the completion of the one before it and aiming at the completion of the next one. All this is self-evident and provides another distinction between the surface machinery and the mine machinery which, it would appear, carries out a human task without breaking it down. As the surface machinery breaks down the tasks so it separates those who work and stipulates their praxis: Gouldner's description makes it obvious how the existence of informal groups is dictated by the machine.

As with the miners, the in-work and out-of-work activities of the surface workers may be understood as an interiorisation of their domination by the machine. Their more respectful attitude and their accepted subordination to supervision is a reproduction of their subordination to the machine, the demands of which they must interiorise if they are going to work there at all. Their comparatively privatised existence outside the plant is intelligible in turn as the interiorisation of their separation by the machine inside. It must be emphasised that this is not a straightforward technological determinism: there is always some 'room' in the interiorisation of the demands of the practico-inert: they may be lived in various ways, happily, bitterly, angrily, etc. at various times. What is important is that they are *dominant*, the limits they set the individual worker are narrow. They may be overcome but this requires a group praxis and we have not yet reached that stage of intelligibility. Nor is it being argued that the specific machines in the plant are responsible for the determination: the demands of the machine are dominant in any society at a certain stage of industrialisation, throughout its institutions and culture, and they may be interiorised from birth and throughout childhood, insofar, for example, as family life patterns are limited and conditioned by the industrial occupation of the parent(s). 'Attitudes to work' may be brought into the work situation or developed there depending on specific circumstances. In this case, given the fairly recent dominance of an agricultural economy in the area and the strength of the indulgency pattern, it would appear that perhaps the machines in the plant played an important conditioning role. We will see that their demands were interiorised through several mediations again modifying any crude determinism that could be read into the argument.

d. Management and workers

'Interest' both unites and divides management and workers. The practico-inert – the gypsum rock, the machines, buildings etc. – is the interest, the being-outside-of-themselves of whoever it is that owns the plant and the company, and, so far as we know, nobody inside the plant shares in the ownership. The practico-inert thus represents the destiny of all those who work there, management and workers alike, its demands map out their lives. The two groups, however, meet different demands of the practico-inert. The machine, for example, not only demands to be operated, it demands to have this demand expressed, it requires human beings to articulate and enforce its demands. The division between those who do this and those who simply comply is the division between management and workers.

Insofar as the machine is the being-object of the owners, each member of management makes himself in some sense the representative of the being-object of the owners. Because of his position in the wider society (education, class background etc.) the manager has found himself in a position to assume his destiny in a way not always open to the ordinary worker;[1] he assumes it as a quasi-interest, allowing the interest, the object-being of the owners to objectify and 'humanise' itself in him. Again the interiorisation is made through various mediations. This view enables us to escape both the complete identification or separation of management and owners; the relationship we have suggested leaves the latter dominant but indirectly, through what they own in its material form (i.e. machines, not shares) and it leaves the former an area of independence in their interiorisation of the owners' interest. It also enables us to distinguish between levels of management. Whereas 'low level' management simply articulates and enforces the demands of one machine or group of machines, the higher management in the plant mediates between all sectors of the practico-inert around which it is built, and the top management mediates between the plant and the other practico-inert elements that make up the 'company'. Each level assumes the demands of the machines at a different level of generality and through different mediations.

Management and workers, then, comprise a whole insofar as the

---

[1] We do not intend to deny the possibility of movement from one group to the other; seeking promotion to a supervisor may be seen as an attempt to assume one's destiny in a particular way.

quasi-interest of one group is the destiny of the other, insofar as they are both grouped around the same practico-inert entities and insofar as they both interiorise – at different levels – its demands; they are united in the practico-inert but divided through their different relationships to it. Here, we discover the unity of the miners and surface workers, since although they are grouped around and comply with the demands of different 'sectors' of the practico-inert, the latter is the being-object of one group (the owners) and the quasi-interest of another group (management) and to this extent both groups of workers are facing the same destiny. Another source of unity comes from the 'market,' another practico-inert entity, which, as we shall see, mediates the relationship of owners and management to their object-being and through its demands embraces both groups of workers in the destiny it creates for them. The material form that unites management, surface workers and miners in this respect is, as Gouldner notes in a rather different context, money.

e. Bureaucracy

We can now look at some of the ways in which the demands of the practico-inert are mediated. Each mediation is always more than simply a mediation, it may be a practico-inert entity or an individual project, and part of our purpose is to draw out the multiple nature of these various elements.

'Bureaucracy', as employed by Gouldner, refers to the existence of rules clarifying or stipulating certain mutual rights and obligations of those who work in the plant. To the extent that these are directly dependent on the division of labour, we can see them as the expression of the requirements of the practico-inert, the articulation of its demands. To the extent that the rules define the mutual obligations of workers and management in relationship to each other, they may also be seen as the articulation of the unity/conflict relationship we have just described, and a mediation of this conflict. Bureaucracy is a mediation, then, when it intervenes as a coherent body of rules between the two groups and when it intervenes in a similar way between both or either of the groups and new demands from the practico-inert resulting from a change in the market situation or the introduction of new machinery.

As an articulation of practico-inert demands, bureaucracy is better suited to the machine than to nature. Like the machine, bureaucratic rules stipulate the ways in which a task is to be carried out, breaking it down into its component parts, its analytic detail. The first aspect of Gouldner's study rendered intelligible is the comparative absence of bureaucracy in the mine and its comparative dominance on the surface. Gouldner explains the divergence in terms of the miners' belief systems, the management's conception of them and the general nature of their work, all of which he would seem to regard as being externally and causally related (1954a: Chapters 6 & 7). The centre of his explanation is 'cultural' or 'social' whereas the present interpretation refers us back to the practico-inert and the interiorisation of its demands. Gouldner does in fact suggest a relationship between the degree of bureaucracy and what we have called the practico-inert but again he envisages it as an external causal relationship and dismisses it:

Diffuse work obligations may be thought to derive from the physical and technical peculiarities of mining; that is since the amount of gypsum rock available is beyond control, and not entirely predictable, this might be the basis of vague work responsibilities in the mine. Track layers, however, were much less frequently confronted with natural resources over which they had no control. Nevertheless they adhere to a relatively unspecified work programme. On the surface, by contrast, specific workers were instructed to do a particular job in a definite time... (pp. 110–11)

This is a very simple view of the relationship between bureaucracy and the practico-inert. We have suggested a more complex 'definition' of work by the practico-inert and our description of the types of machines used in the mine would suggest that the track layers are responding to a general demand of the 'sector' of the practico-inert in much the same way as miners.

More generally our view of bureaucracy enables us to situate and unite Gouldner's analytically distinct three types (Chapter 12). They are united through their relationship to different 'sectors' of the practico-inert and the way in which they mediate the interest/destiny relationship. Indirectly Gouldner has already classified them in this last respect, according to who initiates the rules and whose values they legitimate.

His first category, 'mock bureaucracy', is typified by the 'no smoking' rule. This rule only marginally expresses a demand of the plant itself as a practico-inert entity since the fire hazard would appear to be minimal; it is rather the demand of another practico-inert structure, the 'state' or 'society' which is mediated through the groups in the plant whose immediate interest/destiny does not re-inforce it. In a very minor way, both management and workers experience the 'no-smoking' rule as their destiny, created for them by processes over which they have no control, but it is a destiny that they are easily able to avoid. The superficial solidarity found by both groups in the face of this rule thus becomes intelligible. The rule, of course, is not entirely unconnected with the demands of the machine, since smoking was allowed in the office; perhaps it would be best described as the whispered request of the machine. The attribution of its violation to 'uncontrollable needs' or 'human nature' may be seen as an affirmation of the human (albeit contingently human) over matter.[1]

Gouldner's second category, 'representative bureaucracy' is typified by the safety regulations. They are initiated and legitimated by both management and workers and their infringement is regarded as due either to ignorance or well-intentioned carelessness. These rules refer more directly to the demands of the machine; the safety regulations, for example, refer fundamentally to the demand of the machine that there be somebody there to work it, although there are as well various mediations such as legally required safety standards, and established views of managements' obligations (i.e. ideology). It is a demand made on everybody in the plant, whatever their specific relationship to the machine, and corresponds – self-evidently – to the demand of the organism for its own safety and survival. Since it represents a 'shared interest' of each individual in his own body and of the machine in the body of each individual, the absence of conflict becomes intelligible. Once established, this 'type' of bureaucracy acts as a mediation of conflict occurring around other issues (pp. 187ff.).

It is with 'punishment centred' bureaucracy that the articulating and mediating roles of the rules become most apparent. The demands of the machine are at their most specific and most dominating when they concern the immediate praxis that works it. The extent of this domination depends in part on the nature of the machine – which in this case does not demand permanent operation – and on the market situation which has its own mediations; the important point here is that there is a 'space', a determined (by the practico-inert) 'area of freedom', in which the machines' demands may be interiorised. This includes hours of work, rest periods and the number of men needed to carry out one operation – the type and range of issues covered in a trade union rule book. We can see the eventual interiorisation of these demands as mediated on three levels: firstly there is the mediation of the individual, the length of

---

[1] This is merely a suggestion; a full description would be much more complex; smoking itself is one form of domination of man by matter and at the same time may also be understood as an attempt to possess Being through destruction. See in particular the last sections of *Being and Nothingness* on existential psychoanalysis.

time he wants to work; secondly the mediation of one specific group – the length of time members should be allowed or made to work in view of the wage rates etc.; thirdly the mediation of everybody who works in the plant: we can assume for example that there was a general agreement that nightwork was not necessary. The second level of mediations, those concerning groups, are important at the moment: since one group interiorises the demands of the machines as to-be-enforced, and the other group experiences the same demands as being-enforced-by-others, we have the basis for the intelligibility of conflict between groups in this area of 'freedom'.

The bureaucratic rule in this context mediates at the same time between the demand and its fulfilment and between the two groups, one of which enforces the demand, the other of which has to comply. At the general level the machine demands to be worked: the rule articulates that demand, puts it into language; insofar as the working of the machine is the destiny of one group and the quasi-interest of the other, the rule mediates this difference by stipulating, for example, maximum shift times, maximum breaks, minimum rest periods, etc. Once established the rule will mediate intensified demands from new machines or from the market situation. Any new agreement will be negotiated on the basis of the old one.

This description has now accounted for the central features of Gouldner's 'punishment-centred' bureaucracy: the fact that it is initiated by one group, and that one group experiences it as imposed. His examples, the 'bidding system' and the 'no-absenteeism' rule are directly concerned with the general demand of the machine that there be someone there to work it and with the organisation of the way in which this demand will be complied with.

The three types of bureaucracy, then, find their unity in the practico-inert demands they articulate and mediate. The rules themselves, once established, take on the nature of the practico-inert, produced by past praxis and conditioning present praxis at the same time as they fulfil their articulating and mediatory roles. The demands of the practico-inert are mediated by three other major features; we have not yet developed the theoretical tools to deal with the first, the market, but we can go on to look at the others, the indulgency pattern, and the individual project.

f. The indulgency pattern
The indulgency pattern appears first as a collective way of living the demands of the practico-inert shared by management and

workers; it is a mediation on the third level mentioned above, an interiorisation of the demands making use of the area of 'freedom' permitted by the practico-inert and the market. This interiorisation is itself mediated by the way of life and relationships existing in what had until recently been a rural area. Perhaps the most obvious link between the indulgency pattern and the rural way of life is the method of recruitment employed by 'Old Doug' (Chap. 2 & pp. 63ff.), but the general 'leniency' in the plant, described in the first part of the study, seems to be very much in line with the relationships of independent cultivators to each other. Once established, the indulgency pattern mediates new or changing demands from the practico-inert, it sets the terms in which they are judged by the participants.

The mediation by the local life-styles or 'culture' opens up another course of investigation with which we can deal only in outline. The local way of life is an interiorisation of demands of another sector of the practico-inert, the 'agricultural economy', in turn mediated by the way of life of the immigrant groups who settled in the area. This is a more specific historical situating of the events beyond the general one of the development of the economy as a whole,[1] and it has resulted in the creation of relationships which those involved reproduce as far as possible inside the plant. This is implicit in Gouldner's description of what the workers regarded as leniency:

. . . workers do not define management's role as entailing obligations of
lenient behaviour. 'Leniency' is a judgement rendered by workers
when supervisors temper their performance of the managerial role by
taking into account obligations that would be relevant in other
relationships. (p. 55)

During the war it would appear that the nature of the practico-inert allowed rather more 'space' in which to interiorise its demands. Hitherto we have called this an 'area of freedom' (in inverted commas) but it is certainly not the 'freedom' of the first part of this study. It is *allowed* by the practico-inert, it is one form of the latter's domination; further, the way in which the 'space' is used is in terms of the conditionings of other 'sectors' of the practico-inert. In this sense it is best considered as a mystifying freedom, a freedom which is part and parcel of domination.

[1] This would be what Lefebvre calls a 'vertical complexity' of a
community which must be studied in conjunction with its 'horizontal'
complexity. The latter is the present structure, the former the historical
structures which have developed into and can still be found in the
present structure. See Sartre 1963b; 51.

As the industrial sector demands increasing priority over the agricultural sector, the demand is mediated through the indulgency pattern, to be experienced initially as 'strict' and then as 'to be resisted'. (The intensification of this demand is personified in Peele and in the other successors and bureaucracy first becomes a tool in their hands and then in the hands of at least some of the union leaders.) As the demands of the machine take precedence, the most important mediation changes from the indulgency pattern to bureaucracy. The fundamental alienation that this involves for the workers will become apparent later.

g. *The machine-man*

Through whatever general or group mediations there may be, the demands of the machine are also mediated in the project of each individual. In the *Critique* we find an infinitely more elaborate 'situation' than we did in *Being and Nothingness*. The material world is structured by past praxis and presents the individual not only with pre-created meanings but also with pre-created *demands*, a notion not incompatible with the system of *Being and Nothingness* and even implied in it, but which produces a more restricted view of what practical 'freedom' comprises.

These pre-created meanings and material objects, then, demand with varying intensity their own assumption by consciousness and the organism. The choice presented by the machine for large numbers of people is in the last analysis one which involves starvation or a life of comparatively unpleasant poverty as its alternatives. Many of those working in the gypsum plant seem to have attempted to reject its demands and failed (Gouldner, 1954b; 42ff.). But just as language, once interiorised, becomes a tool by means of which a project is formed and lived, so the demand of the machine, once accepted, becomes a tool in a project, if only in that it lets itself be lived in a number of ways: in fact there are as many ways of living it as there are people to live it. This is an 'area of freedom' in the true sense of *Being and Nothingness*; its roots are in the nature of consciousness.

From the information in *Wildcat Strike*, we can look briefly at the project of Spiedman, the engineer. To begin with we can see that at some stage in his past he has chosen to assume the demands of the machine in such a way as to make himself inessential. To the extent that he has special managerial responsibilities, he has assumed the demands of the machine as to-be-enforced; he has made the machine his quasi-interest, and himself the objectification of the machine, the expression of its demands. Insofar as he is involved in the development of new machinery he makes himself the in-essential mediator between two states of practico-inert matter, and insofar as he is responsible for the installation of new machinery in such a way that it operates smoothly at an optimum speed with maximum productivity, he is not only responsible for ensuring that its demands are complied with by others but also for questioning it on its demands and formulating them for others. He is not only responsible for the simple recreation of the machine's demands, but for translating them from the language of the machine (articulated in the way in which its parts mesh together and the nature, quality, and quantity of its products) into human language. From the start he is in a closer relationship to the machine than most others.

Gouldner's description of Spiedman's character (1954b: 71ff.), although couched in terms of substantive character traits, can help us to understand his project if we look at them as most certainly oversimplified objectifications of some of its features. He notes Spiedman's devotion to the Company, his desire (rarely fulfilled) for acceptance by top management and the isolated nature of his work, his different jobs in different plants. Gouldner concludes:

Spiedman is thus an excellent example of the dynamics of sadistic rationalism, where intelligence and work become instruments of aggressive domination, where they are used for status and ego inflation rather than for the sake of accomplishing the task itself. This, of course, outraged the workers who were more 'task oriented' and who expected that authority would be used mainly to facilitate work rather than having work used to enhance authority. (pp. 71–2)

Management was quite aware of all this: '. . . [but] Since they tended to define "success" technologically rather than socially, the main office thought of Spiedman as "a good man with eccentrici-ties"' (p. 72).

There is a wealth of information in all this. We have already seen how management has made the practico-inert, the machine, its quasi-interest. Success, for them, will be defined technologically. Spiedman's devotion to the Company may be seen as a manifestation of his devotion to the machine: the Company and the machine merge, this is no more than saying that he was an ambitious engineer for the Company. His desire for acceptance by top management may be seen as a desire for recognition, through the highest human personification of the machine, by the machine itself. The contradiction lies in the fact that the very thing that prevents his recognition by top management is the nature of his relationship to the machine. Gouldner describes his activity in conventional

psychological terms as using his power with and from the machine
to enhance his ego; in our analysis 'machine' and 'ego' are the same
thing. His 'ego' is his being-outside-of-himself-in-the-machine, the
more powerful the machine, the more powerful he himself, and
vice versa.

The origins of this project, of which we have examined just one
aspect, lie back in Spiedman's past; all we can say from the
information available is that he has chosen to invest his being in the
machine, perhaps to seek an identification with it as a means to
achieving Value. But in no way was this project as such demanded
of him. He could have assumed the demands of the machine, made
himself inessential in relation to it in a number of ways. We will see
later that the assumption of the demands of the practico-inert
involves a fundamental alienation from oneself, one makes oneself
Other than oneself. Spiedman however lives this alienation by
embracing it, by welcoming it. This is what appears as a product
of his free choice and a personal mediation of the practico-inert
demands.

Given the nature of his project, he may be seen as expressing
perhaps more than any other member of management, the
'machine's eye view' of the worker. He addresses the worker as
the machine addresses him, in his generality as labour power, the
inessential appendage by means of which the machine completes
its essential task. Spiedman makes explicit what remains implicit so
long as the machine has not been able to find its full human
articulation. At one point, Gouldner hints at, only to reject, a
Freudian analysis of the workers' resentment of management as it
is expressed in abuse (p. 73). In the light of the above discussion,
it is possible to suggest an existential psychoanalysis of one of the
major complaints against Spiedman, his swearing (p. 45ff.). The vast
majority of swearwords reduce their target to his physical immanence; if nothing else, it draws attention to his status as physical
object, his contingency ('bastard' in particular) removing the
human possibility of transcendence. In this respect it expresses and
re-inforces in brutal human terms, the attitude of the machine.[1]

h. The unity of the study
We can now make more explicit the aims of the 'dialectical reconstruction' that we are attempting. It has, of course, been carried out
in very general terms, partly because of the nature of Gouldner's

---

[1] This is self-evidently crude and only a suggestion; there are
undoubtedly context-bound and cultural factors that would need to be
taken into account if the point were to be established properly.

study and partly for reasons of time and space, but the ways in which it has modified Gouldner's work should now be apparent. To begin with we have tried to render intelligible as the product of human praxis various features in the study left unintelligible by Gouldner, in that he attributes them to what are eventually contingent facts. We have gone beyond this in attempting to render intelligible the unity of the plant and its various parts and the relationships between them, taken for granted by Gouldner.

We have tried to show the plant as comprised of mutually mediating 'parts' (or structures) comprising the unity of the whole through their reciprocal mediations, whereas Gouldner presents it in terms of analytically distinct categories – his three types of bureaucracy – or in terms of an externally causal series, as in his analysis of bureaucracy and the problems of the succession, or the indulgency pattern. We have thus begun to give priority to some structures over others, insofar as the intelligibility of some can only be achieved on the basis of others: thus, for example, the indulgency pattern is only intelligible given the nature of the machine's de-mands, and the unity of the miners and surface workers is only intelligible on the basis of the general unity of the plant split by the interest/destiny division. Self-evidently, the dominant structure is the practico-inert and, within it, the demands of the machine.

We have also tried to fix the points at which we have to leave the 'whole' of the gypsum plant in order to understand what is happening inside it. At one end, as it were, this happens when we reach the market and the economy as a whole, and at the other we have to take account of the individual project. In the 'middle' we find the historical development of the local community. Each is treated by Gouldner as an external 'causal' factor; we have tried to show how they are interiorised into the plant, reproduced there in a particular way; the relationships of the local community appear as the indulgency pattern, Spiedman's project appears not as a 'character', something there as one of the givens, but as something which is only possible because the plant is there and organised in a particular way; he 'reproduces' the plant in his interiorisation of it, he contributes to what is specific about it.

Finally, we have begun to indicate the complexity of the plant structure; it is in no way reducible to a series of hypotheses. Any particular hypothesis of the type advanced by Gouldner in both parts of his study must involve at least two separate entities that vary in relation to each other, but we have attempted to show in the re-analysis that the elements mediate each other in such a way that they are inseparable, each finds its meaning *in* the other and not simply in connection with it. Their full unity comes from the praxis of each individual in the plant, including the sociologist; we have looked at the plant as a 'detotalised totality' (with the exception of our description of Spiedman's project); it has been seen as a structure of interrelated elements on the basis of its general unity and this unity has appeared through the praxis of the re-analysis, and it remains a formal unity in relation to that which it receives in the everyday praxis of those who work there.

C. CONCLUSION

1. The being of the class

We have now reached the first stage of the intelligibility of 'class' and class relationships, the point at which most Marxists begin. Class as it has been understood so far is a practico-inert structure, a material relationship of matter to matter in which men are the inessential mediations. The material relationships upon which classes are based are those involved in the production and circulation of material goods, the relationships of machines to other machines, of one sector of the practico-inert to other sectors.[1]

The 'industrial system', 'technology', or whatever one likes to call it, does not dominate all men in the same way. It is the product of past praxis, a praxis which has met scarcity through the construction of a system of exploitation; exploitation itself is intelligible in the context of scarcity, as the result of a specific historical development, not as an *a priori* category of the theoretical analysis. This system has always dominated a majority, drawing them off the land into towns, defining their life styles and living standards and limiting their possibilities. In the course of its creation it comes to dominate those who create it, in one sense, in fact, it *becomes* those who create it. The accumulation of capital, technological development, is demanded by matter through the mediation of the market system and it dominates owners, managers and workers but in a different way in each case.

But we have only understood classes so far as collections of separate units, united only by the form of their relationship to matter, the interest/destiny relationship. This is close to Marx's class-in-itself, a structure of relationships to matter, dominated by matter. The precise nature of this relationship as a relationship of individual to individual mediated by the dominating practico-inert

---

[1] Geoffrey Pilling (1972), although he bases himself on Hegel rather than Sartre, seems to offer one way in which it might be possible to combine a Sartrean and a conventional Marxist economic analysis.

is to be determined in the next stage of the theoretical analysis, but it is the material existence of groups united by the practico-inert that provides the foundation from which History is made.

11. Analytic sociology

The remarks on the relationship between the demands of the machine and bureaucratic rules enable us to make some further comments on the nature of analytic sociology. Analytic logic may be seen as the formal (or 'abstract') logic of bureaucratic rules: a logic which breaks down into parts and seeks identities and distinctions related through relationships of exteriority (Lefebvre, 1968). In this sense it is also the logic of the machine, a logic which perhaps found its most complete expression in Taylor and scientific management.

To the extent that the sociologist is analytic in his method and his argument, then he is seeing what he studies from the point of view of the practico-inert, and to the extent that one class has its interest in the practico-inert, he is seeing from the point of view of that class. This should not be taken as a crude identification of sociologist and employer, but neither should its fundamental importance be underestimated. Analytic logic is a form in which praxis is thought, a praxis dominated by the practico-inert thought in terms set out by the practico-inert. To the extent that this domination extends to everybody, it is a way of thinking common to all classes and groups. But it is not a strictly determined way of thinking, rather it is a form that may have several contents. The content depends on, amongst other things, the nature of the collectives of which the individual is a member, his specific relationship to the practico-inert and his own particular ends. Thus within the limits set by analytic logic there is room for disagreement and oppositions and it is here that we find the provision for 'objectivity' and 'bias'. The important point is that the employer, insofar as he has his being-outside-of-himself-in-the-thing is trapped in analytic logic, he can conceive of alternatives but only as 'abstract' and formal possibilities; both sociologist and worker are capable at various times of going beyond an analytic logic and it is because of this that the sociologist's use of analytic logic identifies him at a fundamental level with the employer, independently of his intentions. In many cases of course the identification is likely to be apparent at a more superficial level as well and the identification of social science with the practico-inert and eventually the dominant class is open to a concrete historical substantiation (see Anderson, 1968).

8

The series

1. Theoretical description

The 'collective', men united in and dominated by the practico-inert, is the basis upon which these same men make history. It is a state of 'being' and not a project or praxis, and before we can understand the group praxis that depasses it towards history, we must look at the relationships of the collective as interpersonal relationships mediated by matter rather than, as we have done up to now, simple relationships to matter.

The relationship of *seriality* between each member of the collective is, in Sartre's terms, one of 'exteriority–interiority'. To reveal its fundamental features he uses the simple example of a bus queue (1960a: 308ff.): a line of individuals, with the same purpose, each solitary, unconcerned with the others. The 'solitariness' of each is a provisional negation of a reciprocal relationship with the others, originating in his involvement with other groups and other individuals, and the reverse side of projects only connected with those around him at the most general level of the social structure. It is this general level – the division of labour, the social and geographical organisation of the city, socially constituted hours of work etc. – which renders the presence of each at the bus stop intelligible as activity (i.e. the mediation of these general determinations by individual projects) based originally on reciprocity. It is the social organisation of the city, as the praxis of those who live in it, that is reciprocal, either positively or negatively, and that involves relationships of interiority on which the absence of reciprocity, the exteriority of the relationships of those in the queue is based.

The common-being-outside-of-themselves of those in the queue is the bus: it provides them with a common future and designates each as interchangeable insofar as no specific intrinsic qualities determine who shall or shall not get on; the only differentiating factor is their physical separation as organisms. The bus, then, provides them with an 'abstract' future identity and a present identity as physical organisms.

However, there is only a limited number of seats available: a scarcity as a feature of the practico-inert. Each individual, because of his simple physical identity to the others, becomes a rival to each of them. The practice of taking numbered tickets on arrival at the bus stop (or simply of queueing in order of arrival) uses this simple alteriority (the physical differentiation) as a means of structuring the queue in a certain way. Each individual, then, is determined by the Other (I am determined as third by the two who came before me) insofar as he is Other than them and at the same time he is Other than himself (my being third is not my action or decision, nor does it depend on any of my personal 'traits'; it is determined by others and I make myself Other than myself by accepting their determination and acting accordingly). He is also Other than himself insofar as his being-outside-of-himself is in the future in the bus and demands his waiting at the queue.

We have now reached the heart of seriality. *Simple* alteriority, the physical separation of organisms, is common to all relationships, it is a contingent feature of existence. *Serial* alteriority is the use of simple alteriority to structure my relationships with the Other in a particular way. The series is demanded by the practico-inert object which is our common being; we can in fact reverse the perspective and view the series as the being-outside-of-itself of the practico-inert. It is through the series that I grasp my identity with the Others as an identity of alteriority: we are each Other than the Others. There is a serial way of acting and a serial way of thinking, the serial relationship is a mediation through which praxis is thought. What Sartre calls the 'Reason' of the series is this determination of each by all and of all by each as Other than himself and the Others. There is a serial unity which appears through the interiorisation of the common-being, but it is a unity which is always elsewhere. It is only through the Others that there is a queue (otherwise I would be alone) and thus the unity of 'the queue' only appears through the presence of Others never through my presence alone. Our unity, for example in complaining about the length of the wait or the standard of the service, depends upon the reaction of the Others as Others and on my own reaction as Other. The odd, dispersive nature of this unity should become more apparent as we continue.

The example of the bus queue is an aid to the description of the series but not necessary to it; similar descriptions of other series will be attempted as we proceed. The advantage of the example is its simplicity: in most cases we will discover elements of group or institutional praxis, the intervention of 'personal' characteristics and so on (although these latter are themselves likely to be serialised) which complicate the picture. The core of the series, however, is the use of alteriority to structure the collective. This marks the end of the description of what Sartre calls the 'social object'; the worked material object and the multiplicity of individuals united around and by it, according to Sartre, is the proper object of study for sociology.

A series may either be direct or indirect, defined by the presence or absence of its members to each other – a bus queue or a radio audience – but its unity is always elsewhere, in its common being-outside or in Others. The theoretical description of a structured alteriority provides for an alteriority in content: each individual will react as Other to the Others and, insofar as his action is conditioned by his alteriority, as Other to himself. By looking at some serial reactions we will perhaps get a better idea of the collectivity. They can, on occasions, become vast social upheavals, but in the form of turbulence rather than revolution: the 'rash' of factory occupations and strikes in France in 1936 and again in 1968 are good examples although obviously there are strong elements of group and institutional praxis involved as well. Each group sees the action of the other groups as a possibility for itself, but itself as Other than the others, so when it acts it does so not in conjunction with the groups that are already acting but in addition to them. It is not a matter of simple 'contagion' but a recognition of that-group-over-there which has just occupied its factory as 'the same' in alteriority: that group is 'like' this group but it is Other as well and acting as another group with nothing to do with us; but because it is 'like' us, it is showing us one of our possibilities, we can act in the same way but as Other than them, independently of them.

A 'purer' example is provided by Edgar Morin (1971) – although not in terms of seriality. A rumour develops in Orleans to the effect that some Jewish boutique-owners are spiriting girls away to a white-slave traffic after drugging them in their fitting rooms. It spreads until at its peak, threatening crowds are gathering outside their shops. It only disappears – and then not completely – after the press, the local administration and various political groups have been mobilised or mobilised themselves to combat it. There is no discoverable source, everybody hears it from somebody else, the Other – sometimes even allegedly a policeman or the father of one of the girls who has disappeared (in fact nobody was reported missing during the period in question). Each hears it as Other from the Other; the unity is elsewhere: 'people say' or 'they say' but never 'I say'. When the inaccuracy of the rumour was insisted on, it came to be attributed to some absolute Other: the Jew, the Communist, the Fascists.

A serial reaction, then, is not undirected, or contagious. It has its focal point but each participant acts as Other to the Others, in addition to them rather than with them; and insofar as he is conditioned by the Others he acts as Other than himself: the crowds in front of the boutiques were there because 'people say that'; we occupy this factory because others are winning concessions through the use of the same tactic. The theoretical possibility of the transformation of such a serial reaction into a group praxis will be explored in the next chapter. Initially, however, within the serial reaction, each individual experiences his impotence: the effectiveness or otherwise of his own reactions always depends on Others, and this impotence becomes a shared link with the Others. After the initial serial outburst, the collectivity may sink back into passivity as a consequence of directly experienced impotence. The initial reaction itself may be an attempt to force the reaction of Others.

At the level of the concrete, there is a vast complexity of series and any one refers to a multiplicity of others. Each individual belongs to a number of series – family, work-group, class, geographical community, etc. – which comprise what Sartre calls a 'milieu', experienced as an exterior social force, a container within which he lives and which exerts pressure on him at various points and at various times. His serial isolation is grasped as a consequence of the milieu as such rather than of its structure: I see the solution to my problems as a change in my milieu, a new job, leaving home, moving to a new district, rather than as a restructuring of my present relationships. The conditions under which such an attempt at restructuring might take place will be examined later; for the moment, however, the milieu is grasped as an exterior unity, a force acting upon me from the outside, but with no focal point: the human agents of the force are always Other, the origin of the force remains a mystery (except in those instances when the series is being directly manipulated by an institutional grouping, but these will be considered later). Thus, to take a minor example, nobody forces me to call my colleagues 'Mr So-and-So'; if I asked, they would tell me to address them by their Christian names; yet nobody uses Christian names: the pressure is experienced as a power over me but as a power with no source. Such serial power, with its roots in alteriority, a relationship between consciousnesses mediated by matter, may be reified as a 'social conscience' or 'social consciousness', as 'society' or even 'social structure' and used as an analytic tool, or it may simply be referred to as the notorious 'system'. The series, then, is not the simple ordered dispersion of individuals:

what marks it off from the ordered dispersion of objects is this strange unity which always escapes my attempt to pin it down.[1]

The being of the class may now be grasped as a series of series united by different sectors of the practico-inert. As such, it may be defined as an 'objective system' determined by relationships to the means of production and studied as an object.[2] The problem of 'marginal groups', such as some white-collar workers, may be seen in this context as arising from the too literal treatment of series as 'objects': marginality is a feature of seriality in that nobody 'belongs' to a series, the series envelopes him as an-Other; in a series of series whole collectivities are enveloped in this way and the relationships of certain collectivities to the class may be rendered intelligible in terms of seriality but not in terms of the class as simple object.

This description completes the moment of the practico-inert and takes us from individual – or constituting – praxis to group – or constituted – praxis, the latter being an attempt to take the destiny imposed by the practico-inert and transform it into interest through depassing seriality. We will see that the constituted as well as the constituting praxis is dialectical in structure; the moment of the practico-inert, however, is the moment of the anti-dialectic, the combination and alienation of the free praxis of individuals by the passive action of inert matter, set in motion by free praxis. It is not matter as such that alienates praxis but matter worked by the praxis of other individuals as well as myself: one peasant cutting down trees will not create disastrous floods. In this way, Sartre maintains the principle of *Being and Nothingness* that only freedom can limit freedom. But the anti-dialectic remains intelligible on the basis of free praxis.

It is thus the following collection of structures which must be recombined in each case, according to the rule of the particular process, to find the desired schemes of intelligibility: (1) the univocal relationship of interiority at the heart of the free praxis as the unification of the field; (2) the equivocal relationship of a multiplicity of practical activities each of which seeks to steal the freedom of the Others by the transformations that it causes the objects to undergo (the practices are *at the same time* negative reciprocal relationships, thus relationships of interiority, *and*, by the mediation of inert objects,

[1] There have, of course, been many literary expressions of this phenomenon – Kafka being the most obvious and probably the best.
[2] The debate on the young/old Marx relationship may be seen as involving the movement from praxis to the practico-inert. Sartre seems to offer a way of thinking the gaps between the earlier and later works of Marx, but a scholastic exercise of this type would not interest him. It would not, however, by any means, be an easy task.

indirect relationships of exteriority); (3) the transformation of all free praxis (insofar as it is absorbed and returned by the object) into exis; (4) the inevitable transformation of each exis of the worked Thing into passive activity by the free praxis *of an Other*, . . . whose projects and perspectives *are Other*; (5) the transformation of each one into active passivity by the passive activity of the object. (1960a: 362)

The practico-inert and seriality are maintained by a free praxis which alienates itself in the very act of interiorising the demands of the practico-inert in order to go beyond it:

the manual worker robs himself and produces the wealth of others at the expense of his own life in the very work which he carries out *to earn that life*. But all these tricks, which make freedom a damnation, suppose that the relationship of man to matter and to other men resides, before everything else in *doing* as synthetic and creative work. (p. 366)

In these circumstances, freedom is experienced as the realisation of impotence and impossibility. Impotence may only be experienced on the basis of potential power, lack of freedom on the basis of freedom. The occasional individual may succeed in moving up the social structure or in improving his material condition in some way, but this apparent power and freedom is a statistical probability determined by the practico-inert. The moment of free choice, to improve one's position through one's own efforts, is precisely the moment of alienation in that by so doing free praxis confirms the continued existence of the material structure from which it has decided to escape.

We have already pointed out that in this perspective alienation is not an estrangement from some ideal being, but an observable process. Insofar as it implies impotence it also implies seriality, that each is acting as Other. This is not a 'state of mind' nor a matter of estrangement from one's fellow human beings in the usual sense of the phrase,[1] but a particular way of acting, conditioned by alteriority.

11. Sociology as a serial relationship

Given the description of the 'sociological totality' we can look at the way in which that totality structures the interpersonal relationships of sociologists. Sociologists as a collective may be

---

[1] For a 'psychological' interpretation of alienation, see R. Blauner (1966). In terms developed in British sociology, both 'traditional' and 'privatised' workers may be equally serialised and alienated. The overcoming of seriality would involve a restructuring of the relationships of both groups.

seen initially as falling into Sartre's category of 'indirect series': each individual is more or less absent from the others (working in his own office or in different institutions). His isolation is, to some degree, the reverse side of his project as a sociologist: he is working on 'his own' research problems in 'his own' way. What unites him to other sociologists is the more or less clearly defined 'body of knowledge' known as sociology, the common-being-outside-of-themselves of sociologists. The individual's relationships to the common being may be generalised, in that he teaches and works within its general categories, or be mediated through his own contribution to it, his own being-outside-of-himself.

The main exception to this preliminary description might appear to be the research team, the internal structure of which might not be serialised. We will examine this problem later; for the moment, however, we can note that in the research team's external relationships to other sociologists and other research teams, there are all the elements of seriality. Stein's research report at the end of *Patterns of Industrial Bureaucracy* (pp. 260–3) indicates that the team involved made every effort to separate themselves from other students, deriving much satisfaction from their increased 'status' as members of the team. 'Status', in this context at any rate, may be seen as a measure of alteriority, used by individuals and groups within the series to order themselves.

In 'his own' research, each individual acts as Other than his colleagues: this is the meaning of 'originality'. He acts as Other because he looks for problems, approaches and ideas that have not been conceived of by others or simply because his object of research – his factory, school, community or whatever – has not been investigated before or has been investigated in a different way and/or at a different time. Insofar as he acts as Other, then his work has been conditioned by Others to the extent that it is demanded by the sociological totality. However, this is as much a product of simple alteriority as of serial alteriority: the problem is to discover how this alteriority is used to structure the relationships of sociologists to one another.

Entry into and progress in the profession, at least at University level, may be seen as depending, formally at any rate,[1] on the establishment of alteriority. A Ph.D. thesis must be original research,

---

[1] In all the following analyses of seriality, it should be remembered that all types of relationships may form on the basis of the series, some of which may be regarded as a particular form of serial relationship, some of which may depass the series. What the analyses will try to do is to grasp the fundamental seriality rather than its complications.

i.e. it must be Other; to the extent that there is always more than one applicant for a job then it is alteriority, the established Otherness of the candidate, that structures the collectivity of applicants into the successful and unsuccessful. Alteriority here, of course, means alteriority within the limits set by the practico-inert; there is a sense in which an individual may be too Other, 'too way-out'.[1] Movement 'up' the profession also depends upon the individual's 'own' work as assessed by Others and as conditioned by the work of Others, i.e. it depends upon his work as Other.

Any formal educational activity – at least so far as existing societies are concerned – seems to depend upon and use simple alteriority. Ideas and information are passed on to Others from the Other; classes are held specifically to discuss the ideas of one Other and criticisms are made as Other to the ideas of that Other. Insofar as classes are ranked according to marks and grades then simple alteriority is used to structure the collective: marks are given according to each individual's ability to grasp the ideas of the Other and to criticise as Other. The teacher/student division (which in some respects may be regarded as an interest/destiny relationship, depending on the relationship between the student and what he is taught, his way of interiorising knowledge – as a chore, as a duty, a means to a career, a means to understanding, etc.) results in a rather different serial structure of teachers compared to that of students. Students are addressed as Other in their generality, again at least in principle, although certain other relationships may be formed on the basis of the seriality. The student has, in this sense, a general Other-ness; the staff member, however, is more fundamentally serialised in his relationships with other staff and with students. He has specialised in a specific field, is engaged in one particular project and is addressed by his superiors and the 'system' in his specific alteriority. The demand of the practico-inert comes to each individual as Other than the Others, situated at a certain particular position in the structure, rather than to the individual as a 'general' Other, occupying the same place in the structure with many Others. The demand is for a specific piece of work which will establish its author as Other rather than for work reaching a standard which will be shared by many Others.

However, the fundamental serialisation of staff as compared with students is a matter of degree rather than of quality, although in terms of the content of alteriority, the individual reaction as Other, there might quite possibly be a qualitative difference. The formation

[1] Thus, for example, ethnomethodologists may have problems establishing their relationship to the sociological totality.

of other relationships which depass seriality is however always possible and it should certainly not be concluded from the above description that group praxis is unattainable for staff and easily attainable for students. The serial structure of a collective is its skeleton, expressed in terms of each individual's activity as Other, but even without depassing this structure in any significant way, it is possible to arrange its 'flesh' in various shapes.

Thought is an individual activity to the extent that consciousnesses cannot merge, but this does not make it necessarily serial in the way described. We will see later that there is a group relationship in which the Other makes himself both the same and Other at the same time and it is in comparison with this that the full meaning of serial isolation will become apparent. Thinking as serial praxis is not only thinking in one's contingent isolation from other consciousnesses but thinking as completely Other than those consciousnesses, conditioned by them, and thus thinking as Other than oneself. Again all thinking may be seen as conditioned by Others insofar as it involves the thoughts and words of the Other, but this is no more than the use of common tools which I may use either as Other or in the movement of a joint praxis as Other and the same at the same time. Thinking as Other than oneself means in this context thinking as Other than the Others rather than as the Other who is the same as the Others in any respect but shared simple alteriority. The serial relationships of the sociologist and his self-exclusion from his study must obviously re-inforce each other. In one sense, he uses his alteriority, his Other-ness to those studied, to claim a superior ('objective') understanding.

III. The market as a series

The theoretical description enables us to extend some of our earlier analyses of Gouldner's study and to incorporate something hitherto only mentioned in passing: the market. To begin with, we can look at the relationships between surface workers and between members of management (although not between miners) as serial relationships. We have seen that the surface workers and each member of management is designated as Other by the division of labour, the practico-inert. This designation is a means of structuring each Other in relation to the Others; this is particularly so in the case of the management hierarchy: each is Other than the one above and the one below and it is these Others who condition his praxis. His praxis – that of the Other insofar as it is conditioned by Others – fixes his place in the hierarchy; his ability to meet the requirements of Others, as judged by the Others – i.e.

his praxis as Other – determines his movement up or down the hierarchy.

The ordering of the surface workers is in terms of their physical spacing in the plant as determined by the practico-inert. This is an ordering by means of simple alteriority which conditions their relationships to each other, ranking them in importance to the continued working of the machine at different times. They are also serially ordered by such factors as length of service, insofar as this is taken into account when there is a question of redundancy or promotion. Each is employed as Other to the Others and alteriority becomes a quality in assessment.

The miners present us with a different type of organisation. Although, as we have seen, their praxis is demanded by the practico-inert, the division of labour amongst them is minimal. Each is addressed in his generality as labour power but not necessarily as Other than the Other miners, except insofar as they are recruited individually and only a certain number are demanded to carry out the work. In the face of the matter that they work on, each is both Other than the Others and the same: this is not the 'abstract' identity of alteriority in their designation as dispersed organisms, but a concrete identity of labour power. It is an identity based on seriality (they are employed individually) serialising their relationship to other groups in the plant, but uniting them in an amorphous anonymity rather than individual distinction. We can now root the differences in attitudes, organisation and militancy not only in the practico-inert structure of the Company, the machines that it employs and the matter that it works on, but also in the way in which the members of different collectivities grasp each other. Whereas the surface worker grasps his co-worker as Other than himself and himself as Other than the Others and conditioned by them, and thus Other than himself, the miner grasps his co-miner as both Other and the same as himself and thus Other than the Other workers in the plant. This last alteriority is perhaps the most important serialisation as far as the intelligibility of the miners' activities are concerned.

We can understand what Gouldner calls the 'Rebecca Myth' (1954a: 79–83) in terms of a serial reaction. The 'myth' is the 'idealisation' of 'Old Doug' in comparison to Peele. Both are judged as Other than the Other, in terms of each Other, and the present situation is judged as Other than the previous one, making the present itself Other. That the explanation of the change should be sought in the alteriority of two individuals rather than in, for example, an economic analysis of changing market conditions indicates not only the lack of intellectual tools available to the workers to think their present situation but also an immediate tendency to think and judge in terms of alteriority alone. Peele's characteristics are not judged solely for themselves but in comparison to 'old Doug' and the latter's characteristics take on a new value in the light of Peele. What each is 'in himself' is judged in terms of the Other.

However, the most important feature of the study that seriality renders intelligible, is the effect of the 'market situation'. To begin with, we must take the plant as a whole and place it in relation to other plants and other companies. The market is the particular structure of relationships between these units, particularly between the companies as individual units but also between different plants. The market, the 'free' market, the 'perfect' market in particular, displays the essence of seriality. The determination of price, the being-outside-of-themselves of all participants in the market is, on the surface, arrived at by a process of negotiation between buyer and seller; in appearance bargaining involves an area of freedom with both parties acting as independent agents, the price, undetermined beforehand, being settled on the spot, but this freedom is only an appearance insofar as both parties are conditioned in their bargaining by what is being demanded and offered elsewhere by others. The market 'allows' perhaps a range within which the price may fluctuate, but the final price is decided not by free agents but by profoundly alienated agents, each acting as Other than himself to the extent that his offers are conditioned by Others. This is precisely what the workers discovered when they were negotiating with management. Gouldner talks about the inhibitions that operating in a market economy places on management's powers to take decisions: the need to work out long term consequences in advance, to assess the meaning of an offer in monetary terms and its effects on the Company's competitive position and so on (1954b: 113–16): all these contributed to slowing down the negotiating procedure and thus encouraging the workers' frustration.

In a bargaining situation, management sit opposite workers: each side puts its case and argument ensues. Workers are apparently arguing with management: but management gears its arguments and offers to what other companies, or the management in other plants, are arguing and offering, on the short and long term forecasts of what is likely to happen to the market, the likelihood and cost of a strike. Although face to face with *this* management the workers are arguing with other managements both as concrete others and as the anonymous Other of the market, and eventually with themselves, or rather themselves assessed as Other by the Other. Similarly, management, while face to face with *these* workers, is arguing with every other group of workers in the company, with workers in other companies, and even with other managements who have perhaps granted higher wages from a superior market position. The negotiations are not between those who do the talking but between people who are not there, perhaps between people of whom the participants are unaware beyond the simple knowledge of their existence in 'the market'. In the free space left by this Other-determination, the people opposite each other make themselves mediations of the demands of the Other as it is expressed through the market, the inessential mediation of forces which have their being everywhere else, in all plants and companies, and nowhere else, in no particular plant or company at any one place or time.

Thus the inhibitions on management's power to make decisions are not the simple 'effects' of the exterior market system on the interior events in the plant; they are rather the specific manifestation of the market uniting management and workers in a series in which 'things happen' always elsewhere. The market is both 'inside' and 'outside' the plant at the same time. Insofar as it is interiorised by those inside as the profound conditioning of their behaviour, they make themselves the inessential mediation by which what is 'outside' is made 'inside' and vice versa. Their inessentiality is revealed by Gouldner on another occasion:

The main point here is that, for management in a market economy, political ideology as such is not a crucial criterion of the acceptability of a partner to a contractual agreement. A group of unionists who champion a dissident programme may expect to be dealt with by management, providing that they can gain leadership. Thus market assumptions and arrangements provide an elastic framework in which leadership competition and circulation can take place among unionists. (1954b: 105)

Of course, the 'essentiality' or 'inessentiality' of the negotiating individuals may vary; what is important is that they are designated as Other by the market in which they operate and this designation is interiorised and personified through those with whom they negotiate. In this case what is important to management is that there be some Other to negotiate with. The support of this Other for a dissident programme is only important insofar as it reflects the support for the same programme by Others, i.e. the 'ordinary workers' in the plant. Thus throughout, there is a constant reference to the Other: the crucial factor is never 'here and now' but always lies with Others elsewhere, and each Other refers to still more Others. In this example, the support of the mass of workers in the plant for the dissident programme takes its meaning from the militancy of workers in other plants, other wage rates, other available workers, etc.

So far, we have talked about the market in which the 'Company' as a totality may be seen as one unit, even when we have been referring to the negotiating process between workers and management. Implicit in the latter description, however, has been another market: the labour market; the negotiating session lies at the intersection of these two series. It is in terms of the second series that another feature noted by Gouldner on yet another occasion becomes intelligible, again not in terms of external cause and internal effect but as a fundamental structure of the series in which those in the plant are 'contained'. Gouldner notes that, in a market economy ' . . . pressure is exerted to withhold legitimation from claims which are not *explicitly* agreed upon by both parties and thereby contractually established' (1954b: 87).

The analysis is complicated in that there is neither a simple series of individuals selling their labour power, nor a group or series of groups selling the labour power of its members. Presumably each worker enters the plant individually and sells his labour power as an individual, on entry becoming a member of an institutionalised group, the trade union, which will sell his labour power for him in the future and which in effect sold it for him in the past, previous to his entry. At present we lack the theoretical tools with which to understand the structure of the trade union, but we can look at the workers as individually contracted. Each is recruited because the practico-inert demands his recruitment to keep the plant in operation, or at any rate, to keep it operating at a particular level of production. He is recruited as Other in that his future work is conditioned by the Others in the plant, he is filling a vacancy for a worker at a specific point in the production process to complement and continue the work of Others. He is recruited as Other because Others have created the vacancy and as Other than himself in that he has nothing to do with the creation of his job.

We have already looked at the seriality of management, and the written contract, explicitly stating obligations and duties, is the objectification of this strange relationship between Others (i.e. management and workers), a relationship in which each term is always elsewhere. The articulation of rights and duties becomes necessary because neither side has any rights or duties to the other as such but is submitting himself to an infinite series of impersonal forces that we call 'the market'. The relationship of negative reciprocity that centres on the Interest/destiny relationship is one of negative reciprocity with an Other who is always elsewhere. The contract, in this context, takes on the meaning of a mutual protection which to some extent makes the behaviour of the 'absent Other' predictable, and, as it were, pins it down to the bodies of *this* management, *this* group of workers. Any area of the relationship not pinned down by contract is constantly open to question and dispute because it is always under the influence of the Other elsewhere, rather than the Other here. In this way the labour market and the market for gypsum become further factors in the intelligibility of bureaucratic rules, mediating the earlier mediations of the rules.

The pinning down of rights and obligations to specific Others enables each side to try to force the other to grant or assume further rights or obligations through the use of one market force against another, for example, a strike versus competition from other firms which inhibits this Company's ability to grant wage increases. It thus provides for the conflict at which we will look in the next chapter. Here we have tried to grasp market forces not as external factors which 'intervene' at certain points and in certain processes, but as a general conditioning the specific interiorisation and reproduction of which must be grasped if we are to discover the intelligibility of the plant as a dialectical unity in which conflicting parts are united in a whole.

9

The group-in-fusion and the organised group

Beginning with the description of free individual praxis and the human relationships thereby implied, we have seen how praxis is alienated by matter and how matter unites and dominates men. Each stage has developed a 'mode of intelligibility' which helps us to understand some aspect of the concrete as the product of human praxis, each theoretical stage increasing the complexity and depth of the understanding. We have now reached a sort of 'platform'; whereas individual praxis was self-evidently an abstraction, the picture of man dominated and serialised by matter appears closer to the 'real world'. However, if we left the discussion here we would still lack the intelligibility of History which would appear as a blind process dominated by an amalgam of 'natural laws' that govern matter and the chance dispersion of human beings. If History is intelligible, and intelligible as made by man, then we can say that it is not created by men acting 'individually' in isolation but by men acting together from the basis of the unity they find in the practico-inert and their serial relationships. As the description proceeds we will find that all the previous moments reappear but as depassed in a more inclusive movement.

1. Theoretical description

The problem now is to render intelligible the formation of the group as the depassing of the series. It should be emphasised again that this is not an historical but a logical genesis, still an abstract moment on the way to the totality. The following description is of a 'pure' movement from series to group, at least in the first stages, ignoring the complexity of group-formation in the concrete, surrounded by other social formations.

In the series, the real is defined by the impossible, from a position of serial impotence. The transformation occurs when the impossible itself becomes impossible, when, as Sartre puts it, the impossibility of change becomes the impossibility of living. The group is formed on the basis of common needs and common dangers and is defined by its common praxis and whilst we cannot predict or lay down clear preconditions for its formation we can render its appearance and structure intelligible, initially by looking at the way in which the group is grasped by the outsider.

To the non-member, the group appears immediately as an organism: he grasps it as an object which he totalises in his own praxis and he understands the group praxis on the basis of the dialectical structure of his own praxis, in much the same way as the Third unites the two workers engaged in a joint praxis. This is the first mediation involved in the formation of the group-in-fusion: the collectivity, the series, is totalised as a group, an organism, by an outside agent and the unity is re-interiorised by the series. The outside agent may take several forms. Most frequently, Sartre states, it is a hostile group, the example he employs throughout the section being the rising of the Paris people and the storming of the Bastille (1960a: 379ff.) but the mediation may also come from the being-outside-of-itself of the collective: thus, for example, an elected body deliberating on laws might appear to the collectivity that elected it as its being-outside-of-itself-in-freedom, as an active power which is re-interiorised by the series. Finally, and less likely, the mediation might come through the practico-inert which threatens those it unites, designating them as a group sharing a common danger.

Given the outside mediation, the definition of the series as a group, we can now look at the interior transformation of structures which take place as the unity is re-interiorised. The series contains within itself the seeds of its own depassing: we have seen that free praxis remains free at origin, even if it is immediately alienated. Thus each individual remains a Third, able to totalise the series through his free praxis. Whilst seriality remains, however, the Third is immediately absorbed back into it, he becomes simply the Other Third. The unity of the series is always elsewhere.

If we take the example of an outside group threatening the series, the reaction will be a serial one: I try to protect myself as Other than the Others, as separate from them, and each Other in the series does the same. The outside group grasps this reaction not as a serial but as a group reaction: rioting is seen as organised subversion. This definition releases each Third in the series from his seriality: through the outside group I grasp the series as a group, I unify it as a Third. At the same time since the outside group defines me as a member of the group I have just unified and since it threatens me in the same way that it threatens all of us, I must include myself in my totalisation of those around me. The external mediation is necessary at two points in this double movement: it enables my first totalisation, a depassing of the series towards the other group and it refers me back to that totalisation as a member of it: without it the depassing would have to be included in what was depassed, which is impossible.

In the first totalisation, I place myself as a Third outside the group I totalise; the threat of the Other group reveals my isolation to me as a personal danger. At this point, my contradictory aspects as Third and Other are united in one praxis: because I am Other, i.e. one of the series, I cannot exclude myself from the totalisation, but since I am at the same time a Third, unifying the series through my free praxis, I cannot fall back into seriality. I am trying to avoid the outside threat and so are all the Others: I grasp the group-as-object all around me and the group-as-subject in my own praxis. It is not completely a group-object since I am part of it, nor a group-subject since that would mean that I was its object, whereas I am totalising it through my praxis. In my own individual praxis I freely create the group praxis (obtain arms, put up barricades etc.) and each other member of the group – who is also a Third – is doing the same. In such a situation, each of my actions is a command to the others and vice versa: my praxis becomes the group praxis and I make the group praxis mine. This is the 'spontaneous' movement of the revolutionary crowd.[1] Of course, the group-in-fusion does not take everybody in the series up into itself, but it forms itself in the midst of the series: there are latecomers, people who fall back into seriality, even enemies, and these condition the development of the group.

For the moment, however, we are still concerned with the intelligibility of the internal structure of the group. Each is a totalising Third: my relationship with every other Third is one of mediated, reciprocal interiority: in a group of 100, I am 100th to every Other Third and vice versa. To the group itself, which is the mediation between each Third, I am in a relationship of transcendence-immanence: as a Third I totalise the group, and each other Third totalises me into the group. The Other Third is neither identical nor Other to me, we are, rather 'the same':[2] we

---

[1] For a particularly good description of such a movement see the first interview in A. Willener (1970). A more complicated but equally useful description of the rising of Madrid in 1936 can be found in A. Barea (1972).

[2] It should be emphasised that Sartre's use of the 'same' (le même) here is rather different from its conventional use: it implies a relationship which is neither identity nor alteriority. The word will be used in this sense throughout the rest of the section.

are both 100th to each other, he is my action objectified in another, but objectified as the same, not as Other.[1] The relationship of immanence-transcendence is the foundation of the group-in-fusion: each one can at any moment become the Regulating-Third, commanding the group through his own praxis and revealing his quasi-transcendence and my quasi-immanence. Tyranny and evasion are, in this sense, possibilities open to each, but only temporary possibilities since at any moment I may reaffirm my own quasi-transcendence and the other Third's quasi-immanence.

The group-in-fusion is entirely new and irreducible to the simple collective, although it includes the latter in its movement of depassing. The group praxis is intelligible as the revolving totalisation of each Third in turn and the group itself is essentially praxis: it is created by each of its members as a *means*, and its formation is intelligible in the light of ends; it is the constant reorganisation of 'itself' through the interiorisation of the external totalisation, and the re-interiorisation of its own objectification. On this foundation, the problem for the social scientist or historian is to:

interpret intelligibly the fact that *in these circumstances* some individuals believed themselves able to dissolve the collective and invent a common praxis. This problem . . . refers us to the abstract status that we come across in the first moment of the dialectical experience: the failure of his attempt refers the individual to his solitude and is explained by his negative relationship to the Third, i.e. to a relative non-integration which is explained, in the framework of the totalising movement and of History, by the circumstances of his personal life. Precisely because of that the transformation of the collective into the group, wherever it takes place, carries its own intelligibility for the historian: i.e. it is interpreted positively as the most concrete relationship of the Third to the circumstances and to the circumstantial objectives insofar as this relationship is manifested without being either obscured or determined by the specific behaviour of each individual *as such*. (1960a: 414)

The totalisation of each Third does not realise the synthetic unity of the group, nor is there a simple series of totalisations: each conditions the other through a relationship of interiority, each recognises itself in the others and the others recognise themselves in each. Insofar as I totalise the group in my praxis, then the unity of the group is always *here and now*, and *everywhere* in the praxis of all others, rather than elsewhere in the series. It is an internal unity which is practical, based on the reciprocal recognition of each Third, and not a state of Being. Like individual praxis, group praxis is

---

[1] Sartre places this relationship at the source of what is usually called 'projective' behaviour.

dialectically intelligible both in its creation and in its operation on the external field.

Within itself, under the pressure of circumstances, the group differentiates, but insofar as I am assigned a specific task, it is as a member of the group incarnating the common praxis in my own praxis. In this sense, my task is the 'same' as that of the others, and the circumstantial differentiation disappears immediately into the common objectification of the group praxis. If, however, the group must survive its immediate objectification, for example, to meet a future danger, a counter-attack by the enemy, then it must make itself its own object, it must work on itself to maintain itself. It has achieved a being-outside-of-itself – its success – and now becomes reflexive. From pure praxis it must change itself, give itself a Being, an inertia, in order to survive. At this point the *Oath* appears as a guarantee against future dispersion.

The Oath, it must be emphasised, is not a form of social contract: it does not mark the movement from a state of 'natural' individualism to a social organisation, but rather the transformation from one type of social formation, the group-in-fusion, to another, the organised group. It is a reproduction at the level of constituted praxis of the movement by which individual praxis makes itself into an inert instrument in order to act upon the surrounding environment: the group makes itself inert as a means of transforming itself into its own permanent instrument.

In the group-in-fusion, each Third, by virtue of his transcendence, manifests the possibility of becoming the Other Third, of removing himself from his immanence in the group: there is the permanent possibility of disintegration. My Oath is an undertaking not to remove myself from the group, but since this only removes the responsibility for disintegration onto the others, it must be a common act; in fact, I swear to make the others swear and vice versa: 'To swear is to give what one has not in order that the other will give it to you' (p. 443). My freedom, by its nature, cannot be surrendered: through the Oath, I swear to surrender it to cause the others to surrender their freedom to me. The Oath gives them the right to punish me if I should attempt to reclaim my freedom and in this sense it is a protection against my freedom which threatens the group; at another level it is a means of maintaining the freedom that I have gained through the group. It is also a source of alteriority, insofar as when I have sworn away my freedom I discovered myself as Other in the group which is now a quasi-object and we will see that this is important when we look at the institution.

For the moment, however, this Being-Other is common to each Third, we are each 'the same' Other.

The Oath is intelligible on the basis of fear: the danger against which the group was formed remains but more distant and the fear experienced by each Third is the fear that each, including himself, is not fearful enough. The Oath substitutes a new fear – the *Terror* – for the more distant fear of the enemy: the group exercises violence on itself, threatens itself to keep itself in existence.[1] The Terror unites men, it is a means by which they take control over their destiny and endow each other with reciprocal rights and duties to maintain the group in existence.[2]

The organised group is still praxis, but not a praxis immediately transparent to itself as was individual praxis or that of the group-in-fusion. The group still acts dialectically on its environment, but it does so through the mediation of each individual separately; each individual on the other hand acts on the external environment through the mediation of the group, insofar as the latter has assigned him a specific task. His practical relationship to the object is conditioned by his functional relationship to the group, 'function' here referring to a function of the fundamental relationship of the group to its object. The sworn group becomes a determination of individual praxis as a right and a duty, one of an infinitely complex network of rights and duties.

When I discover myself as Other in the sworn group, it is as a 'common individual': I have established my permanent immanence but I must always discover it from a position of transcendence; despite my Oath, I can never be completely inside the group. When I carry out my assigned task I rediscover myself as an organic individual insofar as the tools I use and the objects on which I work demand that I make sovereign choices. My praxis is intelligible in terms of the group organisation but it only achieves its full intelligibility in terms of my free individual praxis in front of the object. Whereas perhaps conventional sociology would tend to see role-making and role-taking as alternatives or at least as different elements in the same activity (e.g. Turner in A. Rose, 1964) Sartre's description indicates that role-taking *is* role-making and vice versa, the 'role' being my position in the group praxis. We see here a reversal of my serial status: whereas the demands of the practico-inert

[1] Barea gives a vivid description of the Terror in Madrid during the siege, the product of a combination of a group praxis and a serial reaction.

[2] Sartre sees this as the source of law and jurisdiction. See Nicos Poulantzas 1966.

dominated me, they now reveal my freedom. In my immediate praxis, I depass myself as a common individual, but my activity, as a function of the organised group, finds its meaning in the actions of others. The alienation here is only apparent, at least at first, since through the Oath I have freely made myself a common individual and my organic praxis inessential in relation to the group praxis. Free individual praxis here becomes a mediation which deliberately suppresses itself.

However important individuality might be at the moment of praxis, the act is objectified in the common object and the work of the group: the individual player scores a 'brilliant' goal, but it is the team that wins. In the common objectification, I recognise my action both as Other, since it is the objectification of the group, and as mine insofar as I am a common individual. Whereas in the series I cannot grasp the reason why my neighbour is Other, my under-standing is also trapped in seriality, in the organised group, I recognise my neighbour as Other in the same way that I recognise myself as Other: as a common individual, related to him through a mediation of inert reciprocity created by the common Oath. These inert reciprocities may be isolated and studied as 'structures', and may even be studied mathematically, but they only achieve their full intelligibility in the light of praxis and the ends of the totalising group, of which they are a sort of 'skeleton'.[1] This is a different sort of structure to that provided by the practico-inert: the latter is the structuring of individuals around and their domination by matter, the working of 'passive activity', whereas the structure of the organised group is originally produced and constantly repro-duced in everyday activities by free praxis, it is more appropriately called an 'active passivity'. Praxis freely makes itself passive to maintain its freedom: 'active passivity' is the interiorisation and negation of 'passive activity'. We can find here a fairly crude distinction between the structures examined by different types of sociology which will, perhaps, enable us to situate Sartre's work more clearly in terms of conventional sociology. Marxist sociology can be seen as being primarily concerned with structures that are intelligible in terms of the practico-inert domination of man by matter, classes as we defined them earlier, and tends to see all 'structures' as being of that type; in other words it tends to a materialist determinism. On the other hand, American sociology – i.e. structural functionalism plus many of its critics – can be seen

[1] Here again is a central point in Sartre's argument with Levi-Strauss; for an elaboration concerned with primitive societies see Sartre: 'Détermination et Liberté' in Rybalka & Contat 1970.

as primarily concerned with structures in the sense of the structure
of the organised group, they tend towards treating all structures
as if they were the product of a group praxis; in other words they
tend towards 'idealism' or 'voluntarism'. This is only a rough
cross-reference doing little more than situating Sartre and giving
an idea of the way in which a dialectical argument can unite
different approaches as two of its moments.[1]

The inert structure of the group, freely produced and reproduced, produces itself as knowledge:

if we reconsider all the characteristics . . . of knowledge in the
organised group, we see immediately that the organic individual
produces and knows himself as the common individual: (1) insofar as
the object reflects the group to him as practice and practical
knowledge, i.e. *at the same time* on the basis of the common objective as
the future revealing the present situation in the practical field and on
the basis of the grasp of his work on the object as a particular detail in
the common objectification; (2) insofar as the whole as the practical
totalisation, which is also operated by him, imposes on him, in the
functional determination, the practical grasp of the transcendent object
as common and the practical field as the common situation to be
modified . . . The structure . . . as knowledge is nothing other than the
idea that the group produces of itself (and of the universe insofar as it
is practically determined as the field of objectification). And this
reflexive idea, in its turn has no other content nor foundation than the
common organisation as an objective system of relationships.

The idea of man, in an organised group, is only the idea of the
group, i.e. the common individual, and the fraternity-terror, insofar as
it is expressed by specific norms, takes this particular colouration from
the real objective, i.e. the needs or dangers. The material organisation
of the group is no more than the organisation of its thought, the
system of logical relations which constitutes for each the indepassable
principles of each mental operation, is no more than the system of
inert and worked relations which characterises the functions in
exteriority. (1960a: 502–3)

The group, insofar as it 'lives', i.e. reproduces, these structures
in its everyday praxis, has a specific knowledge of itself not immediately available to the outsider, who can only understand it on the
basis of his own experience as a member of other organised groups.
At the same time, those groups or individuals within the organised

[1] This comparison was inspired by a rather less useful comparison made
between Gouldner and Althusser by Robin Blackburn and Gareth
Stedman-Jones in their article 'Louis Althusser and the Struggle for
Marxism' (1972). Jean-Claude Girardin (1972) offers an excellent
situating of Sartre in the Marxist tradition.

group whose work is specifically concerned with internal organisation, have a knowledge of the group as a structure; the totalisation which renders these structures intelligible remains implicit in the group praxis that determines the functions of the specialists, and the knowledge of the specialists appears as analytic thought within the group.

The praxis of the organised group still finds its intelligibility on the basis of individual praxis: the constituted praxis rests on the sworn inertia of the Oath freely produced by the constituting praxis to depass its own limitations, but it is always more complicated than the constituting praxis and when we situate the group in the world, rather than looking at it in isolation, we see that it takes on a new opacity. The group has to operate in the context of external series and institutions that surround it, and the original interiorisation of its own seriality and its depassing of its serial status may begin to be re-exteriorised as group members become separated spatially and temporally and the groups may begin to fall back into the series. Any such threat makes necessary new organising sub-groups within the organised group, at least to maintain communications between the group centre and its members. As the Oath falls back into the past, the necessity for such organisation increases. It is at this point that we discover what Sartre calls *processus*: the common action loses its immediate transparency and takes on the appearance of a drift; it still has an end, the maintenance of the group, and is still dialectical in its structure, but as a common individual, I experience the processus as Other than myself. I do not reincarnate it in my praxis and make it mine, rather it 'happens' elsewhere because of what is happening elsewhere and reacts back to condition my praxis. This is the point at which dialectical intelligibility becomes most obscure. In terms of conventional sociology, the processus may be seen as one of the elements that Weber and Michels handle in a different perspective when they talk about the 'inevitable' spread of bureaucracy, of rationalisation insofar as implicit in their work there is a feeling of 'fate', of the inability to do anything about it. More central to the processes that they talk about is the institutionalisation of the organised group that we will look at in the next chapter.

II. Sociology as group praxis

As we move towards the totality on both the theoretical and the concrete levels, the complexity of the analysis should be increasingly clear. For example, the descriptions of serialised individual praxis and of individual praxis as a moment of a group praxis are opposing descriptions which might or might not be applicable to any one activity; in one praxis is dominated by matter, in the other praxis finds its freedom in matter. How is it possible to decide which offers the greater intelligibility?

In almost every case, it is likely that both (and possibly more) descriptions are useful; specific activity which is not free solitary praxis has different levels of intelligibility, it may be understood through different modes of intelligibility. It must be emphasised again that the theoretical description makes no claim to represent any historical genesis: at the level of the concrete we find a complex network of series, groups-in-fusion, organised groups and institutions at various stages of development and in various relationships to each other and any one formation may itself be split by the Interest/Destiny division. Excluding the possibility of a 'true' apocalypse, a world-wide group-in-fusion that maintains itself as such permanently, any one individual is, or can be simultaneously a member of each type of social formation. The empirical problem is to examine the combinations, fusions and contradictions of these formations, the ways in which they change over time and space, the nature of the dominance and subordination of formations to each other and so on; the concrete is eventually rendered intelligible through the employment of all the modes of intelligibility developed in the theoretical description. We have now reached the stage of complexity where this point must be emphasised.

The problem of the sociologist's personal experience has received increasing attention with the recent development of 'reflexive sociology' following Gouldner's work.[1] The categories developed in the theoretical description can provide an understanding of the experience as a project, as praxis situated in certain social formations, and of the way in which the experience is thought. The two are obviously very closely connected: we saw that sociology as a serial praxis was related to the exclusion of the sociologist from what he studies and that serial praxis is therefore likely to be thought in analytic terms. The problem now is the extent to which seriality dominates sociological praxis and the extent to which we need to refer to other social formations to understand the sociologist. Leaving aside for the moment the question of the group-in-fusion, we can ask to what extent the sociologist may be considered as a member of an organised group, bearing in mind that the formations we will examine are by no means 'pure' organised groups of the type dealt with in the theoretical description.

At the most general level – excluding 'humanity' as a whole – any

---

[1] See for example Barnard 1973, Dawe 1973, Gouldner 1973.

one society (i.e. nation-state) may be considered as an organised group, a number of individuals jointly facing certain problems in a context of scarcity and organising itself to overcome them. Membership is achieved initially through the interiorisation of language and this in itself may be considered an implicit oath, a commitment to the group, although some societies have more explicit oaths taken at some time (or times) during childhood, adolescence or even adult life: the American Oath of Allegiance is an obvious example. The sociologist may be considered at one level as belonging to his society as an individual belongs to an organised group: the group has assigned him a task within a sub-group charged with investigating its structure and with providing information to be used directly or indirectly by other sub-groups to act upon those structures and change them towards given ends. In this light sociology may be regarded as an element of processus,[1] and to the extent that it is the moment of analytic thought in the totalising movement of the society as a whole we have added another dimension of intelligibility to the exclusion of the sociologist from what he studies.

This does not mean that our discussion of sociology as serial praxis was in some way deficient. The serialisation of the sociologist may be understood as a serialisation *on the basis of* this group membership. The complexity of the group in question, its internal divisions of interest and destiny and its internal serialisations all indicate that there are innumerable processes eating away at the 'group' structure. Most modern societies, insofar as they can be considered as organised groups at all, have existed for several generations, been objectified and alienated in the practico-inert, have re-objectified themselves and been re-alienated. When we make ourselves a member of a society through the interiorisation of its language we are at the same time interiorising the demands of the practico-inert dominating the activity of that society. We increase our practical freedom in the sense that the alternative is total exclusion, but at the same time we are subordinating our praxis to the practico-inert, we are joining an already organised group and not a group-in-fusion. The relationships of reciprocal interiority implied by group membership have only a formal importance, providing only a framework eaten away by the relationships of alterity that have been formed,

[1] As 'processus' sociology (and academic organisation and work as a whole) tends to develop 'out of sight' of large numbers of people. The periodic calls for greater public control over what happens in Universities and attacks on developments in the educational system may be seen as responses to this aspect of educational systems.

as it were, 'on top of them'.[1] For this reason, in the developed
Western nations at any rate, it is inadequate to talk in general terms
about the 'social responsibility' or its equivalent of the social
scientist (or, for that matter, of any other type of scientist) in any
sense that implies membership of a simple organised group. In such
societies, 'universalistic' values tend to conflict with each other or
have contradictory interpretations attached to them: 'social responsibility' may conflict with 'scientific neutrality' in a way that
implicitly points to the inadequacies of the simple use of either of
them. At the same time, we have added another dimension of
intelligibility to the general humanism or populism expressed by
some sociologists, including Gouldner: from a position of serial
alteriority, any group identification will be on the most general basis
available, that of the particular society or humanity as a whole.

To the extent that their existence is the result of previous group
praxis, then any of the formations described in the last chapter as
'social objects' may be considered as to some degree intelligible in
terms of the organised group, although the role of that particular
mode of intelligibility might be minimal or have disappeared
altogether. Within the 'society' however, there will almost certainly
be organised groups which correspond more closely to the description of the theoretical section, and the sociologist may belong to any
number of these: political parties, trade unions, 'pressure groups',
all fall to some extent within the category. Perhaps the most
important formation on this level is the sociological association,
whether in a national (or even international) form or a local or
subject-specialist group.

Initially, the intelligibility of such an organisation lies on the level
of the series. It acts as a mediation through which Other exchanges
ideas with Other as Other via journals and meetings. It is certainly
a means, but a means created serially in response to the demands
of the practico-inert, which determines the subjects discussed and
the need for their discussion; insofar as the activity of its members
is objectified in magazines and other publications, then the association itself contributes to the extension of the practico-inert totality.
It is formed as an expression of serial relationships rather than as
an attempt to dissolve alteriority through group praxis insofar as
its object, on formation, the object of those who form it, is to
provide a medium for discussion.

---

[1] This need not always be the case: in, for example, nationalist wars of
liberation, or even in some socialist countries at certain stages of
development, the sociologist might be very much a member of an
active organised group that is also his nation.

This basic serial structure might change if for some reason, sociologists as a group were to be threatened by an external agent; the serial structure would provide a base for its own dissolution, but the extent to which this is possible is debatable. In such a situation the group would assign specific tasks to its members involving acting on an external object; whereas within the serial structure, insofar as specific tasks are assigned, they are assigned to internal organisational work. We argued earlier that there is no *a priori* reason why sociologists should be permanently trapped in seriality and alteriority, but in practice the non-serial groups in which they are involved appear to be external to sociology: students' groups or the 'working class' with its own complex of series, groups and institutions, and the nature of the sociologist's relationships to these groups may change from situation to situation. There is, of course, always the possibility that a group might arise on the basis of and in opposition to the serial structure of the sociological association: there seem to have been several such groups formed out of the American Sociological Association for example, but again, it would appear that these usually reproduce the serial structures of the organisation in opposition to which they appeared (cf. Barnard, 1973).

The remaining formation that ought to be discussed is one already mentioned: the research team. Such teams form and break up periodically: we are not any longer dealing with an organisation that has been in existence over a long period of time into which individuals are recruited from generation to generation and which has progressed through a series of objectifications and re-objectifications. What is significant in the first place, then, is the way in which the group is formed.

Perhaps one of the firmer generalisations possible here is that it is highly unlikely that the research team will be formed 'spontaneously' in response to an external threat or event through which the team grasps and interiorises a definition of itself as a group. Rather, the team is organised from the start by an individual or individuals who may be considered as 'constituting Thirds' in a non-reciprocal relationship to those whom they recruit: 'non-reciprocal' in the sense that they are in a position of transcendence to those who are potential members of the team, and there is, at least initially, no corresponding relationship of immanence, and in the sense that it is the 'constituting Thirds' who provide a definition of the team as a team which is interiorised by members when they become members. The intelligibility of the formation of the research team, then, lies in the activities of a specific transcendent

Third rather than in the activity of a Third who is both 'inside' and 'outside' the group and who grasps himself as the 'same' as all other members. The actual formation of the team may take place in various ways: it might proceed through advertisement and interview or through informal channels. Gouldner's team would appear to have been recruited informally; Edgar Morin, for his Orleans study (1971) recruited whoever was known to him and available at short notice, including one non-sociologist, and Willener (1970) in need of a research team for the May events in Paris in 1968, seems to have used his immediate students and colleagues; even in this last example, perhaps the closest to a 'spontaneous' formation to be found, there was still a controlling Third from the beginning.

The team is not formed as an attempt to overcome the domination of the practico-inert nor in response to an external threat, but in compliance with a practico-inert demand, to study something falling within the field allotted to sociology which cannot be studied adequately by one individual. In this sense, joining a research team does not involve the destruction of seriality but rather a move from one series to another. The student member of Gouldner's team, for example, recruited perhaps on the basis of the serial processes described in the previous chapter, manifests a double alteriority in his activity: we have already seen that his relationship to the workers whom he interviews is one of alteriority and at the same time he is Other than himself insofar as he is the inessential mediation between the worker and the research team, which in turn finds its being in the individual or organisation that formed it. The interviewer is not manifesting a common individuality in the sense given the term in the theoretical description; he has freely subordinated his own individuality to whoever it was who formed the team. The team leader, on the other hand, finds his 'common individuality' in the subordination of the other members to his organic individuality (which in turn is itself serialised in various ways). This does not imply any sort of military discipline, it is equally appropriate to the most relaxed atmosphere, such as that which seems to have existed in Gouldner's team. What is important is that the team has been formed by specific individuals recruiting others, and that the power of decision be invested ultimately in those who formed the team or who supplied the money for them to do so.

The structure of the research team becomes apparent in the case of Gouldner, and to a lesser extent in that of Morin, in the eventual research report: the former's results are presented and commented on in his name alone (with the exception of Stein's report and the obligatory acknowledgements) and in the last analysis, the content is presumably his responsibility alone. Whatever the nature of the research team's discussions and the ideas suggested by other members, these ideas appear to their authors in the end as Other, even if they are acknowledged in the text. They appear in a context which is other than that of their original development and they receive their meaning from the Other who writes the report. Morin's report is different in that it includes extracts from the field diaries of the other team members, but it is apparent from the text that where there was a major disagreement, it was Morin's ideas that went into the main report, which was, of course, published in his name.[1]

If this description is adequate and if the experience of the sociologist, as a sociologist, is, for most of the time, conditioned by serial relationships, then we can add a further dimension to the intelligibility of analytic thought in sociology. We have already noted that serial relationships put the sociologist in the relationship of the Other to what he studies, that he is excluded from what he studies. We saw in the theoretical description that as a member of the series I cannot totalise that series as a group to which I belong without the mediation of an external agent. Thus I can recognise myself as one sociologist amongst others, but this remains only a formal recognition, a recognition as Other, I have no group experience of my own through which I can grasp the praxis of the group I am studying. I am, then, initially and immediately excluded from an understanding of the group I am studying insofar as I have no access to the idea of itself that the group lives in its everyday praxis,[2] and this exclusion is further reinforced by the lack, in my own experience, of relationships that would indicate to me the nature of relationships inside the group. From such a position, I can grasp the group as an organism 'sui generis' or as an inert structure, in other words I can grasp it analytically, but I cannot grasp the necessary totalising praxis and thought that would render the group fully intelligible.

[1] There are of course other types of research-team structure: for example two individuals working together on the same project with no other help. The intelligibility of such a team would have to be determined in each specific case, but in the light of the argument pursued in this section, it is likely to be based on seriality.
[2] Whether a full access is available to the outsider in any situation is debatable and the denial of this possibility is, of course, one of the means by which the group defines itself against others. See R. Merton 1973.

III. Wildcat strike

Gouldner's information allows us to approach the intelligibility of the strike, if not to reach a final conclusion. We can begin by looking at the organised groups within the plant and then at the 'preconditions' of the strike. The description of organised groups will follow the lines pursued in the previous section: we will begin with the most general and work towards the most specific.

At the most general level, each individual in the plant may be seen as belonging to the same 'society' in which he has been 'assigned' a certain function to do with gypsum production. As we indicated earlier, however, the society has been eaten away to a considerable extent by seriality and it is dominated by the practico-inert. It is the practico-inert itself, the form of demographic structure, the class system and the education system which has in fact 'assigned' each individual his function, not direct praxis or an organised group. Each individual is born into this already organised and alienated group and to some extent his future is mapped out in the practico-inert that dominates it. Through membership of the group each individual in the plant shares the same language and to a minimal extent a similar experience.

Within the wider society, we can see the Company as an organised sub-group set the task of producing gypsum board and most of what was said about the wider society also goes for the Company. There appear to be no activities which could be rendered intelligible as the praxis of either of these two 'organised groups', whereas, as we have seen, we are presented with activity that can be rendered intelligible by seeing them as practico-inert entities. Gouldner does talk about 'Company loyalty' but in connection with the old management and the indulgency pattern, and we have already discussed these in terms of seriality. The third 'organised group' at this level, the local community, seems to be equally unimportant. To the extent that the original immigrants can be considered as an organised group building a new life for themselves, then the present community could be regarded as the decayed structure of that group; the 'Oath' here would take the form of the interiorisation of a minority language and certain other relationships but little more.[1] Again we have already looked at the local community as a practico-inert entity interiorised into and reproduced in the plant mediating other practico-inert demands. There seems to be no grounds for looking at it in any other way.

[1] Gouldner tells us that until recently some of the Church services had been held in German.

Beyond these general groups, the most important specific organised group is the trade union. It is certainly both eaten away by seriality and institutionalised, but it would appear to retain some important features of the organised group insofar as it receives a commitment from each worker in the plant and the commitment is followed up by practical action. The trade union is important in that it is the only group so far discussed that is not cut across by the Interest/Destiny division; it also provides, insofar as it includes all the workers in the plant, at least a formal definition of each as 'the same' as his co-workers, a definition which may have an everyday relevance not present in the definition offered by the other organised groups. The way in which the worker recognises his fellow as the Other or the same is by no means pre-determined or predictable. The trade union is important in that, insofar as it has demanded and received the commitment of each worker, or insofar as it has been at some time in the past or promises to be in the future the means by which they make some attempt to control their Destiny, it indicates to each that he was, is and will be at least potentially the 'same' as the Others even if he grasps himself as Other at the moment.

All these social formations (and others) provide the 'milieu' of each worker and each offers to some extent the ossified structure of an organised group which may be taken up and reformed in certain situations. The trade union is certainly the most important of these 'potential' weapons and insofar as it is always active in some way through its officials then it is perhaps the structure most likely to be taken up in a group praxis.[1]

We can now look at the 'causes' of the strike. We need to discover the way in which they are 'causes' and we must examine them as designating the workers as a group and threatening them, presenting them with a definition that is interiorised through the strike; if the causes can be seen as 'pointing' towards the workers as a group then the trade union structure is the immediate and obvious structure to be taken up as a means to self-protection. Rather than seeing the 'causes' as externally acting upon the workers to create the strike, we will try to show them as an integral part of a network of relationships of interiority between the individuals and groups in the plant which develop into the strike.

Gouldner discusses the more immediate points of conflict in the period leading up to the strike and the longer term processes. Under

---

[1]   There are many such ossified structures, which may be brought back to life again. A good example is the rejuvenation of IRA structures in Northern Ireland since 1969.

the heading 'Zones of Disturbance' he deals with five items covering the immediate and longer term events: the export order, the 'cursing supervisor', management's broken promises, the speed-up of the machines, and the problem of working foremen (1954b: Ch. 3). The plant had recently handled a priority export order originally intended for another plant, but delayed by a strike. As a direct influence, Gouldner considers this unimportant (although management regarded it as a contributing factor). There seems to have been no sense of solidarity with the workers on strike, and the official trade union hierarchy was happy to see the order handled by the plant; the incident was not mentioned by the workers during the strike and its importance, he argues, lies in the fact that it indicated the company's weakness at that particular time and in its indication of the strike as a potential weapon for the workers. The importance of the event is indeterminable, the workers were likely to have been aware of the strike as a potential weapon without the help of the export order, but Gouldner's proffered explanation of its effects would indicate in part a long drawn out serial reaction; insofar as the order indicated the Company's vulnerability and pointed out the strike weapon to the workers, the ideas of 'vulnerability' and 'strike' became, as it were, an 'exis', a permanent implicit condition of their praxis which was not realised for some time, and eventually used as Other to the original strikers.

Two other factors have already been discussed to some extent: the 'cursing supervisor' and the speed-up of the machines. The former as the immediate 'cause' of the strike finds its intelligibility in the nature of the organised group. We have already noted that the act of swearing implies a reduction of the one sworn at to his simple physical immanence, that it denies his transcendence. The man sworn at – Tenzman – was the chief steward at the time; insofar as the union organisation at the plant is intelligible as an organised group, then Tenzman's authority – his 'function' – was invested in him by virtue of his common individuality. In his union activity, he revealed himself as a common individual, his free individual praxis subordinated to the common praxis. Spiedman might very well have sworn at him as a specific individual calling on specific elements in his personal history in the process, but insofar as it was an attack on Tenzman as a free individual, it attacked what he, and the other workers in the plant, had made inessential through their membership of the union; it was grasped as an attack on his common individuality and thus as an attack on each other worker. If other workers in the plant had also been victims of Spiedman's tongue, then their common individuality had been emphasised. Insofar as Spiedman merely articulated the way in which the workers were being subordinated by the practico-inert structures in the plant, then the attack upon Tenzman was an attack upon them as a group.

We have probably not reached the full intelligibility of the outbreak of the strike and it seems likely that the event was not as straightforward as the above explanation would suggest. The union had inevitably been eaten away by seriality and in such a situation it is likely that Tenzman grasped himself as to some extent transcendent to the group without a corresponding and balancing immanence; it is likely too that the workers also grasped him as transcendent; this would almost certainly be the case during a quiet period when the involvement of the mass of the workers in union activity was comparatively low and much depended on the initiative of the leadership. In such a situation, Spiedman's attack would be taken as a 'personal' attack rather than as an attack upon the workers as a group and would elicit a personal response, perhaps an attempt to use his position in the union to gain revenge. We do not yet have the theoretical tools to discuss fully Tenzman's relationship to the group or the idea of serial manipulation ('extero-conditioning') but the time lag between the swearing incident and the walk-out would indicate that both modes of intelligibility are applicable: there was a moment of serial manipulation and at the same time, perhaps engulfing it, there was a group reaction; within an established and partly serialised union structure, the workers were coming increasingly to grasp themselves as a threatened group and as the same as each other.

The appearance of new and faster machinery is important in designating the workers as a group in opposition to management. We have already seen the speed of the machines as an element in the practico-inert demands made on the workers and the speed-up is an intensification of these demands which, insofar as it touches or threatens each worker, designates him as the same as the others; insofar as the speed-up finds its inessential mediation in the management which organises it, then it divides the plant along the Interest/Destiny division, and the 'broken promises' of the management are in turn intelligible in terms of the inability of management to control the demand of the practico-inert, their position of serial impotence in the market system, in other words their very inessentiality. The working foreman, in this context, appears as a combination of management and machine which threatens both the working conditions (i.e. speed of work) and implicitly the jobs of the workers.

This discussion covers many of the factors that Gouldner later lists as 'causes' of the strike: technological changes, changes in management personnel, the effect of both of these on the informal relationships between workers and management and 'market forces' (Chapter 5). They cover the decline of the indulgency pattern and represent a change in and intensification of the practico-inert demands, which in turn emphasise the divisions of the groups that find their unity and the source of their conflict in their relationships to the practico-inert. The decline of the workers' motivation to obey and to work may be seen as the initial serial response: an individual attempt, as Other, to achieve some control of the situation from a position of serial impotence which is immediately alienated by closer management supervision. Closer supervision in turn emphasises the worker/management division and contributes to the final movement that overcomes seriality. Under closer supervision, the serial reaction becomes increasingly difficult and each worker as Other becomes increasingly impotent, increasingly conscious of his impotence and increasingly aware of each Other as suffering the same impotence; the impossibility of increasing impotence is finally revealed by Spiedman's curses.

From Gouldner's discussion of the 'images of the strike' (Ch. 4) we can examine the way in which the group praxis of the workers and the activities of the management (the latter, as far as it is possible to tell from the available information, still serialised) were thought by those concerned and it is here that the survival of seriality in the workers' actions becomes apparent. We can also deepen the intelligibility of the strike. We are told that top management saw it as a deliberately planned strategy on the part of the workers and as a struggle for the control of the plant; an alternative view of it was as an irrational emotional outburst. In these apparently contradictory views we find a common definition of the workers as a group acting either as a conscious organism or as an organism driven by some powerful collective unconscious, precisely the view of the group from the outside which provides a definition to be interiorised into a group praxis proper. If management made this view apparent after the strike had started then we can understand its solidarity and its continuation in terms of an interiorisation of the definition.

Gouldner also suggests that the management view of the strike as a power struggle or an emotional outburst enabled the immediate claims of workers to be disregarded, at least as 'moral' questions of right and wrong. It becomes either a straightforward power struggle or a state of affairs needing some sort of 'therapy'. He suggests that this was useful to management insofar as they had serious doubts about the moral rectitude of some of their own actions. This attitude is intelligible in terms of the seriality of management, and adds another dimension of intelligibility to their view of the workers as an 'organic' group.

'Moral' action is itself a serial activity insofar as morality is not innate but received as Other from Others and used to judge (i.e. to order) actions;[1] if management's actions were possibly 'immoral' then it is because the dominant series in which they were placed was itself 'amoral'. The 'practico-inert' of moral behaviour is a body of laws, conventions etc. around which individuals are serialised; the market, as practico-inert entity can threaten those who comprise it in an immediately more fundamental way than can written or unwritten moral standards; it can threaten their very existence. Management's doubts about the 'rightness' or otherwise of their actions is intelligible as an immediate recognition of their serial impotence in the market system which demanded actions in some way 'morally wrong'. This indicates that their view of the strike did not so much fulfil a 'psychological' tension-reducing function as form an intelligible unity, a serial means of thinking their seriality in the market, which does not allow 'moral' activity, and their seriality in relation to the workers which does not allow them to grasp the full complexities and nature of a group praxis. The 'moral problem' is not something through which we can understand or explain their view of the strike, but an integral and minor part of that view.[2]

The workers' 'image' of the strike would indicate that, although it is intelligible in part as a group praxis, it was thought in serial terms. The way in which an action is thought must be mediated by the categories of thought developed during previous activity, there is not always an immediately lucid self-consciousness of the group praxis at any level but the practical one (i.e. people 'know' what they are doing even if they can't express it in a suitable way). It does indicate, however, that there were elements of seriality which remained undepassed in the strike. On the other hand, the workers'

---

[1] This excludes the morality of the organised group, which originates in the Oath.

[2] This should not be regarded as a full analysis of the relationship between the market and 'morality'; they represent two different types of practico-inert entity, the 'market' being dominated by 'inert' matter, morality by man-made matter (language) and various relationships between them may be envisaged in addition to the simple separation and opposition assumed here. There may, for instance, be a 'market' in morality and a morality of the market. The two are more completely unified at the level of the society as a whole.

emphasis on the 'rightness' of the strike would indicate a grasp of their action as freely undertaken even if the standard by which 'rightness' is judged is a practico-inert entity. They were not claiming that the strike was a moral duty but rather that it was a 'justified' assertion of their transcendence.

The ends posited by the strike – an assertion of at least a limited control over their Destiny – were thought in distinctly serial terms. Gouldner discerns two attitudes on the part of the workers: one is 'tradition' oriented, desiring something like a return to the indulgency pattern, the other 'market' oriented, emphasising the necessity for clear contractual agreement and the elimination of 'trust' as a factor in worker-management relations. The 'traditional' attitude may be considered as a serial reaction along the lines of the 'Rebecca myth': it judges the present by the past, making the present Other and aiming at the Other, in this context the other, past situation. The 'market' attitude on the other hand is a direct interiorisation of the seriality of the market situation and an acceptance of its demands as a protection against the serial alteriority of management and the consequent unpredictability of the latter's activities. In both cases the group praxis is alienated by the serial structures in which it takes place and within which it is thought; it is alienated immediately insofar as its demands are thought and expressed in serial terms.

In the same way that the prediction of the group upsurge is not possible, a prediction of its success in interiorising and dissolving the seriality on which it is based is not possible; all we can do is suggest the intelligibility of the failure. In this case we can offer a list of relevant factors: the dominance of the seriality described in the previous chapters, the established serial structure of the trade union, the fact that the workers involved were one group in a series of series or groups of workers, the fact that the tools with which they could think their group praxis in dialectical terms were not available to them, and the fact that the Company as a practico-inert entity included in its recognition of the union and its negotiating machinery the means by which a group praxis could be immediately alienated into a serial process. We have discussed most of these elements at length. In the next chapter we will look in particular at the trade union structure.

The institution and the intelligibility of the concrete

Towards the end of the *Critique* there are a number of long analyses of the concrete,[1] too long to be reproduced here even in summary form. Instead we will concentrate on carrying the theoretical description through the institutionalisation of the organised group and its decay. The last moment has little to offer the description of sociology as it has hitherto been developed, and therefore the pattern of the previous four chapters will be broken and we will move immediately from the theoretical description to the re-analysis of the Gouldner studies; as a conclusion, we will examine the general intelligibility of sociology, tying up the strings of the argument and leading on to the final chapter.

1. Theoretical description

The organised group may be seen in terms of its being-for-itself or its being-for-others. The latter is important not only for its contribution to the intelligibility of various concrete phenomena but also, on the theoretical level, as an element in the institutionalisation of the organised group. The serialised non-group member, when he enters into relationship with a member of a group to which the series is in a practical relationship, grasps the group member as the inessential mediation of the group as a whole, the 'group-object'. The free individual praxis of the group member is unimportant to the serialised individual, except insofar as it hinders the effective completion of his group-function – there are complaints about inefficiency but complements for doing one's job and nothing else are rare. To the extent that the group member interiorises this definition of himself, he loses the ability to understand either his own praxis or that of the group: he no longer recognises that he

---

[1] These include an analysis of the mass-media in terms of extero-conditioning (pp. 614ff.), of imperialism as praxis-process (pp. 671ff.) and of the relationship of the individual to his class (pp. 690ff.). Each contains a wealth of ideas for the sociological study of the respective areas.

mediates the group praxis in his own free individual praxis and the group praxis appears to him as Other, an external determination of his own praxis. We shall see later that this is a factor of the 'creeping institutionalisation' of the group, but as long as the institutionalisation has not progressed very far, the outsider's definition is dissolved in the group member's relationships to other group members.

In the last chapter, we saw that in its internal organisation, the group is a quasi-object to which each member is in a relationship of immanence-transcendence. The 'Regulating Third' appears through his totalising praxis to be sovereign within the group, totalising and determining the group praxis through his own individual praxis, but insofar as the member who complies with the command of the Regulating Third mediates that command with his own free totalising praxis, then he makes himself sovereign in the very act of his obedience. The group is, in this sense, a constantly detotalised totality, a constant movement towards its own ontological unity, towards a completed totality, which falls back at each moment that each Third in the group makes himself a Regulating Third. The inability to achieve an ontological unity is experienced within the group as a permanent danger of disintegration, a malaise, felt by each member whenever he acknowledges his membership of the group, for such a recognition can only be made from a position of transcendence.[1] Complete immanence in the group could not be conscious of itself any more than a leg is conscious of itself as a part of the body. The Oath and the creation of the sworn group has failed insofar as the group has not achieved an ontological status: 'I am inside the group and I fear at the very heart of the inside that I am outside.' (1960a: 510) The malaise is reinforced as geographical and temporal dispersion increases and the original multiplicity, interiorised in the formation of the group, begins to reappear. The threatened serialisation which was part of the original stimulus to organisation remains, and in some ways increases after the organisation.[2]

An immediate response to the danger is the ritual recognition of group membership and ritual organisation. At this point, Sartre's

[1] The statement 'I am a member of . . .' implies the same gap between the 'I' and what follows as does the statement 'I am . . .' discussed in Chapter 3.
[2] It is the emphasis on the impossibility of the organic unity of the group that distinguishes Sartre in an important way from the early Lukács and from Goldmann, and which gives his analysis more depth. For a comparison in which the difference emerges clearly, see Lucien Goldmann: *Power and Humanism* (1970b).

description is very close to that of Durkheim in *The Elementary Forms of the Religious Life*, with the important and fundamental difference that the ritual never achieves its end, the group never realises itself as a totality and cannot be understood as such. For Sartre as for Durkheim, the group can invest its desired unity in some object, be it its direct objectification (the Bastille after it was taken) or a 'totem', a symbol and it may develop a 'social conscience' (which is implied by the Oath) but the objectification is never successful, the 'social conscience' can never account for all activities, it can never be any more than an 'inertia' at the heart of the group.

The long term response is institutionalisation; initially it appears through an intensification of the Terror, each member attempts to determine the Other as an inorganic tool, to eliminate the moment of transcendence in his relationship to the group. The movement is born from the re-appearance of alteriority in the organised group and attempts to interiorise that alteriority as a means of maintaining the group's existence. The institution is still praxis, it still acts on an outside object, but it is also an object itself insofar as it bases itself on its internal alteriority; the movement of institutionalisation occurs on the basis of the serial impotence of its members. Under the permanent threat of dissolution, any manifestation of my transcendence is received with mistrust and suspicion by the others and is alienated insofar as its meaning depends on its reception by Other members. Thus I experience my impotence insofar as I can no longer make myself the Regulating Third and reveal my transcendence; the group praxis comes to me as Other, an external determination. At this point the group's internal structure coincides with the serialised outsider's view of the relationship of the group member to the group and the two reinforce each other.

At this point also we discover authority for the first time. Authority has its origin in the sovereignty of free individual praxis as it totalises and acts upon the surrounding environment: it is transformed into authority by the interiorisation of this sovereignty by Others as the determination of their praxis, and this is rendered intelligible by the re-appearance of serial impotence in the group. The interiorisation is based on impotence, inability to reject rather than on positive acceptance.

The sovereign becomes the indepassable Third. In the group-in-fusion and in the organised group, each is Regulating Third in turn, even when he complies with the commands of another Third. His relationships with the Other Thirds are mediated either directly by each in a face-to-face situation, or indirectly through the group as a whole. In the institutionalised group, the sovereign is himself the mediation between the members: he destroys direct mediation since all communication must pass through him and indirect mediation is alienated insofar as the sovereign controls what is communicated. He becomes the only Other-Third, incarnating the group praxis in his own individual praxis and manifesting it as Other to the group members. The freedom of the group member no longer depasses his own common individuality to suppress itself immediately afterwards, but rather becomes the free interiorisation, based on impotence, of the will of the Other-Third:

at this level a double transformation is operated: (1) at the level of *the common individual*, I receive my powers from all, but *by the mediation of the Other*; the reciprocal organisation remains but is expressed univocally and without reciprocity, the common praxis is manifested in the form of the indepassable praxis of *an individual in freedom*; (2) at the level of my individual operation, my freedom is whisked away and I become the actualisation of the freedom of the Other . . . My freedom freely loses itself and casts off its lucidity in order to actualise here, in my body, the freedom of the Other insofar as it is lived here by me as an alienating signification, as the inflexible absence and as the absolute priority *everywhere* of interiorised alteriority. (Sartre, 1960a: 583)

The institutionalised group remains effective constituted praxis acting on its object, but the threat of serialisation also remains; in fact it is increased insofar as it becomes an integral part of the institution.

The sovereign still tries to achieve the organic unity of the group but there is a fundamental contradiction in his project: he attempts to create the group as his inorganic tool but this reintroduces and cements the alteriority within the group and the institution becomes further serialised. He believes that he has a synthetic view of the group, that he synthesises it in his person and in his praxis, but the information that reaches him and on which he bases his praxis comes to him through serialised channels of communication and is thought and expressed in serial terms. His dominance is thought in one of two ways: the organisation is seen as an inorganic tool operated by the sovereign (which, as thought, manifests the triumph of alienation and serialisation) or it is seen as an extension of the sovereign's own body (which may more appropriately be called mystification). It becomes difficult, in rendering institutional praxis intelligible, to decide whether the result of that praxis is the result of the group praxis mediated by the sovereign or of the sovereign praxis mediated by the group. Each particular result is probably intelligible in both ways at the same time.

The individual or individuals who become sovereign[1] emerge
from the specific historical circumstances in which institutionalisation takes place. At the level of the concrete, the institution is, of
course, situated in the midst of other institutions, groups and series
at various stages of development and we have seen how the interior
organisation and the exterior grasp of the institutionalised individual reinforce each other. In a long analysis of the State and
bureaucracy (pp. 608ff.) Sartre elaborates the idea of extero-
conditioning, the control of the series by the sovereign.

In his personal organic unity, the sovereign manifests the unity
of the institution; to the series, he can provide a phantom unity.
The member of the series – for example the individual businessman
– finds in the institution, or more specifically its sovereign (the
political party and its leader) his unity with others in the series,
other businessmen, a unity which he nonetheless experiences as
Other in serial impotence; by himself he can do nothing, the party
and its leader can gain power; at the same time the sovereign would
be there without his support, and whatever the sovereign might do,
he is preferable to the alternative (the party of the other class) and
the serialised individual can create no alternative of his own. In this
way the sovereign blocks the serial flight: the unity of the series is
no longer elsewhere and nowhere, but simply elsewhere, in the
sovereign.

To act upon the series, the sovereign must extend seriality to the
limits: he presents the unity of the series to each serialised individual
as laying in his alteriority. To affirm my unity with the Others, my
membership of this 'group', I must exercise my own praxis on myself to become increasingly Other, increasingly like the Other. In
this activity, we can find at least one of the modes of intelligibility
of a range of activities from advertising to electioneering, and of
phenomena such as 'fashion', 'youth culture' etc.[2] We can also
render intelligible serial reactions which superficially appear to have
elements of group praxis about them. A pogrom for example, is
sparked off by a sovereign action: a Jew is punished for some
capital crime, a politician attacks immigration, and that by itself may

[1] The sovereign is not necessarily an individual although Sartre implies –
and this would follow from his description – that there is always a
tendency towards the organic unity of the individual. Where a
sovereign group or groups is concerned the analysis is more
complicated but runs generally along the same lines. See Section II of
this chapter.

[2] Sartre, apparently, was astonished at the existence of the 'hit parade'
when he visited the USA in the late forties and this provides one of his
favourite examples.

be sufficient; there need be no organisation by members of the institution who are in direct contact with the series. Whoever is attacked or punished is designated as Other by the sovereign and is thus Other than the series which grasps itself as a unity in alteriority. The Other, the Jew, the black, is however, in the midst of the series, in the same street, in a ghetto in the same town; I find my unity with Others in the series in my own alteriority, I must make myself more like them and thus less like the Other designated by the sovereign. The sovereign's activities are thus grasped as an instruction to remove the Other from our midst, or at least, if somebody should start to remove them, then it becomes my duty to participate, to manifest my alteriority by making myself like the Others who began the pogrom, to affirm my membership of the 'group'. In a pogrom nobody experiences his own responsibility, he acts to make himself like the Other and it is always the Other who is responsible; insofar as I do recognise my responsibility, I do so as Other. We are presented with a serial, distorted reflection of the group-in-fusion.

To the extent that the sovereign attempts to make each member a tool with which to act on the series, then he creates and extends the series within the institution. The group member who is in direct contact with the series finds himself serialised in relation to the other group members as well as to the series on which he is supposed to be acting. At this point we discover the creation and the problems of bureaucracy. Information flow, for example, is distorted insofar as the bureaucrat no longer understands his own praxis, that of the institution or that of the series. Those with direct contact with the series interiorise the definition of their activity offered them jointly by the members of the series and the institution itself and see themselves as simple tools of the sovereign (the pretentiousness of petty officials) or they become to all intents and purposes members of the series. In the latter case, the sovereign has to use the techniques of extero-conditioning on his own officials as well as on the series: the subordinate is urged to act on himself to make himself Other (e.g. through pep talks about the standards of the profession, duty etc.). In this way seriality creeps back up the hierarchy of the institution, even approaching the sovereign.

With the institutionalisation of the organised group and its decay towards seriality, we have reached the end of the regressive theoretical movement. The new seriality is different to that of the earlier, more abstract moment of the movement, it has been brought into relationship with other series, institutions and sovereigns and various forms of groups; we are left with the social formations out of which men make History. History itself is the group praxis, its successes and failures, its alienation over time, its effects upon and the responses it elicits from other groups, institutions and series. The writing of a History intelligible as man-made, as the totalising movement of all social formations and all praxis, is the task of the progressive movement. The regressive movement has taken us to the theoretical totality, the point closest to History that it is possible to reach without moving to the concrete.

However, the theoretical description is circular in the sense that it has revealed a constant movement from man as his own product (free individual praxis) to man as the product of his product (the moment of the practico-inert) and back to man as his own product (through group praxis). History is intelligible in terms of this constant movement, but not as a straightforward cyclical process. There is no regularity in the movement, and it can move through any combination of transformations. The practico-inert may dominate for generations, groups may find themselves in opposition to existing institutions and finally transform themselves into institutions, or they might form on the basis of institutions; groups may arise from and fall back into seriality without reaching the stage of institutions or even of organisation; organised groups or institutions may transform themselves into groups-in-fusion. From the theoretical analysis we have discovered a number of what we have called 'modes of intelligibility' which should enable us to understand these movements in their complexity. Briefly, we can look at one such movement: the formal intelligibility of class and class praxis.

Insofar as the class has a Being, it lies in the series, a collectivity dominated by and finding its Destiny in the practico-inert; it gains its Being from the practico-inert, and in this sense is In-itself in Sartre's, rather than Marx's, sense of the word. The groups and institutions formed on the basis of the series are praxis; insofar as they have a Being it is the series they have interiorised in their formation and then re-exteriorised to maintain themselves in existence as praxis.

If this is the sense in which we can talk about class, then what about the class praxis? If this is intended to mean the working class (or any other class) acting as some tremendous group-in-fusion, then we cannot talk about class praxis at all; such a situation has self-evidently not occurred. On the other hand, insofar as the class has a Being, insofar as it is united through the practico-inert, then any attempt by a group formed in the series to gain control of its destiny implies, beyond its immediate aims, the action of the whole class; the praxis it is undertaking is the only praxis available to the class, i.e. to transform its Destiny into Interest. From the basis of the Being of the class, any praxis is a particular manifestation of the class praxis. We can, then, talk about 'class praxis' in the sense of a constantly uneven development, in different places and at different times, of the same praxis. Within this same praxis, there will be moments of success, failure, alienation, mystification and conflict, for example, between new groups in their first upsurge and institutions and between both and the series. The group-in-fusion and the organised group will have a different relationship to the series to that of the institution: the group-in-fusion will demand its dissolution, the organised group will work on it to dissolve it and the institution will work on it to maintain and control it, and of course, any one of these relationships may change. However, each situation is at least formally intelligible, initially through the praxis of the Regulating Thirds and then through the structures of the various formations and their dialectical interrelationships. In any concrete situation each mode of intelligibility refers immediately to the others, the only limit to intelligibility comes from the position of the observer.

These limitations have hitherto been discussed in terms of the observer's isolation from the group and his consequent inability to grasp its interior knowledge of itself. At this point in the theoretical description we come across a more fundamental limitation. The class cannot be seen 'from the point of view of History', we are not looking at a completed Historical movement but at an ongoing, totalising movement. Even from the interior of the class, it is impossible to grasp its full complexity: there is an element of processus, something always happening elsewhere which appears to the observer, even from the interior of a group-in-fusion, as Other, as a development over which neither he nor anyone has any control. Sartre argues that it is this element of processus which has been taken by some thinkers as the 'hidden laws of society', to be discovered by the theorist.

Insofar as there is a limit to intelligibility, the totalising movement of understanding cannot be achieved by one thinker or group of thinkers alone. At this point we come back to Sartre's situating of himself in the development of Marxist thought. Each totalising movement of understanding, whether it be from within or outside the working class, falls back into the In-itself on its completion, it becomes a 'detotalised totality', a structure of concepts related in a particular way, rather than an ongoing development of relationships between concepts. It remains to be retotalised into another synthesis by another praxis.

11. The strike leadership

The mode of intelligibility of the institution and sovereignty is most useful in extending our understanding of the union leadership and its changes, already discussed briefly in terms of market forces. At this level the circulation of leadership groups was seen as made possible by the demands of the practico-inert which subordinates individual 'characteristics' to the serial relationships in which the individual is involved. However, this does not render the full intelligibility of the disagreements between the leadership groups or the existence of groupings in the first place, or the changing balance of power between groups.

Gouldner seems to see the explanation in terms of a conjunction of personal characteristics and the development of a situation in which differences between personal characteristics become important (1954b: 95–100). To an extent we can endorse this, but with the proviso that it makes personal characteristics into contingent givens of the situation whereas we have already seen that such characteristics are intelligible in terms of the project of the individual concerned, a specific interiorisation of practico-inert demands. Such a project is a continuous development: the very act of interiorisation changes the situation in which the project is worked out. In this sense, the relationship between 'character' and situation is variable: we cannot tell, without more information, eventually the sort of personal information that is unlikely to be available, whether the personalities of those in Byta's group, for example, are intelligible in terms of their position in the union leadership or vice versa. In the absence of further information, all we can do is show the complementarity of the two, and on this basis, we can extend the intelligibility of the changing relationships of the leadership groups to each other and to the other workers in the plant.

A union leadership, whether local or national, find their intelligibility as sovereigns or sovereign groups within an institution. The established union leadership in one plant, if it has been in office for a comparatively long period at a time when industrial relations have been fairly stable and routine, is certainly intelligible in such a way, and in the plant in question, although there had been problems, the strike seemed to erupt into a fairly well established leadership.

The processes of election from the series (the workers), recognition by and negotiation with the management establish the leaders as the 'representatives' of the workers – 'representative' in the sense that the serial unity of the collective or institution is manifested in the unity of the union leadership. To the extent that the leaders' power is based upon recognition from serial impotence by both management and workers, then the maintenance of that power is also the maintenance of seriality within the institution of which they are the head. The leader in such a position grasps himself as separate from both management and workers; he is separate from the workers to the extent that he is elected as the Other who will 'represent' and he manifests their unity in his personal organic unity. He relates to the grievances of the workers as to the grievances of the Other, independently of whether he holds his office full-time or continues working; in the latter event, his institutional position involves at the same time a different understanding of his own grievances, i.e. he understands them as Other to the extent that he is sovereign. In his role as sovereign, he becomes less the one who experiences grievances than the one who judges the grievances of Others, the one who decides on their legitimacy and the action to be taken. The extent to which he makes the grievances of Others his own depends on the extent to which he assesses them as legitimate from his sovereign position.

On the one hand, then, the leader's position is based on the serial acceptance of the union members, on serial impotence. On the other, it is based on recognition by management, who, in relation to the union leadership, are the mediation of the serial power of the market. In relation to the seriality of the workers the leadership has power; in relation to the serial organisation of the market it is at least comparatively impotent. To an extent, however, the former power is based on the latter impotence insofar as the impotence is mediated by the management who recognise their power. We have seen that written contracts are an attempt to gain some control over the market situation and it is precisely in those contracts that the leadership's power is recognised by management. Here we find the intelligibility of the 'market orientation' of the Byta group, its willingness to submit to authority, since it is to an extent that authority which recognises their power and saves them from complete impotence in the face of the market.

Disputes within a sovereign group can occur for various reasons. Divisions between the classes that make up or control the State, for example, are intelligible in terms of practico-inert contradictions interiorised by the classes concerned, and the State is at least in part intelligible as an institution through which these disputes may be mediated. In the case of the union leadership under consideration the only practico-inert contradiction which might possibly be interiorised by the sovereign group is fairly remote and appears to have been experienced as a contradiction in thinking the conflict rather than as a fundamental cause of the conflict.[1] Nor does the division seem to have been the result of a previous upsurge of a group from amongst the workers.[2] Gouldner seems to imply that it was primarily one of personal characteristics and individual viewpoints; from the point of view of intelligibility the important thing is why it should be possible for such differences to become important.

When we are concerned with a sovereign group rather than an individual sovereign, the unity of the institution must be manifested in the unity of the group. But a sovereign group is as incapable of achieving an organic unity as the institution itself. There is, then, a constant strain rooted in the threat to the existence of the institution presented by members in a position to manifest their transcendence.[3] Within a sovereign group whose potential power is derived, for example, from periodic elections, power is a permanent possibility for those who are not at the moment at the head of the group; hence different personalities represent different possible unities for the institution. There is no 'desire' or 'need' for power as a characteristic of those involved, rather the nature of institutional power is such that there is a permanent strain towards individual power which takes up each individual in the sovereign group. To understand why specific individuals lead or join factions within the sovereign group would require reference to the historical growth of the institution and the individual projects of those concerned. What is important is that a degree of 'personality conflict' is a permanent possibility in an institution ruled by the sovereign group.

Given that such conflict occurs, each group will attempt to act on the series in a different way. The faction that holds power will attempt to maintain its seriality; this does not necessarily involve an exercise in extero-conditioning, but rather the simple maintenance of serial impotence. The faction that does not hold power, if it cannot achieve its aims through operations within the sovereign group, will act on the series to unite it against the present leadership. This does involve an exercise in extero-conditioning insofar as each member of the series must recognise his unity with the Others

---

[1] This of course is the 'contradiction' between the industrial and agricultural sectors of the economy that was discussed in Chapter 7. Whereas the contradiction was seen as mediating the conflict in the plant, it was not seen as the origin of the conflict.

[2] Gouldner (pp. 37–8) discusses a previous incident, but this seems to have followed a course similar to the strike itself.

[3] It should not be thought that the union is being portrayed as some sort of 'Stalinist' or even potentially Stalinist organisation; the strain towards individual power is common to all institutions but for various reasons by no means always completed.

against the ruling faction, but he must recognise it as manifested in the opposition faction, i.e. he must recognise his unity with his co-workers itself as Other. The problem for the faction attempting to gain power is that in certain situations the collective may create an authentic group out of itself through the interiorisation of the unity that it finds in the opposition faction. It is in this sense that extero-conditioning perhaps adds a new dimension of intelligibility to the strike.

There was, of course, no direct overthrow of the sovereign faction; rather the strike 'displaced' it and left power effectively in the hands of the rival faction. Thus the group formed on the basis of the collectivity of the workers did not manage to overcome the seriality of the institution, which would have involved the disappearance of both sovereign factions into the mass of the workers or the displacement of both. This adds a further element of intelligibility to the previously noted fact that the strike was thought in serial terms. The individuals who thought the strike at its effective point of contact with management, insofar as they were members of a sovereign group, were caught up in the seriality and the serial thinking of the institution. The failure to overcome seriality cannot be made fully intelligible: the sort of information that could help (although not decisively since the success of a group praxis is no more determined than its appearance) would be detailed information about the interactions between the workers between Tenzman being sworn at and the walk-out and a fairly detailed account of interaction between leadership and workers and between members of the leadership groups during the strike.

III. Conclusion: the intelligibility of sociology

The discussions up to this point have dealt with sociology in terms of the abstract moments of the theoretical description, and each succeeding description, to the extent that it has depassed the previous one, has taken us closer to the complexity of the concrete. Taken together as a synthesis – the full operation of which would extend and deepen many aspects that in this context have had to be dealt with superficially – they give us a synchronic description of the structure of the 'sociological field' and sociological praxis. It is not, however, a full description of sociology: that would require the integration of a diachronic description of the development of the structure that has been described – i.e. a history of sociology – and an understanding of the specific interiorisations of the sociological field by individual sociologists, the sociological 'project' in the sense in which the term was used in the first part of the study.

A study of the historical development of sociology is obviously beyond the scope of this work, but it is possible to comment upon the formal intelligibility of that development. The second aspect, the sociological project, if it is to be explored in its full complexity, would require studies of specific sociological careers and is again beyond our scope. What is possible is a general discussion of choices open to the sociologist.

The historical development of sociology is conventionally handled in various ways: it is sometimes seen in terms of the sources of development in and conflicts between ideas and concepts;[1] sometimes this is combined with more direct references to the position of the sociologist in his own society, either generally in class or group terms or occasionally in more immediate individual terms.[2] Rarely, if at all, is there a comprehensive discussion of the development of sociology as a university discipline, and the consequences of its integration in to the university for the nature and structure of the subject. All of these approaches have something to offer, but what is demanded before all' else is a conceptualisation which enables them to be thought as a unity, and a grasp of the intelligibility that such a unity would offer. The conceptualisation being suggested here is that which is in general outline available from the theoretical totality.

The 'Founding Fathers' of sociology were created as such by their contemporaries and by those who came after them, and to an extent the creation is still continuing,[3] but this does not mean that we have to begin with the process of the acceptance and integration of their thought into the academic world and the world at large. Rather we must begin with the individual thinkers themselves, recognising that they were not necessarily attempting consciously to create a new discipline (although many of them were) and looking at them as choosing to relate to the world and to possess it through knowledge and understanding. To understand the form and content of their work as well as its consequent acceptance and importance within the discipline, we are, from this starting point, referred in two directions.

To grasp their choice of themselves, their project, we are referred

---

[1] There are many examples of studies whose approach is 'idea-oriented'; see in particular R. A. Nisbet 1967, R. Atkinson 1971; R. W. Friedrichs 1970; Alan Dawe 1971.
[2] See in particular Gouldner 1971; Perry Anderson 1968.
[3] For example, Andreski's work on Spencer can be considered in this light.

to their origins, to their birth and their relationships with their parents and those around them, through whom the rest of the world including their class position, relationships and ideologies were mediated. The terms in which they produced their thought are understandable through the ways in which the dominant systems of thoughts were mediated directly and immediately through the family and the education system. At the same time we are referred outwards to the general development of the society in which they lived, which offered them the choice they made and was at such a stage of development that totalising theories about society and human behaviour were being demanded and accepted by certain sections of it.

The individual we are trying to understand must be grasped as a unitary and developing project which manifests itself in, and is, all of his activities. Weber's personal 'peculiarities', his long depressions, for example, are not irrelevant to his theoretical or his empirical work but are elements in a relationship to the world through which we can grasp the full meaning of his sociology, and his sociology is a relationship to the world through which we can grasp the full meaning of his 'private life'.[1] We must then, initially, understand what can be called the 'necessity of Weber': his necessity in general terms, why it was possible for him to become a sociologist in late nineteenth-century Germany and his necessity in personal terms, why he became a sociologist rather than, say, a Lutheran parson, and the necessity of his sociology, why he developed the sociology that he did, rather than Durkheim's sociology or Marx's sociology. The development of a particular thought may be studied in terms of the contradictions and necessities of its own categories,[2] but if we are to understand the *precise* constellation of categories and why these categories and no others were employed, then we need to grasp the individual project of the thinker. It is only through reference to what is outside the system of thought, to the society and to the individual, that we can grasp the precise meaning of that system for its author, those who received it, and its consequent alienation and institutionalisation, i.e. its 'interpretation'.

The regressive movement, then, is from the wider society to the

[1] Alan Dawe (1973) attempts to distinguish between personal experience which is important for the sociologist and that which is not. This may be seen as a serial thinking of what is in the context of the article a group experience insofar as it implies the division of experience according to a practico-inert division between 'sociology' and 'non-sociology'.
[2] This can be done fairly rigorously in isolation; see in particular Paul Hirst 1972.

individual project through the mediations of family, education system, teachers, etc. The progressive movement is from the individual project through its work on the world and the effects of that work, the way in which it is taken up, by whom and when. At this level, a thinker may be regarded as thinking the world for the particular class or group which takes up his thought. To the extent that it is taken up, we are referred to the class relationships in which it takes its place, the 'need' of the class for an ideology or system of thought, and the systems of thought with which it finds it necessary to argue. The movement from the individual thinker back to the world is mediated by the techniques available for the publication and distribution of his work, which in turn refers us to the technical development of the organisation of publishing and printing, the general educational level, the real and potential size of the reading audience and the way in which his work is read or, perhaps more accurately, the social formations within which it is read,[1] and the financial arrangements that allow a thinker to survive through writing or demand that he take some other sort of work as well. By tracing the process through to the wider development of society, we can begin to render intelligible the spread of a particular writer's ideas and the transformation of their meaning in the hands of others. In the case of sociology we can begin to grasp its development as a University discipline with a particular structure.

The first mode of intelligibility, then, is simply that of the Third, totalising the world with a particular end in view, what in the first part of this study we called simply the project. From this mode of intelligibility we move to the others: the institutional development of the universities and the sovereignty of the state in relation to the ruling class or classes of the period in question, and to the intelligibility of the institution, organised group, the group-in-fusion and the series insofar as these modes of intelligibility are required to understand the movements of history and its effects on the development of sociology. At the same time we remain on the level of the Third and of the practico-inert insofar as each 'external' development is interiorised through individuals in a certain relationship to the practico-inert totality that sociology becomes.

What is important about the development in this context is that the project of a number of individuals to understand and know the world is transformed into the practico-inert conditioning and determination of the everyday praxis of the individual sociologist. We

---

[1] For example, the reading of Marx in a University or in a political party or group will involve different interpretations and consequences.

can, in a very general way, outline some of the consequences. We are not claiming that the 'founding fathers' tried to reach a *total* understanding of the world, or even that their work shows the dialectical structure that such an understanding would imply, and certainly it was itself conditioned by a practico-inert totality of previous philosophical and sociological work, but on the other hand, their work was an attempt to grasp a totality of relationships. The topics covered in most undergraduate courses as separate units – sociological theory, sociology of religion, the family, deviance, industrial sociology etc. – if they are found in the work of the classic sociologists as identifiable topics at all are dealt with in a more general totalising framework. The last major 'totalising' theorist of academic sociology in the twentieth century would appear to be Parsons.[1] The totalising attempt of sociology has declined and insofar as it remains it is directed at sociology itself rather than at the outside world, or confines itself to the elaboration of the founding fathers. As the attempt to grasp the world has become fragmented, so sociology's attempt to grasp itself has intensified.

Insofar as this is an adequate description of the transformation then it has certain consequences for the nature of the 'understanding' that modern sociology attempts. Understanding, by its nature, is not a fragmentary movement, even the most minor movement of understanding refers itself to an ever widening area: my friend crosses the road to buy some cigarettes; I understand his end – buying cigarettes – on the basis of the situation which he is going beyond – his lack of cigarettes – and vice versa. But at the same time my understanding, if it remains alive, is referred to the existence of shops selling tobacco, the use of money as a medium of exchange, the necessity to cross the road carefully, the effects of tobacco on the human physical and nervous systems etc. etc.[2] An act of understanding, an act of consciousness as described in Chapter 2, implies any number of previous and future acts if it is not to remain a partial and therefore inadequate understanding.

The fragmentation of sociology, then, originating in its institutionalisation and growth as a university discipline, the requirements of teaching and the dominance of analytic thought, which in turn has its origins in the wider society, this fragmentation would indicate that the knowledge of understanding sought by the modern

---

[1] This does not take into account the development of Marxism, which although it obviously has its place in the study of the development of sociology, is intimately connected with many other factors.

[2] I.e. What Schutz regards as background assumptions, but which cannot remain as such for a living movement of understanding.

sociologist and demanded from him by his 'discipline' is of a very different nature to that sought by the classical sociologists; it is a partial and therefore inadequate understanding, inadequate in terms of its own nature as an act of consciousness. Within each of the sub-disciplines certainly there is what might be called a 'totalising tendency' – in particular such a tendency can be found in the sociology of sociology and perhaps the sociology of deviance.[1] The important point is that what is demanded of the individual sociologist, if he is to be recognised as a sociologist, includes in many instances, although not necessarily all, a limiting of his own effort to understand either himself or the world. The demands are presented to him as 'sets' of knowledge that he must acquire, topics and methods from amongst which he must choose, an acceptable style and form of writing up reports etc. In the face of these demands and their implied limits to understanding, it is possible to discern three very general orientations or projects.

The first and perhaps most obvious choice is to interiorise the demands of the practico-inert system as dominant and to choose oneself as subordinate. Such a choice by a sociologist is one moment of a more fundamental project which would render the choice intelligible, and the simple subordination of oneself can take place in various ways: in resentment, boredom, relief, as a matter of course or as a radical break with the past, and again to understand the particular nature of the subordination, we are referred to the fundamental project. This choice is of an alienation of oneself to an external entity: it may be understood as an attempt to capture my Being through my being-for-others and at the same time through the acquisition of an 'interest', a being-outside-of-myself recognised by myself and others as my Being, but in which I can no longer recognise myself, only myself-for-others. The alienation is a deliberate projection of myself into worked matter (sociology with its implications about life-style, type of work etc.) in an attempt to coincide with Being through my being-outside-of-myself-for-others-and-for-myself-in-the-objectification-of Others.[2] The impossibility of such a coincidence is the contradiction on the basis of which the development of the project may be understood.

Fundamentally this means that I no longer have the ability to understand myself, or, implicitly, anything that I study. I grasp

[1] Examples of the former have already been given; for the latter see Taylor, Walton and Young 1973.

[2] This formulation has been retained to imply the complexity of the dialectic that it encloses; Sartre spends some 3,000 pages exploring the course of such a dialectic in Flaubert.

myself as Other, in exteriority as a 'sociologist' and from a position exterior to myself, I can only grasp others in exteriority. Reciprocal relationships of interiority with those I study are unimaginable because it is not I who study them but myself-as-sociologist and a recognition that those I study are related through relationships of interiority in any more than a formal sense would bring into question my relationship with them.[1] This relationship of the sociologist to himself is the reverse side of the domination by the practico-inert totality described in previous chapters. Its most obvious manifestation is, at those stages in the development of the project when the contradiction becomes crucial, a complete separation between the sociologist's 'work' and his private life: sociology becomes a 'career', a 'profession', a 'job' and the sociologist experiences his own life as fragmented into at least two compartments. Such a conception may even be provided for by the structure of the profession insofar as certain activities are considered beyond the scope of disciplinary action or as not-being-sociology and therefore not contributing to career advancement – for example, the writing of poetry or novels.

The individual sociologist, may, however, interiorise the demands of the practico-inert without subordinating himself to them, but in an attempt to possess the world through understanding by using the tools given him by sociology. Again this choice is intelligible as a moment of a more fundamental project, but it is one which does not necessarily involve a fundamental alienation. The mode of knowledge or understanding he aims at is important insofar as it can be either analytical or dialectical in structure and to an extent his success in 'using' sociology depends on his ability to escape from the analytic knowledge that it offers, since its acceptance is also an acceptance of the major categories of the practico-inert. Such a project will, on the whole, tend to be dialectical.

Initially this will be because there is no longer a 'distance' between the sociologist and his work: it is an integral rather than an external feature of his relationship to the world and there is a constant and reciprocal reference from his understanding of the world to his understanding of himself and vice versa. His choice of himself might from the beginning be one of understanding himself through his understanding of the world, but even if it aims simply at a 'possession' of the world, he will inevitably be referred back to himself through its successes and failures. The very nature of 'sociological knowledge', the simple fact that it is knowledge of the

[1] In this context, 'verstehen' becomes a purely formal recognition to the extent that it is made to depend on formal rationality and observation.

world in which he is living, can be one source of the reference. On this basis, in fact, it would be possible to construct an ethico-political justification of the teaching of sociology and its aims which could give a concrete meaning to the idea of a 'community of learning' insofar as what is being taught refers to and even requires an understanding by both teachers and taught of their relationship to each other and to the rest of the world. If the sociologist either seeks an understanding of himself from the start or is referred to it through his project of possession by knowledge, he will have a grasp of the relationships of interiority through which the world can be understood.

This relationship to his work can potentially produce conflict between the sociologist, his discipline and other sociologists, as well as the administrative organisation of the educational system. If the movement of understanding is totalising, then it cuts across the boundaries of topics within sociology and between sociology and other disciplines. Insofar as the 'sociological totality' is perhaps less clearly defined than that of other disciplines, and insofar as the 'totalising tendency' of sociology is still recognised as acceptable sociology, then perhaps the individual can survive within the discipline without meeting too many difficulties in this respect. At the same time, however, a totalising movement of understanding would cut across other elements of the totality, particularly those that attempt to divorce sociology from personal life and the wider social and political life of the sociologist. From recent reactions to Gouldner's work, it would seem that this is perhaps the area in which conflict is most likely to occur.[1] A conflict over discipline boundaries might possibly be one of the mechanisms that refers the sociologist to himself in his project of possessing the world, insofar as it questions him and his activity directly.

The third possible project is the interiorisation of the demands of the practico-inert in an attempt to use the tools thus gained as a means of furthering the understanding and praxis of some social formation. Again this does not necessarily involve a dialectical understanding, nor does it necessarily involve the sociologist in an attempt to understand himself at the same time as he tries to understand the world. The nature of the understanding that he seeks will depend upon, amongst other things, the nature of the formation to which he belongs and his relationship to it. A member, for example, of an institution or organised group based on a class will be likely to be serialised in relation to his organisation and his

---

[1] cf. *The American Journal of Sociology*, July 1972, and Gouldner's reply in the March 1973 issue.

fellow sociologists and in this situation his work will be produced, in all likelihood, in serial and analytic terms. To the extent, on the other hand, that the group to which he belongs is in conflict with other groups and that involvement in this conflict in turn conflicts with the demands of sociology as a practico-inert totality, he is likely to be referred to a dialectical understanding of his own position and the praxis of the formation to which he belongs; again he will be likely to begin to grasp relationships as relationships of interiority.

It is from such a position, from the interior of a practical group and in a situation where he is constantly referred to his own position that the individual sociologist is most likely to be able to do what was described at the end of Chapter IV as reducing the 'objectness' of those he studies to the minimum. In the terms of the categories developed through the second part of this study, this involves a recognition of the relationships of reciprocal interiority between those he studies and between himself and those he studies; whether this reciprocity is positive or antagonistic is not, at this stage, important. In this context, the attempt to reveal the freedom of those he studies becomes the sociologist's attempt to explore the limits and possibilities of his own freedom.

It should be emphasised that this is a very broad typology of projects and a very general examination of their nature and implications. In the concrete, not only will each individual project be more complex, but elements of each project are likely to interpenetrate as they develop. For example, the thinker who tries to understand himself through understanding the world might be referred back to a group or class external to sociology with which he finds himself in alliance. Perhaps the most frequent inter-penetration is the project which attempts to interiorise the demands of the practico-inert as a moment of a wider project in which sociology becomes, in turn, a means, and fails over a period of time during which the individual subordinates himself to these demands and alienates himself to the sociological totality. Any number of transformations are possible.

II

Conclusion

In the last chapter, we outlined three possible 'sociological projects';
we will now attempt to elaborate the option or options implied in
Sartre's work and to make explicit the relationship between philosophy and sociology that has remained basic to the arguments
throughout. To an extent, of course, the attempted analyses and
re-analyses must stand on their own as examples of a specifically
Sartrean philosophical sociology, but we can add some general
programmatic observations.

1. Summary: philosophy and sociology

In the discussion of *Being and Nothingness*, we tried to point
towards the relevance of its method, descriptions and conclusions
for the practice of sociology: it was seen as providing the tools with
which the sociologist could grasp interpersonal interaction and the
framework within which he could explore the relationship between
himself and those he studies and his way of seeing the world
around him, his way of understanding. In criticising Goffman and
Garfinkel, we attempted to establish that Sartre offers a more
complex and demanding conception of the self and of interpersonal
activity than might, at first glance, be supposed. We also tried to
show that any sociological study of interaction presupposes Sartre's
form of phenomenological enquiry and that it is possible to work
back from such a study to discover the ontological assumptions of
the author; we tried to show how these assumptions are revealed
in the content of the sociological study, in its adequacies and
inadequacies, consistencies, contradictions. Finally, we tried to show
how the categories and method of Sartre's analysis can be employed
in a study of the 'self' or of language use with consequent advantages in consistency and intelligibility.

A central point of Chapters 3 and 4 is that no philosophy is a series
of random ideas from which the sociologist may pick and choose
at will. It is, rather, a rigorous and systematic argument in which
each part is related to and dependent upon the others; to take one

8

element in isolation for use in an empirical sociological study changes the meaning of that element and produces observations and conclusions that can in no way be considered consistent with the philosophy in question or the aims of the philosopher. For example we saw that Goffman argues that the mental hospital defines its patients as certain types of objects, superficially a point that appears to be distinctly 'Sartrean'. Yet we found that in the context of Goffman's work, it was part of a conception of an institutionally defined self crude in comparison to Sartre's and unable to handle as adequately as the latter the complexity of the phenomena that Goffman observed. More significantly, the discussion of Garfinkel and Schutz showed how the idea of 'ethnomethodological indifference', although superficially similar to the phenomenological reduction, has in practice no similarities with the philosophical concept. We also tried to show, in our discussion of the life world and consciousness, how even comparatively sophisticated readings of philosophical work can change the meaning of that work and its original direction. The effective identification of consciousness and the life-world was responsible for a conception of action different to that of Husserl and inadequate in terms of a critique based on Sartre's work. Here, perhaps more than elsewhere, we tried to establish the relevance of what might at first glance seem highly esoteric philosophical debates to the way in which the sociologist conceptualises the world. If sociology is to learn from philosophy, it must treat the philosopher seriously and make the attempt to grasp and employ his philosophy as a whole. These criticisms enabled us to draw out a Sartrean analysis of the relationship of the sociologist to those he studies and the nature of 'doing sociology'. The method we followed is particularly significant: the important point is that Sartre offers a way of thinking the activity and experience of the sociologist by means of a rigorous method with its own established categories and criteria. The importance of this is revealed in a comparison with 'reflexive sociology', most of which attempts an analytically logical and generalised introspection, an 'impure' opposed to a 'pure' reflection.

If the sociologist's 'experience' and 'attitudes' are important in understanding his sociology, then we have to know exactly what 'experience' and 'attitudes' are, and the precise way in which they effect what is produced as sociology. Gouldner offers us few suggestions; certainly, sociologists have 'domain assumptions' and these should be made explicit, but *how* do we make them explicit? And what is the relationship between 'domain assumptions' and the private life of the sociologist, which Gouldner would also like to take into account? The problem of producing answers through introspection must be immediately apparent to anybody who seriously tries it: who can say in black and white terms exactly what he experiences and how it influences his activity and ideas? Alan Dawe (1973) has tried to develop the idea of a 'representative experience', arguing that if reflexive sociology is to be more than a subjectivism denying the possibility of sociology itself, then we need some way in which we can distinguish experience important for the sociologist qua sociologist from other experience. His 'representative experience' however seems to be difficult to pin down: how do I *know* that my experience is representative? I know that I have a common mood, a common excitement, perhaps a common hope, that I live through the same events as other people, but beyond this, if I try to compare my experience with those around me the differences begin to emerge: the experience that in some ways I share with others plays a different part and comes at a different stage in the life of each of us; there is vital dimension of the unique as well as the representative in each experience and what conceivable standard is there for separating the two? We can, perhaps, separate the extremes in a very general way; so, for example, a revolution is a representative experience, my encounter with my grandmother's ghost is probably a unique one, but even here why should one be more important for my sociological work than the other?: the latter might even persuade me to give up sociology altogether. We might, possibly, be able to establish the analytic utility of a particular representative experience, but again this does not establish the representativeness of the experience, it could conceivably be a construction on the part of the sociologist to explain what otherwise cannot be explained. It is only possible to talk about a 'representative' experience by ignoring its unique dimensions, and if the uniqueness is recognised there is no adequate criteria to separate it from the representative, the separation must remain an assertion.

The experiences that Dawe mentions at the beginning of his article, a feeling of isolation after a CND march and of unity and discovery during a University occupation can, however, be dealt with, not as 'experiences' in the sense of substantive feelings or emotions, but as *relationships*, a particular way of grasping oneself in relation to others and others in relation to oneself. To describe experience as a relationship of consciousness to matter and consciousness to consciousness avoids reference to the 'quality' of experience, which must always be open to accusations of subjectivism,[1] and has its own test of 'analytic utility' in its ability to render events intelligible as the product of human action; significantly it can render intelligible the feeling of having shared in a representative experience. We can establish that *these* relationships render *this* event intelligible in a way in which it is not possible to establish that a particular experience is representative. If we grasp the experience of the sit-in as the relationship of a group-in-fusion, we can take into account feelings that are both shared (the 'same') and unique ('Other') at the same time based on the relationship of immanence-transcendence that I have to the group. The more directly 'private' the experiences of the sociologist the more we will have to refer to descriptions of *Being and Nothingness* rather than the *Critique*.

This argument leads us to the definition of 'theory' that we concentrated on in Chapter 5. The terms 'theory' and 'philosophy' have been used synonymously to refer to the investigation of what cannot be grasped and isolated in any way 'outside' of the observer; this investigation refers him directly to his own experience and in this sense all theoretical sociology is reflexive sociology. It is here that we find a fusion of philosophy, in the Sartrean sense of the word, and sociology, a fusion whose product replaces what is usually regarded as 'sociological theory', a field held to be distinct from philosophy and empirical research. The distinction can no longer be maintained: if I am investigating something 'outside' of myself, then I must make it part of my experience in order to be able to talk about it all, and, of course, if I investigate my own experience, then that experience is of what is 'outside' me. In the introduction, Tiryakian was criticised for bringing together sociology and philosophy as separate entities; in contrast, we have developed the argument that when I am 'doing sociology' I am at the same time 'doing philosophy' and vice versa.[2] This requires from the sociologist an honesty different from that usually assumed: for example the expectation that research results should not be falsified, or ideas stolen. The honesty required here is an honesty about himself and his experience and the subjection of that experience to a rigorous analysis in the terms of the theoretical description; it requires the avoidance of its 'easy' assessment in

[1] It is difficult, for example, to see how Dawe could definitively reject the accusation that the experience for which he claims a representative status was no more than a passing depression or euphoria which he has exaggerated or overdramatised for, perhaps, personal or political reasons.

[2] This has been recognised by thinkers as far apart in other respects as Peter Winch (1958) and Merleau-Ponty (1963). The content we are giving the fusion here is, of course, specifically Sartrean.

terms of the morality of the day or of his own group, or in terms of his own image of himself. By its concern with feelings and emotions, reflexive sociology would appear to be prone to the 'easy' assessment: the very concern with 'substantive' experience is perhaps related to the morality of a particular social group in a way in which concern with the structure of consciousness is not.

The theoretical totality built up during the second half of the study is an 'extension' of the theoretical description of consciousness examined in the first part, but one which moves in the opposite direction, towards the concrete rather than towards the fundamental categories of Being. It is in no way a 'representation' or a 'description' of the world; its aim is to establish the possibility of a world which can be understood as the product of human praxis, and the way in which we understand the world is not necessarily the same as that in which we practically construct it. No one social formation has any historical priority over the others, no one 'came first' and the transformations through which the formations pass do not necessarily follow the course of the transformations traced in the theoretical description.

In the development of the theoretical description, we have 'situated' and explored the limits of the absolute, ontological freedom established in the first chapters. The 'freedom' of the earlier work is different to that which Atkinson (1971) argues sociology should assume. If freedom is to be more than a pious acknowledgement, we have to know its precise nature and limits, and we have seen that it may alienate itself at the precise moment it exercises itself, and it may be transformed and turned against itself by worked matter and others. The exploration of freedom is essentially a theoretical task, basic to any understanding of the world.

It must be emphasised that the re-analyses of the Gouldner studies are neither the simple restatement of Gouldner's observations in different words, nor 'examples' of what was dealt with in theoretical description. We have tried to establish the existence of the plant, its organisation and the events inside it as dialectically intelligible as produced by or (more relevantly in this case) maintained by free human praxis. The 'dialectical sociology' proposed here is infinitely more complex than that proposed for example by Friedrichs (1972), involving more than the simple recognition that the sociologist is part of what he studies, although this obviously is an important feature; it is also a way of looking at what is studied to reveal the interrelationships of various phenomena not in terms of external cause and effect but in terms of their mutual interpenetrations and contradictions in and with the totality they comprise. In other words, we have attempted to give each separate phenomenon a different *meaning* to that given it by Gouldner.

Usually, perhaps, the aim of the sociologist is to separate and classify into different categories and then to establish relationships between categories. The procedure followed in the re-analyses here has been the opposite: we have tried to explore and deepen our understanding of the interconnections of each part to the whole. The separation of the three 'types' of bureaucracy becomes one moment in their re-integration as integral parts of the whole. They no longer comprise the conclusion of the study, but are a stage on the way. We are no longer faced with a series of externally related phenomena but with phenomena that are linked through relationships of interiority, firstly through a relationship with the practico-inert and secondly through praxis itself. The relationship of each part to the whole is one of reproduction and contradiction at the same time: thus workers and management are a 'whole', united through the plant, and beyond that the Company and the market, as practico-inert entities, and at the same time, workers are divided against management through the interest/destiny relationship to exactly the same practico-inert entities. In this context, the types of bureaucracy express and mediate different relationships to different sectors of the same practico-inert entities in which they find their unity; they are not caused by the structure of the plant, but express and mediate that structure: there is a relationship of interiority not exteriority. In the same way, we have tried to show how market forces are not 'external factors', something else to be taken into account, but are interiorised and reproduced in the structures and activities inside the plant, they *are* the plant to the extent that they are reproduced there. Similarly, we have tried to explore the interrelationships of 'personal characteristics' to the other phenomena in the plant and to situate the 'causes' of the strike not as external pressures pushing people on, but as a certain structure of relationships which the strike attempts to change. The aim has been to *re-construct* the study, rather than simply *re-describe it*.

The central concern of this chapter, however, is with the description of sociology as it was developed firstly in terms of the sociological project and then in terms of sociological praxis and the practico-inert. Implicit in this description, has been a prescription and this we will now attempt to draw out. Before we do so, however, it should be noted that Sartre himself explicitly, if only briefly, prescribes a role for sociology and it is to this that we will now turn.

II. A structural sociology?

Sartre displays very little knowledge of contemporary sociology. Beyond some comments on Durkheim, the only 'sociologists'
he mentions are Lewin and Kardiner. Furthermore, although he
sees the *Critique* as laying the foundations for the human sciences,
his remarks on the relationship between the foundation and its
superstructures are little more than passing comments. However,
we noted that he sees the objects of study proper to sociology as
being 'social objects', practico-inert entities[1] with the human beings
who are united in and around them; to this object, we could add
another, the structure of the organised group.

A sociology confining itself to either of these two objects would
be structural in the sense of excluding praxis from its study; it would
see its objects as sets of synchronic relationships eventually formu-
lable in mathematical terms. Perhaps the structuralism nearest to
that envisaged here is that of Levi-Strauss, and it is to the latter's
work that Sartre turns when he deals with a social science as
opposed to a totalising philosophy. This sort of study would be no
more than one moment in that totalising movement and it would
depend upon philosophy for its intelligibility.

The problem with the conception of a totalising philosophy
mapping out the objects for and synthesising the work of the human
sciences is that it leaves the latter only a marginal role. The
totalisation is more than a simple addition of the work of the
sciences and whilst there are certainly problems open to this sort
of scientific investigation, the totalising philosophy must always take
pride of place; science becomes a comparatively minor technical
task:[2] Moreover it is difficult to see how the theoretical description
can assign clearly defined objects of study to the social sciences: the
study of 'social objects' for example would involve the sociologist in
economics insofar as they concern the structure of the practico-inert
and would possibly refer him to some of the natural sciences as well.
Any discipline that involves the study of praxis – social psychology,
history, politics etc. would be drawn into the totalising philosophy.

[1] Insofar as the study of practico-inert structures involves a study of
diachronic developments the immediate source of which is not praxis,
then this type of structural sociology might also be termed the study of
'processus'; the two notions – 'processus' and 'practico-inert' – are to
some extent similar and tend to be used interchangeably.
[2] Or, alternatively, it can be argued that the totalising movement
becomes inessential because of its inadequacy and looseness. This is the
position taken by R. Castel (1966) but he asserts rather than argues the
inadequacies of the *Critique.*

The main point here is that Sartre's work is intrinsically totalising, drawing into itself all the human sciences, not only sociology.

Given the fact that the present divisions between the disciplines are unlikely to disappear in the foreseeable future, however, there is a case to be made that sociology is the discipline best able to take this totalising role for itself, and that if there is a Sartrean sociology, then it is a totalising sociology. Whilst now an established and fairly popular discipline in universities, sociology still has a comparatively loose and wide field of study, as a practico-inert entity it is rather less well-defined than other disciplines; it seems to be within sociology, perhaps because of the decline in totalising theory since the founding fathers, that the need for such a theory is most acutely felt. An indication of the totalising tendency within the discipline can be gained from a comparison of sociology as it is with the sort of structural sociology that could be derived from Sartre's work. Although it might do so in a fragmented and analytic way, sociology as it is cuts across all the modes of intelligibility produced in the theoretical description. As a practico-inert entity it includes the work of Garfinkel and Marx, Parsons and Becker, Weber and Durkheim; structural sociology of the sort outlined here would include, of these, only the work of Parsons, some of Marx's work, and perhaps some of Durkheim and Weber, but only to a limited extent.

A totalising sociology based on Sartre's work would draw into itself established analytic sociology, attempting to discover its intelligibility, to make it part of a whole. Sartre argues, in *The Problem of Method*, that the more rigorously analytic the study, the easier it is to incorporate it into the totalising movement. His meaning is fairly easy to discern: a rigorous statistical study, for example, reveals information in terms of percentages, probabilities etc. which need no modification and are taken up as 'given' by the totalising movement. Yet this inclusion does involve a modification of what is included, as Goldmann (1969) points out. It involves a change in the meaning of the 'given', in its relationship to other elements: a statement that was originally a conclusion, the terminal point of an analytic process is now related to an infinity of other elements and it 'points', not as before, back to the process that produced it but forward to the totalisation of which it is part. When the totalising movement questions the procedures by which the original statement was arrived at, its meaning is likely to be even more radically changed, and it might be eliminated from the proposed totalisation altogether, becoming instead an indication of the relationship of sociology to the rest of the world.

Given that a totalising sociology is implied in Sartre's work, we can move on to examine its nature in terms of aims, methods and the activity and relationships of the sociologist.

III. An existentialist sociology

At the end of Chapter 4, it was argued that the theoretical description implied that the sociologist should aim at reducing the 'object-ness' of those he studies to the minimum, that he should aim at describing as many possible futures as possible and revealing the past as the free product of human beings. In the second part of the study we have been concerned with 'intelligibility' implying the freedom of the earlier part. Intelligibility assumes freedom insofar as it means intelligible as the product of human praxis. If praxis were determined externally, by the nature of the environment or organism, it would be unintelligible, contingent, just 'like that' for no particular reason. At the same time, and by the same argument, freedom assumes intelligibility, at least as a permanent possibility.

Implicit throughout the study has been the argument that the intelligibility of what is being studied depends to a considerable extent on the intelligibility of his own praxis to the sociologist, and through that, on his relationships with his fellow sociologists and others; this is most apparent when it concerns understanding a group praxis as thought by the group. If the sociologist is aiming at portraying the intelligibility of those he studies, he is aiming at portraying the freedom of those he studies, even if that freedom is alienated at the moment it is exercised; in the same way that the intelligibility of what is studied is part and parcel of the intelligibility of his own praxis to himself, then in aiming at the freedom of those he studies, he is also aiming at his own freedom. If I find my understanding of others in my understanding of myself and vice versa, then the same is true of freedom.

In the terms of *Being and Nothingness*, then, the project being suggested here is one of possession of the world through understanding as opposed to knowledge, an understanding which aims at the revelation of freedom, the revelation of Being in the form of future possibilities rather than as a determining weight pressing down on human beings. In terms of the *Critique*, the understanding of the other's freedom, and the revelation of our reciprocal freedoms to each other, occurs in the fundamental relationship of reciprocity, in which I recognise the Other both as the sovereign subject of his field of praxis in which I am an object, and myself as sovereign over my own field of praxis in which the Other is an object.

A totalising sociology must aim at the freedom of both the sociologist and those he studies. It entails that the sociologist enters into a relationship of reciprocity with those he studies. If the reciprocity is positive, then it must entail what in conventional terms is called a 'commitment' to those studied: he must make their ends his ends in the process of pursuing his own ends and let himself be used as a means to their ends. This is a 'stronger' relationship than that suggested in the recommendation 'to take the point of view of those studied'; rather it takes the point of view of those studied as to some degree the 'correct' or 'true' view.[1] In the terms of the *Critique*, it involves a rejection of the 'sociological totality' and a totalisation of the world from the position of an individual trying to understand himself through an understanding of others and vice versa. In the case of negative reciprocity, then again the sociologist must make the ends of those he studies his own ends but only as one moment of a struggle in which the aim is to overcome the praxis of those studied; this in fact is closer to 'taking the point of view of those studied', with the vital difference that whereas here it is an important moment in conflict, a matter of tactics, seeing the world 'through the eyes' of those studied as a matter of principle removes the sociologist from his study, and puts him in the position of an outsider as far as what happens after the study is concerned.

The practical problems hardly need pointing out: many studies on the lines of Gouldner's could become impossible, at least as studies involving the conventional face-to-face methods of research since they would be rejected by one of the parties concerned, and there would be problems about the continuation of sociology itself as an academic discipline in the traditional sense, insofar as its position depends on its acceptance by various groups as 'objective', 'non-political' or whatever. To explore the complexity of these problems is beyond the scope of this study, but we are not necessarily advocating a direct clash with various authorities or with academic tradition. The extent to which the sociological totality and the professional ethics it involves and advocates may be 'used' by the sociologist following through the sort of project being suggested here is by no means pre-determined, and it is always possible that the looseness of the sociological totality and the comparative independence of the academic system as a whole will enable the sociologist to survive as a sociologist.[2] Here we can only indicate the

[1] William F. Whyte's appendix to *Street Corner Society* gives a good idea of the problems involved here and in many ways this study comes very close to what is being advocated here.
[2] There are of course many studies which at times come close to what is being suggested here, particularly those employing the methods of

existence of these problems; we can explore in more detail the nature of such a project in terms of what it would look for and what it would do.

It is not necessary for the sociologist to 'go native', to become a gypsum worker or whatever, although in some cases this might be both useful and necessary. A commitment to the ends and freedom of those studied can take several forms, not necessarily a commitment to their *immediate* ends, for example, in the Gouldner studies, to a solution of the strike in the form of a contractual agreement, which we have seen as the alienation of the group praxis of striking. Rather, it means that it is the work of the sociologist to take the current, immediate projects of those studied, to examine them in the light of the structures in which they take place and which they are trying to change and to pinpoint precisely the moments of freedom and alienation and the nature of the group and class relationships of those involved. The project of understanding posits no other end but freedom, and it is the freedom that is expressed and perhaps alienated through the immediate praxis of those studied that the sociologist must elucidate. Through this elucidation, the study must aim at making itself useful to those studied – through the understanding it offers of their activities and the possible futures that it is able to outline; it must therefore be available to those studied, even, and perhaps especially, if it challenges their own serial consciousness of themselves. At the same time, the sociologist discovers through his project his own effectiveness and his own future possibilities: the advantages and disadvantages of remaining a sociologist.

It is impossible to set out programmatically what to look for and what methods to use in the sort of study being advocated here; the simple answer to such a question is everything and everyone. We remarked several times in discussing the Gouldner studies that it was impossible to draw final conclusions about the modes of intelligibility appropriate to certain events because there was not enough information available. This should not be taken to mean that certain features should be searched out in preference to others. Understanding is a totalising movement: any event is in principle intelligible, and intelligible in terms of all other events; in this sense, there is no observation, no information that is irrelevant to the

symbolic interactionism usually in the area of deviance; the point is that most such studies do not have the theoretical tools to integrate their insights with those of more conventional sociology or to be able to understand and control the relationship of the sociologist to those he studies.

study. If this principle were followed rigorously, however, then no study would be complete until it encompassed the world and its history; there must obviously be some criteria for cutting off a study at a certain point, including or excluding certain information. The first criteria is one of sufficiency, a phenomenon, an event, is intelligible when it is self-evident in the terms developed in the theoretical description. It must be emphasised that 'self-evidence' refers always to the terms of the theoretical description, it is not self-evident in the sense of 'What Everybody Knows', but rather of 'What Everybody is', of the conclusions of a rigorous investigation of consciousness and Being. Not all modes of intelligibility are appropriate to every *event* (although they all might be appropriate to every situation): for example, we can render the 'Rebecca Myth' intelligible in terms of seriality alone. The second criteria also refers to self-evidence in the sense that this is achieved when no evidence contradicts the suggested intelligibility: there may be no need to include all available evidence but simply to account for that which does not fall immediately into place in the light of the suggested intelligibility. This again depends eventually on the honesty of the individual sociologist, the only check on which is the availability of recorded evidence to others; in this respect it does not differ from conventional sociology.

It should now be evident that a totalising sociology can aim at a totalisation of a specific event or situation, not in isolation but without attempting the impossible task of a totalisation of History. The investigation of the limited situation must, however, carry within itself a reference to the wider situation of which it is a part. Thus in the reconstruction of the Gouldner study, it was necessary at various points to refer in passing to the general economic and social development of the USA, to the wider structure of the market and the past histories of individuals in the plant. The choice of event or situation contains its own limitations on the evidence that needs to be presented: we needed only to refer to the general economic development of the USA, not to describe it in detail. At any one time, certain problems will be more important than others for the sociologist in the course of his own project and for those he studies in the course of theirs and it is here that the justification for choosing one study rather than another must lie. Thus, for example, the course of industrial action may present itself as a problem to the sociologist insofar as, in his individual project, he has discovered an identity with or a future in relation to the working class. In this case, the events he studies are determined by his group membership in general terms, and in particular terms by the more immediate problems of those he studies. In the case of the Gouldner study, the course, successes and failures of the strike would be more important than the nature of bureaucracy, a problem belonging directly to the 'sociological totalisation'. Bureaucracy would not be ignored but would not be a centre of attention. Specific topics for study are, then, chosen for what are conventionally called 'subjective' and 'objective' reasons: they arise in the project of the sociologist and are presented to him by those he studies.

As far as methodology is concerned, any method is on principle useful, it reveals something. Selection must to some extent be arbitrary: it depends on the availability of those studied, of time and money etc., and perhaps most importantly on the nature of what is being studied. If the aim is, for example, to discover the intelligibility of the strike studied by Gouldner, then in addition to the available information, we would need a blow-by-blow account of the activities of the union leaders and workers between the Spiedman–Tenzman argument and the eventual walk-out, and this would involve a direct observation of events. Lacking this, we were only able to attempt a reconstruction of events and suggest their probable intelligibility.

Whatever method is used, its precise meaning, exactly what it tells us, must be clearly understood. It was suggested that the separation of each worker from his fellows for interview purposes established and emphasised the serial nature of the views received and gave priority to only one of the relationships that each worker had with his fellows, that of a Third (a serialised Third). This does not mean that the information thus obtained is of no use: it must be recognised as a serial expression of relationships, and as such it requires firstly the establishment of its own intelligibility and secondly it must be related to other events and situations in the plant.

Finally, it must again be emphasised that when intelligibility is established, its meaning also lies in the future, in the way in which its illuminations transform the situation of those studied and the sociologist. In this sense, each study, however complete it might be, immediately creates the demand for further study. And, as we have seen, the sociologist himself is involved in a massive ongoing process – History itself – which he can only grasp from his position within it. There will always be elements elsewhere, created and formed by others, which are unavailable to him and which he experiences as processus. The 'final totalisation' is beyond his grasp because he changes it by contributing to it and because of the simple fact that others make History as well. On its completion, it falls back from being a totalisation even of one situation and takes on the form of a 'detotalised totality' which becomes the 'given', part of what is taken up into further totalisations. Insofar as it aims at an unrealisable end, sociology too falls into Sartre's description of man in *Being and Nothingness* as a 'useless passion', but one which is necessary as long as man exists.

Bibliographical note

In addition to works referred to in the text, the bibliography includes a
number of references that I have found particularly useful introductions or
discussions of Sartre's work. As far as Sartre himself is concerned, M. Rybalka &
M. Contat, *Les Ecrits de Sartre* (Paris, Gallimard, 1970) contains a bibliography
exhaustive to 1970 and reproduces several of the rarer texts. This will be
referred to as *RC*.

I have deliberately kept my translations from the *Critique* as 'literal' as
possible in order to convey the general flavour of the work, as well as some of its
problems. The only part so far published in translation (Sartre, 1963b) is a
much easier work and gives little impression of what is to come.

BIBLIOGRAPHY/REFERENCES

Adler, Franz. 1950. The Social Thought of Jean-Paul Sartre, *American Journal of
Sociology*, Vol. IV, pp. 784–94
Alberes, R. M. *Jean-Paul Sartre: Philosopher Without Faith* (New York: Philosophical
Library)
Althusser, L. 1971. *Reading Capital* (London: New Left Books)
1972. *For Marx* (London: Penguin)
Ames, Van Meter. 1950. Fetishism in the Existentialism of Sartre, *Journal of
Philosophy*, Vol. 47, pp. 407–11
1955. Mead and Husserl on the Self, *Philosophy and Phenomenological Research*,
Vol. XV, pp. 320–31
1956. Mead and Sartre on Man, *Journal of Philosophy*, Vol. 53, pp. 205–19
Anders-Stern, Guenther. 1950. Emotion and Reality, *Philosophy and
Phenomenological Research*, Vol. X, pp. 553–62
Anderson, Perry. 1968. Components of the National Culture, *New Left Review*
50, pp. 3–57
Aron, Raymond. 1969. *Marxism and the Existentialists* (New York: Harper and
Row)
Atkinson, R. 1971. *Orthodox Consensus and Radical Alternative* (London:
Heinemann)
Audrey, Collette. (ed.) 1948. *Pour et Contre existentialisme* (Paris: Editions Atlas)
Ayer, A. J. 1945. Novelists-Philosophers V: Jean-Paul Sartre, *Horizon*, Vol. 12,
pp. 12–25, 101–10
Bandyopadhyay, Pradeep. 1972. The Many Faces of French Marxism, *Science
and Society*, Vol. 36, pp. 129–57
Barea, Arturo. 1972. *The Forging of a Rebel* (London: Davis Poynter)

Barnard, Jessie. 1973. My Four Revolutions: An Autobiographical History of the
    ASA. *American Journal of Sociology*, Vol. 78, pp. 773–89
Barrett, William. 1961. *Irrational Man* (London: Heinemann)
Barthes, Roland. 1968. *Elements of Semiology* (London: Jonathan Cape)
    1972. *Mythologies* (London: Jonathan Cape)
Bauman, Z. 1973. On the Philosophical Status of Ethnomethodology, *Sociological
    Review*, Vol. 21, pp. 5–23
de Beauvoir, Simone. 1946. Pour une morale d'ambiguitie, *Les Temps Modernes*,
    Nos. 14–17
    1953. *The Second Sex* (London: Hamish Hamilton)
    1955. Merleau-Ponty et le pseudo-Sartrisme, *Les Temps Modernes*, No. 115,
        pp. 2072–122
    1960. *The Mandarins* (London: Fontana)
    1963. *Memoirs of a Dutiful Daughter* (London: Penguin)
    1965. *The Prime of Life* (London: Penguin)
    1968. *Force of Circumstance* (London: Penguin)
    1972. *Tout Compte Fait* (Paris: Gallimard)
Becker, Howard. *Sociological Work* (London: Allen Lane, The Penguin
    Press)
Bendix, R. 1956. *Work and Authority in Industry* (New York: Harper Row)
Berger, Bennett. 1971. *Looking for America* (Englewood Cliffs, New Jersey:
    Prentice-Hall)
Berger, Peter. 1963. *Invitation to Sociology* (New York: Doubleday Anchor)
Berger, Peter & Luckmann, Thomas. 1966. *The Social Construction of Reality*
    (New York: Doubleday)
van der Berghe, P. 1963. *Dialectic and Functionalism: Towards a Theoretical
    Synthesis, American Sociological Review*, Vol. 28, pp. 695–705
Bettocci, Peter A. 1965. Existentialist Phenomenology and Psychoanalysis, *Review
    of Metaphysics*, Vol. 16, pp. 190–210
Birchall, Ian. 1970. Sartre and the Myth of Practice, *International Socialism* 45,
    pp. 20–4.
    1971. Sartre – Part Two. *International Socialism* 46, pp. 17–22
Blackburn, R. & Stedman-Jones, G. 1972. Louis Althusser and the Struggle for
    Marxism, in Howard & Klare (eds.), *The Unknown Dimension* (New
    York: Basic Books)
Blauner, R. 1966. *Alienation and Freedom* (Chicago: Chicago University Press)
Blumer, Herbert. 1969. *Symbolic Interactionism: Perspectives and Method*
    (Englewood Cliffs, New Jersey: Prentice Hall)
Le Bon, Sylvie. 1967. Michel Foucault: positiviste désespére, *Les Temps Modernes*
    No. 248, pp. 1299–1320
Bondey, François. 1971. Jean-Paul Sartre, in Maurice Cranston (ed.), *The New
    Left* (London: Bodley Head)
Bordieu, Pierre. 1966. Champ intellectual et projet créature, *Les Temps
    Modernes*, No. 246, pp. 865–906
Bordieu, Pierre & Passeron, J. C. 1967. Sociology and Philosophy in France since
    1945, *Social Research*, Vol. 34, pp. 162–212
Burke, Kenneth. 1966. *Language and Symbolic Action* (Berkeley, University of
    California Press)
Burkle, Howard R. 1966. Social Freedom in the Critique, *Review of Metaphysics*,
    Vol. xix, pp. 742–56
Burnier, Michel-Antoine. 1966. *Les existentialistes et la politique* (Paris: Gallimard)

Butts, R. E. 1958. Does Intentionality Imply Being? *Journal of Philosophy*, Vol. 55, pp. 911–12

Castel, Robert. 1966. Un beau risque, *L'Arc* 30, pp. 20–7

Catlin, George. 1946. A Reply to Existentialism, *Proceedings of the Aristotelian Society*, Vol. XLVII, pp. 197–22

Caute, David. 1960. *Communism and the French Intellectuals 1914–60* (New York: Macmillan)

Churchill, Lindsay. 1971. Ethnomethodology and Measurement. *Social Forces*, Vol. 50, pp. 182–91

Cohen, Percy S. 1968. *Modern Social Theory* (London: Heinemann)

Contat, Michel. 1968. *Explication des Sequestrés des Altona par Jean-Paul Sartre* (Paris: Archives de Lettres Modernes)

Cooper, David. 1965. *Psychiatry and Anti-Psychiatry* (London: Fontana)

Coulter, Jeff. 1973. Language and the Conceptualisation of Meaning, *Sociology*, Vol. 7, pp. 173–89

Cranston, Maurice. 1962. Sartre, *Encounter* April & June 1962

Culler, Jonathan. 1973. Phenomenology and Structuralism, *The Human Context*, Vol. V, pp. 35–42

Dawe, Alan. 1971. The Two Sociologies, *British Journal of Sociology*, Vol. 21, pp. 207–17

1973. The Role of Experience in the Construction of Social Theory, *Sociological Review*, Vol. 21, pp. 25–52

Dempsey, Peter. 1950. *The Psychology of Jean-Paul Sartre* (Cork: University Press)

Desan, Wilfrid. 1954. *The Tragic Finale* (Cambridge Mass.: Harvard University Press)

1966. *The Marxism of Jean-Paul Sartre* (New York: Doubleday Anchor)

Dion, Michel. 1972. Philosophie et dialectique materialiste, *La Pensée* No. 166, pp. 3–24

Doubrovsky, Serge. 1961. Sartre et la mythe de la raison dialectique, *Nouvelle Revue Francaise*, Vol. 18, pp. 491–501; 689–98; 879–88

Douglas, Jack D. 1970a. *The American Social Order* (New York: The Free Press)

1970b. *The Relevance of Sociology* (New York: Appleton-Century-Crofts)

1970c. *The Social Meanings of Suicide* (Princeton N.J.: Princeton University Press)

1971. *Understanding Everyday Life* (London: Routledge & Kegan Paul)

Dreyfus, Diane. 1969. Jean-Paul Sartre et le mal radical, *Mercure de France*, Vol. 34, pp. 154–67

Duclos, Denis. 1973. L'Insertion Professionalle des étudiants en sociologie, *La Pensée* No. 167, pp. 22–38

Earle, William. 1960. Phenomenology and Existentialism, *Journal of Philosophy*, Vol. LVII, pp. 75–83

Fanon, Frantz. 1965. *The Wretched of the Earth* (London: MacGibbon & Kee)

1968. *Black Skins, White Masks* (London: MacGibbon & Kee)

1970. *A Dying Colonialism* (London: Pelican)

Faye, Jean-Pierre. 1960. Sartre entend-il Sartre?, *Tel Quel* 27, pp. 75–81

Foss, D. C. 1972. Self and the Revolt Against Method, *Philosophy of the Social Sciences*, Vol. 2, pp. 291–307

Friedrichs, Robert W. 1970. *A Sociology of Sociology* (New York: The Free Press)

1972. Dialectical Sociology: Towards a resolution of the current crisis, *British Journal of Sociology*, Vol. 23, pp. 263–73

Garfinkel, H. 1967. *Studies in Ethnomethodology* (Englewood Cliffs, New Jersey: Prentice-Hall)

Geras, Norman. 1972. Louis Althusser: An account and assessment, *New Left Review* 71, pp. 57–86

Gerth, H. & Wright-Mills, C. 1954, *Character and Social Structure* (London: Routledge & Kegan Paul)

Girardin, Jean-Claude. 1972. Sartre's Contribution to Marxism, in Howard & Klare (eds.): *The Unknown Dimension* (New York: Basic Books)

Glucksmann, Andre. 1972. A Ventriloquist Structuralism, *New Left Review* 72, pp. 68–92

Goffman, E. 1963. *Behaviour in Public Places* (Glencoe: Free Press)
   1968a. *Asylums* (London: Penguin)
   1968b. *Stigma* (London: Penguin)
   1969. *The Presentation of Self in Everyday Life* (London: Allen Lane, The Penguin Press)

Goldmann, Lucien. 1969. *The Human Sciences and Phiosophy* (London: Jonathan Cape)
   1970a. Jean-Paul Sartre: Question de méthode, in *Marxism et les sciences humaines*, pp. 242–58 (Paris: Gallimard)
   1970b. *Power and Humanism*, Spokesman Pamphlet No. 14 (Nottingham: Bertrand Russell Peace Foundation)
   1970c. Problèmes philosophiques et politiques dans le théâtre de Jean-Paul Sartre, *L'Homme et le Société*, No. 17, pp. 5–34

Gorz, Andre. 1966a. De la conscience à la praxis, *Livres de France* XXXIV, pp. 3–7
   1966b. Sartre and Marx, *New Left Review* 37, pp. 33–72

Gouldner, Alvin W. 1954a. *Patterns of Industrial Bureaucracy* (New York: The Free Press)
   1954b. *Wildcat Strike* (New York: Harper Row)
   1964. Anti-Minataur: The Myth of a Value-Free Sociology, in I. L. Horowitz (ed.) *The New Sociology*, pp.196–217 (New York: Oxford University Press)
   1971. *The Coming Crisis of Western Sociology* (London: Heinemann)
   1972. A Reply to Martin Shaw: Whose Crisis?, *New Left Review* 71, pp. 89–96
   1973. Varities of Political Expression Revisited, *American Journal of Sociology*, Vol. 68, pp. 1063–93

Grene, Marjorie. 1970. The Aesthetic Dialogue of Sartre and Merleau-Ponty, *Journal of the British Society for Phenomenology*, Vol. 1, pp. 59–72

Grimsley, Ronald. 1955. An Aspect of Sartre and the Unconscious, *Philosophy*, Vol. xxx, pp. 33–4

Gurwitsch, Aron. 1941. A Non-Egological Conception of Consciousness, *Philosophy and Phenomenological Research*, Vol. 1, pp. 325–48

Hahn, Otto. 1965. L'oeuvre critique de Sartre, *Modern Language Notes*, Vol. 80, pp. 547–63

Hartmann, Klaus. 1970. Praxis: A Ground for Social Theory?, *Journal of the British Society for Phenomenology*, Vol. 1, pp. 47–58

Hindess, Barry. 1972. The 'Phenomenological' Sociology of Alfred Schutz, *Economy and Society*, Vol. 1, pp. 1–27

Hirst, Paul Q. 1972. Recent Tendencies in Sociological Theory, *Economy and Society*, Vol. 1, pp. 216–28

Le Huenon, Roland and Puerron, Paul. 1972. Temporalité et démarche critique chez Jean-Paul Sartre, *Revue de Sciences Humaines*, Oct. Nov. 1972, pp. 567–81

Hughes, H. Stuart. 1964. *The Obstructed Path* (New York: Harper Row)

Jameson, Fredric. 1961. *Sartre: The Origin of a Style* (New Haven Conn.: Yale University Press)

Jeanson, Francis. 1961. *Sartre par lui-même* (Paris: Editions du Seuil)

   1965. *La problème morale et la pensée de Jean-Paul Sartre* (Paris: Editions du Seuil)

Kern, Edith (ed.). 1962. *Sartre: A Collection of Critical Essays* (Englewood Cliffs, New Jersey: Prentice-Hall)

Kline, George. 1967. The Existential Re-discovery of Hegel and Marx, in Lee and Mandelbaum (eds.): *Phenomenology and Existentialism*, pp. 113–37 (Baltimore: Johns Hopkins Press)

Kolb, William L. 1967. A Critical Evaluation of Mead's 'I' and 'Me' Concepts, in J. G. Manis & B. N. Meltzer (eds.), *Symbolic Interactionism*, pp. 241–50 (Boston: Allyn & Bacon)

Kreiger, Leonard. 1967. History and Existentialism in Sartre, in Kurt Wolff & Barrington Moore (eds.), *The Critical Spirit*, pp. 239–56 (Boston: Beacon Press)

Kuhn, Manfred H. 1967. Major Trends in Symbolic Interactionism in the Past Twenty Five Years, in J. G. Manis & B. N. Meltzer (eds.), *Symbolic Interactionism*, pp. 46–67 (Boston: Allyn & Bacon)

Kuhn, Thomas. 1970. *The Structure of Scientific Revolutions* (Chicago: Chicago University Press)

Laing, R. D. 1967. *The Politics of Experience and the Bird of Paradise* (London: Penguin)

   1971a. *Knots* (London: Tavistock)

   1971b. *The Self and Others* (London: Penguin)

Laing, R. D. & Cooper, D. G. 1964. *Reason and Violence* (London: Tavistock)

Leat, Diana. 1972. Understanding Verstehen, *Sociological Review*, Vol. 20, pp. 29–38

Leduc, Violette. 1968. *Ravages* (London: Arthur Barker Ltd.)

Lefebvre, Henri. 1968. *Dialectical Materialism* (London: Jonathan Cape)

Lessing, Arthur. 1967. Marxist Existentialism, *Review of Metaphysics*, Vol. xx, pp. 461–82

Levi-Strauss, Claude. 1966. *The Savage Mind* (London: Weidenfeld & Nicolson)

   1970. Confrontation over Myths, *New Left Review* 62, pp. 57–74

Lichtheim, George. 1964. Sartre, Marxism and History, *History and Theory*, Vol. III, pp. 222–46

   1966. *Marxism in Modern France* (New York: Columbia University Press)

McKinney, J. and Tiryakian, E. A. (eds.) 1970. *Theoretical Sociology* (New York: Appleton-Century-Crofts)

McMahon, Joseph. 1971. *Humans Being: The World of Jean-Paul Sartre* (Chicago: Chicago University Press)

Manser, A. R. and Kolnai, A. J. 1963. Existentialism, *Proceedings of the Aristotelian Society*, Supp. Vol. xxvii, pp. 11–50

Marcuse, Herbert. 1968. *Negations* (London: Allen Lane, The Penguin Press)

   1972. Sartre's Existentialism in *Studies in Critical Philosophy*, pp. 157–90 (London: New Left Books)

Marx, Karl. 1972. Notes on Machines, *Economy and Society*, Vol. I, pp. 244–54

Marx, K. and Engels, F. 1968. *Selected Works* (London: Lawrence & Wishart)

Mead, G. H. 1938. *The Philosophy of the Act* (Chicago: Chicago University Press)

   1952. *Mind, Self and Society* (Chicago: Chicago University Press)

Merleau-Ponty, Maurice. 1947. *Humanisme et terreur* (Paris: Gallimard)

   1955. *Les Aventures de la dialectique* (Paris: Gallimard)

1963. The Philosopher and Sociology, in M. Natanson (ed.), *The Philosophy of the Social Sciences*, pp. 487–505 (New York: Random House)

Merton, R. K. 1967. *Social Theory and Social Structure* (Glencoe Ill.: The Free Press)

1973. Insiders and Outsiders, *American Journal of Sociology*, Vol. 78, pp. 9–47

Mills, C. Wright. 1959. *The Sociological Imagination* (New York: Oxford University Press)

Moore, Asher. 1966. Existential Phenomenology, *Philosophy and Phenomenological Research*, Vol. 27, pp. 408–14

Morgan, D. H. J. 1972. The British Association Scandal, *Sociological Review*, Vol. 20, pp. 185–200

Morin, E. 1971. *Rumour in Orleans* (New York: Random House)

Morris, Phyllis. 1970. Sartre on the Existence of Other Minds, *Journal of the British Society for Phenomenology*, Vol. 1, pp. 17–21

Murdoch, Iris. 1950. Review of 'A Sketch for a Theory of the Emotions', *Mind*, Vol. LIX, pp. 268–71

1967. *Sartre: Romantic Rationalist* (London: Fontana)

Natanson, M. 1951a. *A Critique of Jean-Paul Sartre's Ontology* (Lincoln Neb.: Nebraska University Press)

1951b. Reply to Van Meter Ames, *Journal of Philosophy*, Vol. 48, pp. 95–102

1970. *The Journeying Self* (Reading Mass.: Addison Wesley)

Neisser, Hans P. 1959. Phenomenological Approach in Social Science, *Philosophy and Phenomenological Research*, Vol. 20, pp. 198-212

Nisbet, Robert A. 1967. *The Sociological Tradition* (London: Heinemann)

O'Connor, D. J. 1964. *A Critical History of Western Philosophy* (New York: The Free Press)

Odajynk, Walter. 1965. *Marxism and Existentialism* (New York: Doubleday Anchor)

Olsen, Robert G. 1959. Authenticity, Metaphysics and Moral Responsibility, *Philosophy*, Vol. XXXIV, pp. 99–111

O'Neill, John. 1972. *Sociology as a Skin Trade* (London: Heinemann)

Peyre, Henri. 1968. *Jean-Paul Sartre* (New York: Columbia University Press)

Pilling, Geoffrey. 1972. The Law of Value in Ricardo and Marx, *Economy and Society*, Vol. 1, pp. 281–307

van de Pitte, M. M. 1970. Sartre as a Transcendental Realist, *Journal of the British Society for Phenomenology*, Vol. 1, pp. 22–6

Plantinga, Alvin. 1958. An Existentialist's Ethics, *Review of Metaphysics*, Vol. 12, pp. 216–36

Pollman, Leo. 1970. *Sartre and Camus* (New York: Frederick Ungar)

Pouillon, Jean. 1966. Présentation: Un essai de définition, *Les Temps Modernes* 246, pp. 769–90

Poulantzas, Nicos. 1966. La Critique de la raison dialectique de Jean-Paul Sartre et le droit, *Archives de Philosophie du Droit*, Vol. 10, pp. 83–106

Presseault, Jacques. 1970. *L'etre-pour-autrui dans la philosophie de Jean-Paul Sartre* (Paris: Desclee de Brouwer)

Rau, Catherine. 1949. The Ethical Theory of Jean-Paul Sartre, *Journal of Philosophy*, Vol. 46, pp. 139–47

Reynaud, Jean-Daniel. 1961. Sociologie et 'Raison dialectique', *Revue Française de Sociologie*, Vol. II, pp. 50–60

Rickman, H. P. 1960. The Reaction Against Positivism and Dilthey's Concept of Understanding, *British Journal of Sociology*, Vol. II, pp. 307–318

Ricoeur, Paul. 1967. Husserl and Wittgenstein on Language, in Lee &
    Mandelbaum (eds.): *Phenomenology and Existentialism*, pp. 207–17
    (Baltimore: Johns Hopkins Press)
Rose, A. (ed.) 1967. *Human Behaviour and Social Process* (London: Routledge and
    Kegan Paul)
Roshier, Paul. 1972. Drunk on Syntax, *New Society*, 3 August 1972, pp. 247–8
Ryle, Gilbert. 1971. *Collected Papers, Vol. I: Critical Essays* (London: Hutchinson)
Sartre, Jean-Paul. 1947. *Situations I* (Paris: Gallimard)
    1948a. *Anti-Semite and Jew* (New York: Schoken Books)
    1948b. *Baudelaire* (London: Methuen)
    1948c. Conscience de soi et connaissance de soi, *Bulletin de la Société Française
        de Philosophie*, Vol. 42, pp. 49–91
    1948d. Entretien sur la politique (With David Rousset and Gerard Rosenthal),
        Les Temps Modernes, pp. 385–428
    1948e. *Existentialism and Humanism* (London: Methuen)
    1948f. *Situations II* (Paris: Gallimard)
    1949a. Drole d'amitie, *Les Temps Modernes*, Nos. 49 & 50
    1949b. *The Psychology of the Imagination* (London: Rider)
    1949c. *Situations III* (Paris: Gallimard)
    1950. A propos du mal, *Livres du France*, pp. 13–4.
    1955. *Literary and Philosophical Essays* (Translations from *Situations I and III*)
        (London: Rider)
    1957a. *Being and Nothingness* (London: Methuen)
    1957b. *The Transcendence of the Ego* (New York: The Noonday Press)
    1958. *In Camera* (London: Penguin)
    1960a. *Critique de la raison dialectique* (Paris: Gallimard)
    1960b. *Intimacy* (short stories) (London: Panther Books)
    1961. *The Age of Reason* (London: Penguin)
    1962a. *Altona* (London: Penguin)
    1962b. *The Flies* (London: Penguin)
    1962c. *The Imagination* (Ann Arbor: University of Michigan Press)
    1962d. *Men Without Shadows* (London: Penguin)
    1963a. *Iron in the Soul* (London: Penguin)
    1963b. *The Problem of Method* (A translation of the first part of the *Critique*)
        (London: Methuen)
    1963c. *The Reprieve* (London: Penguin)
    1963d. *Saint Genet* (London: W. H. Allen)
    1963e. *Sketch for a Theory of the Emotions* (London: Methuen)
    1964a. *Situations IV* (Paris: Gallimard)
    1964b. *Situations V, Colonialisme et neo-colonialisme* (Paris: Gallimard)
    1964c. *Situations VI, Problemes du Marxisme I* (Paris: Gallimard)
    1965a. *Lucifer and the Lord* (London: Penguin)
    1965b. *Nausea* (London: Penguin)
    1965c. *Situations VII: Problemes du Marxisme II* (Paris: Gallimard)
    1966a. Jean-Paul Sartre répond (Interview: a critique of structuralism) *L'Arc*
        30, pp. 87–96
    1966b. *Situations* (Translated from *Situations IV*) (London: Hamish Hamilton)
    1967a. *What is Literature?* (London: Methuen)
    1967b. *Words* (London: Penguin)
    1969a. *The Communists and Peace* (London: Hamish Hamilton)
    1969b. Itinerary of a Thought (Interview), *New Left Review* 58, pp. 43–66

1970a. A Propos de l'existentialisme, in *RC*, pp. 653–8
1970b. Bariona, in *RC*, pp. 535–633
1970c. Determination et liberté, in *RC*, pp. 735–45
1970d. Légende de la vérité, in *RC*, pp. 531–45
1970e. La liberation de Paris: une semaine d'apocalypse, in *RC*, pp. 659–62
1970f. Masses, Spontaneity and Party, in Miliband & Saville (eds.), *The Socialist Register 1970*, pp. 233–49 (London: The Merlin Press)
1970g. The Theory of the State in Modern French Thought, in *RC*, pp. 517–30
1970h. Visages, in *RC*, pp.560–4
1971a. *L'Idiot de la famille, Tomes I & II* (Paris: Gallimard)
1971b. *Les Jeux sont faits* (London: Methuen)
1972a. *L'Idiot de la famille, Tome III* (Paris: Gallimard)
1972b. *Plaidoyer pour les Intellectuals* (Paris: Gallimard)
1972c. *Situations VIII* (Paris: Gallimard)
1972d. *Situations IX* (Paris: Gallimard)

Schaff, Adam. 1968. L'objectivité de connaissance à la lumière de la sociologie de connaissance et de l'analyse du language, *Social Science Information*, Vol. VII, pp. 103–30

Schneider, Louis. 1971. Dialectic in Sociology, *American Sociological Review*, Vol. 36, pp. 667–78

Schutz, Alfred. 1962a, b & c. *Collected Papers, Vols. I, II & III* (The Hague: Martinus Nijhoff)
1967. *The Phenomenology of the Social World* (Evanston Ill.: Northwestern University Press)

Seyppel, J.H. 1953. A Comparative Study of Truth in Existentialism and Pragmatism, *Journal of Philosophy*, Vol. 50, pp. 229–41

Shaw, Martin. 1971. The Coming Crisis of Radical Sociology, *New Left Review* 70, pp. 101–9

Silverman, David. 1971. *The Theory of Organisations: A Sociological Framework* (London: Heinemann)

Sinka, D. 1963. Phenomenology and Positivism, *Philosophy and Phenomenological Research*, Vol. 23, pp. 562–77

Spiegelberg, Herbert. 1954. French Existentialism: Its Social Philosophies, *Kenyon Review*, Vol. XVI, pp. 446–62
1960. Husserl's Phenomenology and Existentialism, *Journal of Philosophy*, Vol. LVII, pp. 62–73
1965. *The Phenomenological Movement* (2 Vols.) (The Hague: Martinus Nijhoff)

Stack, George J. 1971. Sartre's Dialectic of Social Relations, *Philosophy and Phenomenological Research*, Vol. 31, pp. 394–408

Sudnow, David (ed.) 1972. *Studies in Social Interaction* (New York: The Free Press)

Suhl, Benjamin. 1970. *Sartre: The Philosopher as Literary Critic* (New York: Columbia University Press)

Talloch, D. M. 1952. Sartre's Existentialism, *Philosophical Quarterly*, Vol. 2, pp. 31–52

Taylor, Laurie. 1972. The Significance and Interpretation of Replies to Motivational Questions, *Sociology*, Vol. 6, pp. 25–31

Taylor, I., Walton, P. & Young, J. 1973. *The New Criminology* (London: Routledge & Kegan Paul)

Thody, Phillip. 1961. *Jean-Paul Sartre: A Literary and Philosophical Study* (New York: Macmillan)
1971. *Sartre: A Biographical Introduction* (London: Studio Vista)

Tillich, Paul. 1956. The Nature and Significance of Existentialist Thought, *Journal of Philosophy*, Vol. 53, pp. 759–78

Tiryakian, Edward A. 1962. *Sociologism and Existentialism* (Englewood Cliffs, New Jersey: Prentice-Hall)

 1965. Existential Phenomenology and the Sociological Tradition, *American Sociological Review*, Vol. 30, pp. 674–88. Discussion, Vol. 31, pp. 58–64

Touraine, Alain. 1969. Towards Actionalist Sociology, *Social Science Information*, Vol. 8, pp. 147–61

Trotignon, Pierre. 1966. Le Dernier Métaphysicien, *L'Arc* 30, pp. 27–32

de Waelhans, Alphonse. 1962. Sartre et la raison dialectique, *Revue Metaphysique de Louvain*, Vol. 60, pp. 79–99

Wahl, Jean. 1969. *Philosophies of Existence* (London: Routledge & Kegan Paul)

Warnock, Mary. 1965. *The Philosophy of Sartre* (London: Hutchinson)

 1970. *Existentialism* (London: Oxford University Press)

Weber, Max. 1949. *Methodology in the Social Sciences* (New York: the Free Press)

Whyte, William F. 1955. *Street Corner Society* (Chicago: Chicago University Press)

Wild, John. 1959. Contemporary Phenomenology and the Problem of Existence. *Philosophy and Phenomenological Research*, Vol. 20, pp. 166–79

 1960. Existentialism as a Philosophy, *Journal of Philosophy*, Vol. LVII, pp. 45–62

Willener, Alfred. 1970. *The Action Image of Society* (London: Tavistock)

Wilson, Nancy (ed.) 1962. *The World of Zen* (London: Collins)

Winch, Peter. 1958. *The Idea of a Social Science* (London: Routledge & Kegan Paul)

Wollheim, Richard. 1953. The Political Philosophy of Existentialism, *Cambridge Journal*, Vol. 7, pp. 3–19

Yolton, J. N. 1951. The Metaphysics of En-soi and Pour-soi, *Journal of Philosophy*, Vol. 48, pp. 548–56

Young, Michael, F. D. 1972. On the Politics of Educational Knowledge, *Economy and Society*, Vol. 1, pp. 194–215

Zimmerman, Don. *Paper-Work and People-Work*, Unpublished Ph.D. Thesis, University of California, Berkeley

INDEX

Index

Index

Index

段# Index

Index 242

Sociology, and existentialism, Chap. 1 *passim*, 223–8; sociological project, 24, 28, 85–92, 207–14; sociology as analytic praxis, 1–16; as reciprocal praxis, 124–5; sociology and scarcity, 132–3; sociology as a practico-inert structure, 140–2, 206–7; sociology as serial praxis, 164–7; as group praxis, 181–7; reflexive sociology, 11, 13, 18, 34, 86, 107, 182, 218, 219; structural sociology, 221–3

Sovereign, 197–202

Spiegelberg, H., 14n1, 15n2

Sudnow, D., 65n

Taylor, I., Walton, P. & Young, J., 211n1

Temps Modernes, Les, 3n1

Terror, 178–9, 197

Thompson, H., 30n1

Tiryakian, E. A., 2, 11, 12, 18, 218

Turner, R., 178

Value, 19, 23, 28, 29, 30, 33, 34, 103, 155; *see also* Being-For-Itself, Nothingness, Project

Van der Berghe, P., 95n2

Wahl, J., 1

Warnock, M., 2, 7n1, 15n1, 27n2

Weber, M., 2, 35, 36, 89, 108, 117, 118, 181, 208, 222

Whyte, W. F., 114n2, 224n1

Willener, A., 175n1, 186

Wilson, T., 29n2

Winch, P., 218n2

Young, M., 64n